D0209772

The Vertical File and Its Satellites

A Handbook of Acquisition, Processing, and Organization

Second Edition

Shirley Miller

RECEIVED

JUN 12 1980

MANKATO STATE UNIVERSITY
MEMORIAL LIBRARY
MANKATO, MINN.

Libraries Unlimited, Inc.- Littleton, Colorado
1979

Copyright © 1979, 1971 Shirley Miller
All Rights Reserved
Printed in the United States of America

No part of this publication may be reproduced, stored in a
retrieval system, or transmitted, in any form or by any means,
electronic, mechanical, photocopying, recording, or otherwise,
without the prior written permission of the publisher.

LIBRARIES UNLIMITED, INC.
P.O. Box 263
Littleton, Colorado 80160

Library of Congress Cataloging in Publication Data

Miller, Shirley.
    The vertical file and its satellites.

    (Library science text series)
    Includes index.
    1. Vertical files (Libraries).   I. Title.
Z691.M55   1979   025.17'2   79-13773
ISBN 0-87287-164-9

This book is bound with Scott Graphitek®–C Type II nonwoven material.
Graphitek–C meets and exceeds National Association of State Textbook Adminis-
trators' Type II nonwoven material specifications Class A through E.

CONTENTS

444203

ACKNOWLEDGMENTS

This book is dedicated to Sophie and Louis Miller, who knew what it was like to struggle against great odds.

I am indebted to the many people in the library, museum, and archival fields who shared their knowledge and experiences with me in the best tradition of these professions. Their number prevents mentioning each individual oy name.

Because of their special contribution to this book, I would like to express my gratitude to Donald Toepfer, Grace Scott, and Jule Fosbender.

INTRODUCTION

PURPOSE AND CONTENT

The first edition of **The Vertical File and Its Satellites** was published in 1971. The warm response it received was proof of the need for a comprehensive contemporary handbook in this area. The decision to prepare a revised edition was made in recognition of the many developments which have taken place since 1971. The second edition introduces new resources, new products, and new techniques that have appeared during the intervening years.

However, the current version represents more than just an updated edition. It is also an expanded edition. Portions of the original text have been enlarged to provide more thorough treatment of certain subjects. The coverage of photographs is one example. The new edition of this book has been broadened in another way. It now includes information about vertical files and related resources in special libraries. This emphasis was added in response to requests from librarians working in such facilities.

The new edition retains the philosophy and approach of the original volume. It demonstrates how supplementary materials can add variety and depth to a library's holdings. As well as presenting the merits of various types of auxiliary materials, the book focuses on how to acquire them. It also deals with the organization, processing, housing, and circulation of these resources.

The title of this book, **The Vertical File and Its Satellites**, was carefully chosen to reflect its wide range of coverage. The "vertical file" is a familiar term in the working vocabulary of most librarians. Traditionally, it has denoted a collection made up primarily of pamphlets and clippings which are housed vertically in filing cases or similar containers. The potentials and problems of vertical file materials are thoroughly treated in this book. As important as the vertical file is, however, it represents only one aspect of the resources covered. The "satellite" collections which reinforce the traditional vertical file also receive detailed examination in the chapters that follow. Typical of such "satellites" are picture collections and map collections.

The structure of this book has also been shaped by the variety of materials it includes. A roll call of these supplementary aids would reveal pamphlets, flyers, clippings, catalogs, annual reports, reprints, bulletins, sample magazines, charts, posters, pictures, postcards, photographs, maps, photocopies, special indexes, and sometimes even manuscripts and archives. This rich mixture of materials means that many new dimensions can be added to library service. But it also means that the processes of selection, organization, and physical management must be flexible enough to take this diversity into account. In developing this book, consideration was given both· to the common elements and the diverse attributes of these resources.

The first two chapters are devoted to an overall view. Chapter 1 is a broad introduction to techniques and tools for locating supplementary materials. Chapter 2 is concerned with technical and mechanical routines which are widely applicable. The remainder of the book offers an intensive survey of special types of supplementary resources. Individual chapters focus on the unique features of pamphlets, clippings, vocational material, local history collections, maps, and pictorial material, as well as indexes and reference folders developed to fill special informational needs.

COVERAGE ELSEWHERE

Librarians looking for other comprehensive guides to the principles and practices of supplementary collections will find scanty pickings.

Lester Condit's **A Pamphlet About Pamphlets**, which was originally published in 1939 by the University of Chicago Press, is now being reprinted on demand by University Microfilms. However, it is of interest as a historical landmark rather than as a current handbook.

Although **The Pamphlet File in School, College, and Public Libraries**, by Norma O. Ireland, is still available from the F. W. Faxon Company, Inc., its 1954 copyright date should be fair warning that the passing years have diminished the usefulness of its contents. A companion volume, **The Picture File in School, College, and Public Libraries**, is even older. It dates from 1952.

In 1968, Geraldine N. Gould and Ithmer C. Wolfe collaborated on a volume entitled **How to Organize and Maintain the Library Picture/Pamphlet File**. The authors directed most of their attention to pictorial resources, with pamphlets and clippings receiving secondary consideration. The book clearly reflects the fact that it is based on experiences in an elementary school library. While the authors have attempted to broaden their outlook to include secondary schools, the needs of public libraries are given only cursory treatment.

1968 also marked the publication of **Readings in Nonbook Librarianship** by the Scarecrow Press, Inc. The collection was edited by Jean Spealman Kujoth. Some of the articles deal with pamphlets, clippings, maps, and pictorial materials. However, they are often directed to very specialized library situations. Furthermore, **Readings in Nonbook Librarianship**—like all anthologies—offers a sampling of ideas rather than an overall, unified approach. There is enough here to whet your appetite, but no more. The collection is now out of print.

A more current title is Donna Hill's **The Picture File: A Manual and a Curriculum-Related Subject Heading List**. Originally published in 1975 by Linnet Books (Shoe String Press, Inc.), it is being reissued in a revised edition. Since it is limited to pictorial resources, it does not meet the need for an overall survey of supplementary materials.

Hopefully, the new edition of **The Vertical File and Its Satellites** will continue to fill that need.

THE REWARD

Before you commit yourself to reading the remainder of this book, you may properly ask, "What do these supplemental sources of information offer in return for my effort, time, and money?"

The answer is "A great deal!" They will help your library earn the goodwill and confidence of its users by increasing the percentage of times you can send those users away satisfied. These materials can also result in savings in staff time by making the search for information easier and quicker. As a bonus, many of these items represent real bargains since they are offered free or for a nominal fee.

These supportive resources are valuable allies in all types of libraries.

In school libraries, they will make excellent instructional devices for teachers and prime research tools for students. A large chart showing ecological relationships may be just what a science teacher needs to dramatize a lesson presentation. Brochures or clippings that deal with the problem of drinking and driving will be eagerly welcomed by pupils taking driver education. A high school senior who wants to compare the programs in oceanography at various universities will be grateful for a collection of college catalogs.

School use of supplementary materials doesn't stop at the high school level. Students in institutions of higher learning can profit from them also. The reports of the World Bank may supply precisely the information needed to complete a project for a college economics class. Pamphlets on the status and needs of the elderly may be important adjuncts to a university course in gerontology.

Supplementary sources of information are equally as important to the broad clientele served by the public library. A pamphlet on making hairpin lace will delight the woman who wants to revive this art remembered from her childhood. A handy map will help you direct patrons to the bird sanctuary in a neighboring county. An old postcard may settle an argument about the height of a building that once stood on Main Street.

Even in special libraries, auxiliary materials have a significant role to play. The vertical file in a business library might feature such items as market surveys, pamphlets on advertising techniques, and reprints of articles on new products and processes.

GROUND RULES

One of the minor but aggravating problems in writing about supplemental sources of information is the lack of a descriptor that is both appropriate and generally accepted. It's misleading to lump all of these varied resources under the heading of "vertical file materials." The traditional definition does not make allowance for some of these informational tools. In addition, some of these resources may be housed in horizontal cases, pamphlet boxes, flat folders, or index drawers rather than in vertical files.

Nor is it accurate to refer to these materials as "ephemeral" or "fugitive." An instructive pamphlet on taxidermy is not really "ephemeral." It will be hoarded longer than many books. Well-organized brochures and clippings are not "fugitive" at all. They are waiting at your fingertips.

Because of this confusion, it was necessary to decide on a substitute expression that would more adequately delineate the variety and nature of the resources covered in this book. The term chosen was "supplementary resources." It is relatively short and reasonably descriptive. Whenever you encounter the words "supplementary resources" in this text, they will be used to indicate the complex assortment of materials that can be found in the vertical file and its satellites.

This volume does not follow the customary pattern of placing a bibliography and roster of suppliers and sources at the end of each chapter. Instead, a composite list of references will be found at the back of the book. Referral numbers will lead you from the text to the proper entry in the master list.

In the chapters of this book, you will find many individual items cited as typical examples. In the list of references at the end of the volume, you will find exact prices quoted. These inclusions were made in the full knowledge that many specifics will have changed by the time this book reaches the reader. Nevertheless, the examples will add flesh to otherwise nebulous concepts, while the price notations will give a relative indication of cost.

In the course of reading this book, you will occasionally encounter such expressions as "in our library . . ." or "we have used . . .". These comments refer to the Kalamazoo (Michigan) Public Library, where your author is currently employed in the Reference Division. To put these referrals in their proper perspective, it is important to note that **The Vertical File and Its Satellites** does not restrict itself to the philosophy or practices of any one library. It is a distillation of many years of working experience in various types of libraries. This experience has been reinforced by extensive research and consultation.

December 1978   S.M.

CHAPTER 1

LOCATING SUPPLEMENTARY RESOURCES

THE SEEKING MIND

Money and professional tools are handy aids in building a collection of supplementary resources, but they aren't nearly so vital as the proper state of mind. To succeed in this endeavor you must become an eager and perceptive gleaner. It is a three-step process. First of all, you must be enthusiastic about the value of supplementary resources. Second, you must develop alertness, ingenuity, and perseverance in searching out choice items. Finally, you must cultivate the ability to recognize riches wherever they occur, even in your own backyard.

To demonstrate how productive a "backyard" can be, I toured my hometown to see what I could find without consulting a single list or sending a single postcard. Here is my itinerary and my crop of discoveries:

Sheriff's department

    State snowmobile act

    Regulations for recreational boats

    Safety tips on boating

    Leaflet on safe use of fireplaces and stoves

    Series of crime prevention booklets

Car dealer

    Gas mileage guide from the federal government

American Red Cross

    Biographical leaflet on Clara Barton

    Booklet on the Red Cross name, emblem, and flag

    Literature on various Red Cross programs such as blood collection and disaster relief

    Publications list of the American Red Cross

    List of films, speakers, and demonstrations available from the local unit

    Flyers and leaflets on first aid procedures, safe swimming, and safe boating

    Pamphlet on drug abuse

Republican Party headquarters

Guide to the proper display of the United States flag

Leaflet on energy conservation

Copy of the Constitution of the State of Michigan

Booklet of facts about Michigan, past and present

Information on candidates and issues in upcoming election

Directory of community service agencies and organizations

Copies of Republican Party magazines

Oculist

Brochure on Michigan Eye-Bank

City Hall

Map of Kalamazoo

Bus schedules

Neighborhood newsletters

Emergency planning procedures for floods, fire, and tornadoes

Brochure on the city's newspaper recycling program

Shopping mall

Exhibit for Fire Prevention Week yielded leaflets on preventing home fires and forest fires, as well as material about smoke detectors

Michigan Heart Association

Pamphlets, leaflets, charts, and posters that cover function and diseases of the heart, high blood pressure, strokes, smoking, and nutrition

Credit union

Credit union quarterly, **Everybody's Money.** Good for clipping and also contains leads to free and inexpensive publications

Easter Seal Society

Handbook on rights, services, and information for handicapped persons in Michigan

Access guide to facilities in Kalamazoo, assessing possible physical obstacles

Newsletter of the Michigan Easter Seal Society

Easter Seal Society (cont'd)

Easter Seal booklet on safe bicycling

Large selection of literature from other agencies and organizations cooperating in services to the handicapped

Savings and loan association

Customer magazine worth clipping for house plans and article on hot tubs

Pamphlet on personal tax-sheltered retirement plans

Charter and by-laws of the association

Annual report of the association

Dentist's office

Booklet on use of fluorides to fight tooth decay

Community college

Set of eighteen brochures on various career programs offered at the college

Series of five career brochures from the American Dental Hygienists' Association

Secretary of State's branch office

Booklet on laws and safe driving information for motorcycles and mopeds

Manual for automobile drivers covering licensing, traffic laws, and safe driving tips

Travel agency

Series of U.S. Travel Service booklets on consumer information for travelers

Booklet of key facts for businessmen traveling overseas

Illustrated brochure on Canadian tourist attractions

Copies of North Central Airlines' customer magazine

American Cancer Society

Description of the American Cancer Society and its activities

Leaflets, flyers, and posters on smoking

Booklets on detection and treatment of various types of cancer

Lists of visual aids and programs available from the local unit

Social Security office

Leaflets on Social Security benefits and regulations

Restaurant

Complimentary magazine informing visitors about what to do and where to dine in Southwest Lower Michigan

County health department

Wide range of publications from the state department of health, the federal government, health-oriented associations, and business firms. Cover all aspects of health from calorie counting to measles

Convention and visitors bureau

Calendar of community events

Series of printed guides for visitors on such subjects as recreational activities and tours in the area

Chamber of Commerce

Official state highway map

Michigan public transportation map and directory

Official highway map of Kalamazoo County

Calendar of Michigan travel events

Guide to making consumer complaints

Travel leaflets on attractions in the Kalamazoo area

Descriptions of services of the Chamber of Commerce

In my tour of the city, I exhausted my available time long before I exhausted the sources of information.

Seeking out materials is like a game that can be played wherever you are. The most unlikely places and occasions can result in happy discoveries. This explains why a good searcher is always on the alert. One of my finds was a paper placemat from a local Oriental restaurant which detailed the history and use of chopsticks. My intention was simply to get a good meal, but I ended up with a potential vertical file item as well. On another occasion I turned on my car radio just in time to hear about a free booklet on genealogy being offered by the Mormon Church (officially, the Church of Jesus Christ of Latter-Day Saints) in Salt Lake City.

Your friends, your family, and your patrons can become helpful in your search for materials. If you are enthusiastic, they will be infected with the virus, too. You will find your blotter well covered with spoils from their trips or from meetings they have attended.

Of course, you can't rely solely on footpower, friendship, and serendipity. Fortunately, there are more conventional devices for locating supplementary resources which you can use in the comfort of your own library.

GUIDES TO GUIDES

Occasionally, a library or educational agency will publish a bibliography of guides to free and inexpensive materials. A bibliography of this sort is really a list to help you locate lists.

A current example is **Free and Inexpensive Materials: A Selected List of Guides to Sources**, prepared by the Library of Congress **(143)**. The latest edition of this free publication was released in August 1977. It includes many excellent titles, as well as a few that are of lower caliber.

The value of such surveys is that they give you an overview of a large number of possible location aids.

It is important to remember that such inventories rapidly become dated. The only solution is to be constantly watchful for the announcement of new selection tools.

COMPILATIONS

One type of selection tool is a compiled list in book or pamphlet form. In the process of collection building, such lists can operate as convenient shortcuts.

Some compilations are like shooting stars, making one appearance and then fading from view. Others have established themselves so firmly that they are revised and reissued at regular intervals. For the novice, it is better to start with time-tested lists. Unfortunately, overblown, overpriced guides appear on the market periodically and promise much but deliver little. Don't invest before you investigate.

General Compilations

There are guides which pull offerings together on a variety of subjects from a variety of sources. Most of them were designed for use by teachers, but they can also be employed successfully by school libraries, public libraries, and even special libraries.

General compilations which cover a wide range of subjects are particularly useful for the brand-new library seeking to start a supplementary resource collection. Other libraries will find them helpful in filling gaps in their collections and in updating resources.

In deciding how much of your budget to invest in these lists, remember that they serve a double purpose. They can be of direct value to patrons as well as librarians. Students writing for free materials for school assignments find them a boon. These lists also have a two-edged usefulness in locating material. They not only record individual items but also include offers of bibliographies, catalogs, and publishers' lists, which will expand your horizons still further.

Where funds are very limited, a group of neighboring libraries can band together to buy these guides and then rotate them among participating agencies. Libraries which belong to systems or cooperatives might request that copies be purchased by the headquarters library to circulate among the member libraries.

The following paragraphs single out general compilations which are promising new endeavors or which have demonstrated their usefulness through the years.

A "granddaddy" among the general compilations is **Free and Inexpensive Learning Materials (106)**, produced biennially by the Office of Educational Services at George Peabody College for Teachers. Although the latest edition was delayed by a change in distribution channels, the guide will resume its normal publication schedule in the future. The new nineteenth edition, released early in 1979, contains over 3,000 instructional aids. All entries have been evaluated for their educational value by the staff of the Office of Educational Services. While the compilation includes a good many paperback books—some of which run well over 200 pages—it also features pamphlets, maps, pictures, posters, and charts. The entries are grouped under 82 headings, which parallel subjects taught in elementary and secondary schools. Cross references are provided between subjects. Size, price, and complete ordering information are given. Grade levels are often noted, and brief descriptions accompany most items. This trusted guide is well worth its modest purchase price. Proof of its usefulness is the fact that it has been published since 1941.

Ruth H. Aubrey's **Selected Free Materials for Classroom Teachers (24)** is now in its sixth edition. Over 500 sources of free teaching materials are listed in the 1978 compilation. The items available from these producers consist of booklets, leaflets, catalogs, posters, charts, periodicals, maps, pictures, and films. Inclusion was made on the basis of appropriateness and usefulness in the classroom. The sources are alphabetically arranged under broad curricular headings, some of which are subdivided. A special section on teachers' aids is included. Under each producer, a descriptive note cites individual titles or the general publishing program of the source. Grade levels are indicated. An extensive subject index is provided. This nominally priced list is a good buy. At the moment, the publisher is undecided about the possibility of future editions.

Another book from the same publisher is Robert Monahan's **Free and Inexpensive Materials for Preschool and Early Childhood (160)**. The second edition was published in 1977. Revisions are planned for every other year. This list includes items for use directly with children, as well as items intended as background or resource material for adults involved with children. In the 1977 edition, titles are arranged under 30 categories such as "Animals and Pets," "Exceptional Children," "Health," "Holidays," and "Language Development." Most titles are annotated. While books, films, flannelboard packets, and even puppets are included, there is a goodly representation of pamphlets, posters, and pictures as well. This list would have its greatest value in elementary school libraries and in libraries serving teacher-training institutions. However, public libraries might also want to screen this list for items about craft projects and for publications that can be used by parents.

Educators Progress Service, Inc. is a well-known name to teachers for the many guides to curricular resources which this firm issues. Among its publications is the **Elementary Teachers Guide to Free Curriculum Materials (82)**. Like all Educators Progress Service productions, it is revised annually, which helps to promote currency and availability. The 1977 edition records 1,875 items from 571 sources. The basic grouping of entries is by curricular categories. There are separate title and subject indexes as well as a source index. Sources willing to supply libraries and schools in Canada and Australia are noted in special indexes. The annotations are informative and often quite chatty. All types of printed materials are represented, including charts, pictures, and maps. One section lists items for the teacher's reference and professional use. This compilation will be of interest to elementary school librarians and children's librarians who want a highly screened list of resources.

Information for Everyday Survival: What You Need and Where to Get It (112) is a publication of the American Library Association. It was developed by the Appalachian Adult Education Center at Morehead State University in Kentucky. The 403 pages of this compilation include over 2,000 pamphlets, books, films, filmstrips, games, tapes, and records. Most items fall into the free and inexpensive range. Although designed for disadvantaged adults, this list offers many leads to vertical file materials suitable for any public. The list is organized under thirteen basic categories, such as aging, community, free time, and education. The basic categories are subdivided into specific subject areas. There is a detailed index. Each entry includes an annotation, indication of physical format, reading level for printed material, and ordering information. The ALA's Subcommittee on Library Service to the Rural Poor and Appalachian People is spearheading an effort to collect titles for a future revision of this practical guide.

A brief but interesting sampling of supplementary materials is offered in **Where to Get Hundreds of Educational Materials—Free! (96)**. It is produced by Frances Press, Publishers. The third edition is to be released early in 1979. The second edition (1975) contains sixteen very general headings under which the entries are informally arranged. While the second edition is only 24 pages long, it contains so many blanket referrals and publications lists that it gives access to much more than its miniature size indicates. Terse descriptive notes are provided.

Laymen, as well as librarians, are delighted to get something for nothing or for a very modest investment. The publishers of trade paperbacks have attempted to cash in on this interest from time to time by bringing out lists of free and inexpensive "things," which include not only samples and services, but printed materials as well. These giveaway guides are fun to read and offer some intriguing clues if you use discrimination in selection. While they won't take the place of the more conventional lists, they are like frosting on the cake. Watch your paperback outlets for new compilations since these lists come and go.

One of the long-term survivors in this area is Mort Weisinger's **1001 Valuable Things You Can Get Free (250)**. The tenth edition was published in 1977. One word of caution! This list contains a number of items which aren't really free. Any charge is described as a postage and handling fee.

Specialized Guides

In addition to general guides to supplementary resources, there are lists which concentrate on special subject areas. These compilations may originate with commercial publishers, educational institutions, organizations, or governmental agencies.

The titles that follow were selected because they are representative of the specialized guides accessible to all types of libraries, from school libraries to special libraries.

From Commercial Publishers

Educators Progress Service, Inc. publishes four lists devoted to specialized subject areas. They are revised annually. These curriculum-oriented compilations are:

Educators Guide to Free Guidance Materials (82),

Educators Guide to Free Health, Physical Education and Recreation Materials (82),

Educators Guide to Free Science Materials (82),

Educators Guide to Free Social Studies Materials (82).

These are reputable lists. The items included are carefully chosen and annotated. The policy of annual revision results in a continual flow of new selections. However, printed materials are heavily outnumbered by filmed items and recordings. The lists do not justify purchase if they are to be used only for the limited inclusion of vertical file materials. On the other hand, they would be helpful aids to any school or public library eager to enhance both its audiovisual services and its printed resources. The lists are available on a 30-day approval plan to allow examination. Since these guides are often represented in curriculum centers, school librarians or public librarians may be able to consult them there.

Media Monitor (151) is a new service intended to alert educators to practical learning resources on topics of current interest. Its range is from kindergarten through grade 12. Four issues of **Media Monitor** are published during the school year. While released under a series title, each issue of **Media Monitor** is an independent list, devoted entirely to a single subject. These specialized lists can be purchased on a subscription basis. Each list can also be ordered individually. The topics chosen for the 1978-1979 lists are "The Oceans: New Frontier," "Our Society of Many Cultures," "Economics for Consumers," and "Mental Health." While filmed resources, recordings, simulation games, and kits appear on the lists, they also cover pamphlets, pictures, posters, photographs, charts, and maps. **Media Monitor** can be recommended to school libraries looking for leads to all types of media in the subject areas surveyed. It would be a more doubtful choice for libraries looking only for vertical file materials. **Media Monitor** is the creation of Mary Robinson Sive, the author of **Selecting Instructional Media: A Guide to Audiovisual and Other Instructional Media Lists (218).**

Each year Dow Jones & Company, Inc. prepares a **List of Free Materials Available to Educators (78)**. Inclusions are based on usefulness to students and teachers in business-related courses. While the guide is primarily directed at college level, some items are suitable for secondary schools. Restrictions on availability are carefully delineated in the entries. A copy of the list will be sent without charge to libraries in secondary schools, colleges, and universities.

Museum Media (245), edited by Paul Wasserman and Esther Herman, provides an introduction to a unique group of resources. This sourcebook was planned to offer bibliographic access to all types of media produced by 732 museums, art galleries, and related institutions in the United States and Canada. Along with other varieties of media there are listings for pamphlets, leaflets, monographs, catalogs, postcards, and color prints. The current edition was published in 1973, but a new edition is planned for the spring of 1979. Its substantial price—presently $62.00—may limit purchase of **Museum Media** to larger public and academic libraries. Representatives of smaller libraries may be able to refer to the list at these centers.

The publishers of trade paperbacks are active in the area of specialized subject guides, too. One of the most recent examples is an Avon Books publication, **A Treasury of Free Cookbooks**, by Patricia Lee Murphy **(166)**. Most of the booklets listed are products of the food industry and its affiliated interest groups. Some come from other sources, such as government agencies. While the publications vary greatly in quality, libraries will find a number of useful items, especially those on ethnic cooking or on the preparation of unusual foods such as buffalo meat.

From Organizations

Organizations offer a fertile field for obtaining specialized lists. The examples which follow are not meant to be comprehensive. They were chosen to illustrate the vast diversity that can be expected in lists from the organization sector.

Clues to some potential acquisitions can be found in **General Aviation Educational Materials (103)**, a free list distributed by the General Aviation Manufacturers Association. It introduces items available from the Association and its members which complement the aviation and science curriculum at all levels. The Association attempts to update the list on a yearly basis.

The Pharmaceutical Manufacturers Association will send you a free copy of **Health Care and the Consumer: A Guide to Informational Materials (200)**. It describes over 200 publications, films, and teaching aids produced by the Association, its member companies, the National Pharmaceutical Council, and the ACT Foundation. There is no charge for most printed materials covered in the list.

The Health Insurance Institute is in the process of preparing a new edition of **Health Education Materials and the Organizations Which Offer Them (121)**. The target publication date is sometime early in 1979. Past editions of this booklet provided librarians with a quick approach to organizations, firms, and government agencies which distribute free or inexpensive literature on all aspects of health. The list will be available free of charge.

Robert Morris Associates produces an annual compilation titled **Sources of Composite Financial Data—A Bibliography (208)**. It can be used to locate statistical materials about business and industry. While some entries carry surprisingly high price tags, there are a number of free or relatively inexpensive items. This list would be of greatest interest to libraries serving businessmen or students of business administration. A fee is charged for the list.

The **Man-Made Fibers Fact Book (148)** has a double usefulness. As well as offering a detailed survey of the industry, it features a list of educational materials from companies and organizations within the industry. Most of the items are free. The **Fact Book** is issued by the Man-Made Fiber Producers Association, Inc. A single copy of the current edition was sent to me without charge, although it carries a price indication of $1.00.

The **Bibliography of Law-Related Curriculum Materials: Annotated (8)** is the work of the American Bar Association's Special Committee on Youth Education for Citizenship. The second edition was published in 1976. It lists more than 1,000 books, pamphlets, kits, newsletters, and journals suitable for grades K-12 or for teacher reference. The annotated entries designate grade level and format. School libraries will find many good vertical file possibilities among the pamphlets covered. A small fee is charged for the list. Although no revision is underway at the present time, the possibility of a third edition within "the next few years" is a good one. In the meantime, new curriculum materials are reported three times a year in a special section of the ABA's magazine, **Update on Law-Related Education (239)**.

Lumber and Wood Products Literature (175) is a list of printed and audiovisual materials available from the federated associations of the National Forest Products Association and from other cooperating organizations. A new edition was published in 1978. This bibliography offers promising suggestions for the vertical file on such topics as forestry, lumber characteristics, and home building. Single copies of the list can be obtained free of charge from the National Forest Products Association.

Critical evaluation is the hallmark of the **Selective Guide to Materials for Mental Health and Family Life Education (153)**. This highly respected list is prepared under the direction of the Mental Health Materials Center, Inc. The third edition, published in 1976, contains some 500 resources which experts have chosen as the best materials in the field. While the list includes books and audiovisual items, it also incorporates many pamphlets and leaflets. The entries are arranged by subject. At least one page is devoted to the description and evaluation of each item. Don't be intimidated because the original purpose of the list was to pinpoint materials for professionals to give to clients or to employ in discussion groups, curriculum planning, or public presentations. The recommended pamphlets and leaflets would make admirable additions to vertical files used by laymen and students. The substantial price of the list may be a deterrent to purchase, but the quality of the list is unquestioned. A fourth edition of the guide is in preparation, with publication scheduled for the spring of 1979. In a departure from past procedures, there will be two volumes—one concerned with audiovisual materials and the second, with printed materials. Distribution of the new edition will be handled by Marquis Who's Who. The time span between future editions will be two years.

From Government Agencies

The Superintendent of Documents is the source of a major set of lists on specific subjects and fields of interest. Called **Subject Bibliographies (226)**, they represent the documents for sale by the U.S. Government Printing Office. There are now over 270 **Subject Bibliographies** covering such diverse topics as minorities, photography, physical fitness, railroads, and oceanography. According to present plans, the number of lists will be expanded. Because of the immensity of the set, a **Subject Bibliography Index** has been prepared to assist in locating specific lists.

Subject Bibliographies are free. Your library can request a full set or check just the lists you want on an order form which the Superintendent of Documents will supply.

Most of the bibliographies are revised on a yearly basis. The policy of regular revisions is a helpful one, since it facilitates the incorporation of new titles, the updating of prices, and the elimination of out-of-print items. You can have your library added to the mailing list to receive revised editions as issued.

No library—large or small—can afford to ignore this series. The lists are important assets for ordering, reference, and interlibrary loan purposes.

From time to time, specialized lists are developed by other units of our national government. One such list is **Selected Federal Publications Concerning the Handicapped (194)**. It is the product of the Office for Handicapped Individuals, U.S. Department of Health, Education, and Welfare. This annotated bibliography presents publications relating to the handicapped which are available from various federal agencies. A new edition was released in the winter of 1978. Single copies of the bibliography may be obtained free from the Office for Handicapped Individuals.

Don't assume that only on the federal level can you find useful compilations in specialized areas. One of the "tried-and-true" standbys is produced by the Department of Public Health of the Commonwealth of Massachusetts. This helpful list is titled **Sources of Free and Inexpensive Health Education Aids (150)**. The latest edition was published in 1978. Single copies are available free of charge.

SERIAL INDEXES AND BIBLIOGRAPHIES

Even the regularly revised compilations mentioned in this chapter involve a time lag. This is where serial indexes and bibliographies can come to the librarian's rescue. They can alert you to new publications soon after their release. Because currency is one of the essential features of an effective collection of supplementary resources, this awareness of new materials is very important. Serial indexes and bibliographies can also keep you informed of changes in publishing programs. Some of these tools include a number of retrospective titles as well as new ones. Such tools perform two functions—informing you of the latest publications and reminding you of significant back titles which are still in print.

From Commercial Publishers

Since 1932, the **Vertical File Index (240)** has been offering one solution to the problem of locating recent publications. The H. W. Wilson Company publishes this list monthly except in August. It presents a rich variety of materials of particular interest to secondary school libraries, public libraries, and libraries in institutions of higher education.

The entries are arranged by subject. Complete ordering information is given. Descriptive notes are included for most items. A title index is provided in each issue for access by the names of publications. At the end of each quarter, the subject headings used during that period are cumulated in a special index.

The cover and introductory portion of the **Vertical File Index** depict it as a guide to pamphlet material. It must be pointed out, however, that some of the so-called pamphlets exceed 200 or 300 pages. From a broad viewpoint, the listing of paperback books might be considered a disguised blessing, since the index can be used as a selection tool for both the vertical files and the book collection.

The publisher's publicity also describes the **Vertical File Index** as a guide to free and inexpensive material. This statement, too, must be accepted with some flexibility. Items for sale far outweigh free materials in the **Vertical File Index**. Even pamphlets of modest size sometimes carry fat price tags. A spot check of 1978 issues revealed a substantial number of items in the range of $3.00 and up.

One final *caveat emptor* is that every entry in the **Vertical File Index** does not represent a new publication. Each recent issue I examined included older titles, which presumably have just come to the attention of the editors. This means that you must watch the publication dates as you make selections.

Despite these cautions, the **Vertical File Index** is an indispensable tool and should be on the subscription list of any library attempting to maintain a thriving vertical file collection. Its longevity is testimony to its helpfulness.

A new experiment in bibliographic tools was launched in 1977 with the appearance of **Sources: A Guide to Print and Nonprint Materials Available from Organizations, Industry, Government Agencies, and Specialized Publishers (222)**. It is a subscription service with three issues a year, scheduled for winter, spring, and fall. Its aim is to provide access to materials published outside normal trade channels that may not be picked up in traditional bibliographic guides. Each issue is to cover some 600 sources, representing about 100 subject areas.

The core of every issue is a directory of sources which gives the purpose of each body, a summary of its information services, and a listing of its print and nonprint materials. The entries are intended to supply the reader with a characterization of each source and not necessarily with a complete listing of its materials. Therefore, the title citations under many sources are representative rather than comprehensive. Among the materials recorded are a number of pamphlets and some posters and charts.

Title and subject indexes are provided in each issue. The subject indexes cumulate throughout the year. Of special significance to the vertical file builder is a separate index of free and inexpensive materials ($1.50 and under), which can be found in every issue. The items in this index are culled from the directory of sources. The $1.50 limit creates some ironic results. There are instances where the index lists a $1.50 pamphlet from a given source, while a similar pamphlet from the same supplier is omitted because it costs a mere $0.30 more.

If a library subscribes to **Sources** for the complete package of information it offers, the leads to vertical file items are welcome bonuses. Purchase is not justified for these items alone, considering the yearly subscription price—set in late 1978 at $60.00. Libraries may want to investigate access through a cooperative network or library system.

Sources is distributed by Gaylord Bros., Inc., in association with Neal-Schuman Publishers, Inc.

Librarians attempting to strengthen their services in the business sector will want to become acquainted with the **Marketing Information Guide (149)**, which is published bimonthly. It is an annotated bibliography of current materials in the fields of marketing and management. Among the entries a careful reader will find some offers of pamphlets, reprints, and special periodical issues which are worth considering. But beware—prices are sometimes steep! I would not advise subscribing to the **Marketing Information Guide** if your only interest is to find vertical file materials. However, if the **Guide** is used as a general purchasing and reference aid, it is worth considering for a business, academic, or larger public library.

From Government Agencies

Since the United States Government Printing Office is the world's largest publisher, it is both a golden opportunity and a real challenge to keep up with the many publications that continuously pour out of the federal presses. Fortunately, the federal government also provides serial indexes and bibliographies that will help you cope with this avalanche of materials.

The most comprehensive listing of newly released federal documents is the **Monthly Catalog of United States Government Publications (162)**. As well as recording publications for sale by the Superintendent of Documents, it also lists publications which are available from the issuing agencies. The expanded and improved indexes have made it easier to employ the **Monthly Catalog** as a tool for selecting and ordering supplementary resources.

Careful study of each monthly issue for possible acquisitions is a process usually limited to the larger library or the special library. Yet even in small libraries, the **Monthly Catalog** will frequently prove useful in running down ordering information for documents that are desired for the collection.

Even the most enthusiastic user of the **Monthly Catalog** will have to admit that there are certain limitations in this serial bibliography. Its listings do not include all publications produced by federal agencies. In addition, there is sometimes a serious time lag between the issuance of a document and its appearance in the catalog. In spite of these drawbacks, the **Monthly Catalog** remains the major tool for tracking federal documents.

Every library should be on the free mailing list to receive **Selected U.S. Government Publications (216)**, which is distributed eleven times a year. Each issue of this annotated guide contains a selection of "newly released or still popular" publications for sale by the Superintendent of Documents. It provides a convenient sampling of documents likely to be of general interest. Brand-new titles rub shoulders with old standard items on its pages.

It should be pointed out that **Selected U.S. Government Publications** does not include materials designed for free distribution by their originating agency. Nor does it list publications sold only through the distribution service of an individual agency.

Selected U.S. Government Publications can be a good jumping-off point in your search for government documents. But it shouldn't be the end of your quest.

Another free serial index of great importance to libraries is the **Consumer Information Catalog: A Catalog of Selected Federal Publications of Consumer Interest**. This guide is issued quarterly by the Consumer Information Center **(60)**. It is crammed with practical publications on everything from automobiles to nutrition. The titles chosen are geared to the layman. A large number of items are free. The remainder are modestly priced. As well as new titles, selected earlier publications of merit are included. Any publication listed can be ordered through the Consumer Information Center. A companion guide to Spanish-language publications is described in chapter 4.

Some individual departments and agencies of the federal government prepare serial bibliographies of their own publications. One of the more ambitious publicity projects involves the U.S. Department of Commerce, which produces a biweekly guide to its publications under the title, **Business Service Checklist (43)** (replaced in

January 1979 by **Recent Commerce Publications**). Another example is the Bureau of Mines, which offers a free monthly listing called **New Publications—Bureau of Mines (188)**.

Serial lists issued by governmental agencies are not limited to reporting federal publications. There are useful serial bibliographies which give access to state documents.

The best-known aid in this field is the **Monthly Checklist of State Publications (163)**, which is compiled by the Library of Congress. It is arranged alphabetically, first by the geographical entity and then by the issuing agency. Frankly, some of the inclusions for university publications are esoteric enough to tickle even a tired librarian's funnybone. However, the **Checklist** also incorporates such practical items as state road maps, cooperative extension service bulletins, publicity brochures, and hunting, fishing, and trapping regulations. As well as introducing you to useful publications from other states, the **Checklist** will also help you to fulfill your special obligation to collect documents of your own state.

As valuable as the **Checklist** is, it does have limitations. Since it is a record of state documents submitted to the Library of Congress, the cooperation of state agencies is essential. If a state neglects to send certain publications or is tardy in sending them, these oversights are reflected in the **Checklist**.

Many states issue serial lists of documents originating with agencies in the state government. The state library is often charged with the responsibility of preparing such serial lists.

Foreign governments also produce serial indexes and bibliographies. An interesting example is a list called **Selected Titles (215)**, which is distributed by the Canadian Government Publishing Centre. It is a survey of priced Government of Canada publications. Many pamphlet-sized items and a number of charts are included. The list is issued three times a year.

From Organizations

Serial indexes and bibliographies can be sponsored by associations. In its issue for the fifteenth of the month, the American Library Association's **Booklist** features a column labeled "United States Government Publications." The entries represent a selection of documents particularly suited for consideration by public and school libraries. Annotations and ordering information are given.

A serial tool for locating business materials is prepared by the Advertising and Marketing Division of the Special Libraries Association. **What's New in Advertising and Marketing (251)** lists both books and pamphlets. The entries are of interest to public libraries as well as special libraries in the business field. The list is published ten times a year.

Even in highly technical areas, there are serial indexes which offer clues to vertical file acquisitions. Three serial publications sponsored by professional organizations in the nursing and hospital fields can serve as illustrations.

The **Cumulative Index to Nursing & Allied Health Literature (67)** has an appendix listing pamphlets at the back of each issue, including the annual cumulative volume. These lists offer promising leads. Unfortunately, it is necessary to backtrack to the journal which originally mentioned each pamphlet to obtain the information needed for evaluating and ordering the publication. The index is published by the Seventh-Day Adventist Hospital Association.

Each quarterly issue of the American Hospital Association's **Hospital Literature Index (130)** contains a section at the back listing recent acquisitions to the Association's library. The list appears in the annual cumulative volume as well as in the three previous issues. The entries are arranged by subject. While books and journals are included, the lists contain enough pamphlet-type material to justify screening for vertical file purposes. Prices are not given.

It may be stretching definitions a bit to discuss the **International Nursing Index (135)** in this section, since it has a trade publisher; but it does exist under the sponsorship of two organizations, the American Nurses' Association and the National League for Nursing. Each quarterly issue, including the annual cumulative volume, incorporates a list of relevant publications from organizations and agencies around the world which are interested in nursing. Some clues to vertical file materials can be found in these lists.

PUBLICATIONS LISTS

Publications lists can be wonderful allies in building your supplementary resource collection. Accumulate all you can. As well as assisting in your ordering activities, they serve other purposes as well. For the patron who wants to investigate a particular group or agency, its publications list offers a quick profile of its purpose and philosophy. The public welcomes such lists, too, for its own ordering needs. No library can afford to stock every item on every list. But if you have lists available, your patrons will be able to select special materials to order for their own collections. Finally, publications lists can be used to initiate interlibrary loans.

Publications lists can be gathered from a variety of sources.

From Government Agencies

At the federal level, there are many agencies which compile lists of their publications. Some are comprehensive in nature. Others are selective. In most cases you can obtain a free copy by writing directly to the issuing office. To give an indication of the wealth of lists available, here are just a few of the United States government agencies which have publications lists for distribution:

> Administration on Aging
>
> Bureau of Community Health Services
>
> Food and Drug Administration
>
> Library of Congress
>
> National Highway Traffic Safety Administration
>
> Small Business Administration
>
> U.S. Department of Agriculture

At the state level, it is also profitable to approach individual agencies for their publications lists. The most obvious use of such lists is to obtain material about your own state which will have current usefulness and possible historical value in the years to come. However, there are publications lists issued through state agencies which transcend state boundaries. Among the best-known examples are the lists of the cooperative extension services affiliated with land-grant universities. These lists are treasure-troves of practical pamphlets for the farm, home, and garden. Further instances are the publications lists of both the Hogg Foundation for Mental Health at the University of Texas and the Rutgers Center of Alcohol Studies at Rutgers University.

Even publications lists from foreign governments may be helpful ordering mechanisms for some libraries. For example, the Canadian Government Department of External Affairs offers a free catalog of its English-language publications. It is titled **Publications Available Outside Canada (46).**

From Organizations

This nation is blessed with an awesome number of organizations dedicated to an equally awesome variety of interests. Many have extensive publishing programs and offer free catalogs of their output. Here are just a few of the many groups that will supply you with lists of their materials:

Alcoholics Anonymous

American Council of Life Insurance

American Humane Association

American Medical Association

League of Women Voters of the United States

National Association for Retarded Citizens

National Concrete Masonry Association

National Wildlife Federation

From the Commercial World

Publications lists from commercial publishers are important acquisitions for any library with a real commitment to its supplementary resource collection. Catalogs or price lists of the better-known pamphlet series should be part of your ordering equipment. Some of these pamphlet series are described in chapter 4 and chapter 6.

In addition, watch for lists from companies that engage in publishing only as a peripheral operation or as a public relations effort. A unique example is the publications list produced by the Eastman Kodak Company. Eastman Kodak's major activity is not publishing, but to complement its manufacture of photographic products, it publishes more than 800 books, guides, and pamphlets relating to these products and to photographic techniques. Each year it issues an **Index to**

Kodak Information (79) listing these publications, many of which are potential vertical file resources.

The publications list of the Metropolitan Life Insurance Company is an example of a more limited publishing program carried on as an adjunct operation. Metropolitan's **Catalog: Health and Safety Educational Materials (156)** includes a number of useful pamphlets and pictorial items.

PERIODICALS

Periodicals can provide invaluable assistance in your efforts to keep up with the changing world of supplementary resources. Some boast of formal lists; others offer more incidental references. However they're presented, all of these clues are worth considering.

Popular Periodicals

The popular magazines are surprisingly rich in leads.

In alternate months, **Changing Times: The Kiplinger Magazine** includes a full-page feature, "Things to Write For." It offers a selection of useful pamphlets, reports, and circulars available either gratis or for a small fee. Annotations are included for all entries.

Family Handyman incorporates a department called "Information: Literature on Subjects of Interest to Do-it-yourselfers." It describes free and inexpensive publications which will appeal to the handyman or hobbyist. Many are good vertical file possibilities.

In its special section, "The Better Way," **Good Housekeeping** sets aside a portion of one page for a listing of booklets which it recommends. Descriptive notes are provided.

The "Right Now" portion of **McCall's** often includes suggestions of places to write for information that would bolster your vertical files. Leads to interesting materials can also be found in the "Mini Mag" section of **Seventeen**.

It would be a mistake to end your surveillance with these patterned listings. Additional hints can occur almost anywhere in a periodical.

Feature articles may mention helpful pamphlets which the reader can acquire or sources to which one can write for literature.

The subject-oriented columns or departments that appear regularly in a magazine deserve particular attention. A pet column, a money management forum, a news roundup, a section on careers for women, or a monthly feature on household hints may contain good leads to significant materials. Question-and-answer columns to which readers appeal for information are especially good hunting grounds.

Even the ads displayed in magazines are worth scanning. Using this technique, I've discovered some unusual handicraft booklets offered by manufacturers of various household products.

Alongside advertisements for vitamins and vacations, you may occasionally find announcements of reprints, plans, catalogs, and booklets which the periodical itself publishes and offers for sale. **Better Homes and Gardens, Woman's Day,**

Family Circle, and **Good Housekeeping** are examples of popular magazines with active publishing programs which announce their wares in their own pages.

Other Periodicals

Periodicals that never appear on the local newsstands can also furnish suggestions for supplementary resources.

Such periodicals may be allied to a profession.

In the library field, a helpful source is the **Library Journal**. It has a regular column called "Checklist" that is devoted to free and relatively inexpensive materials. While some of the entries are of professional interest only, other titles would make excellent additions to vertical files serving library patrons. Special emphasis is placed on bibliographies. A similar column appears in **SLJ/School Library Journal**.

Wilson Library Bulletin each month contains a jaunty newsletter called "The Librarian's Monthly Almanac." It's well worth scanning for leads to booklets, bibliographies, posters, and catalogs.

Periodicals affiliated with the teaching profession can be of assistance, too. Each year the **English Journal** features a listing of sources of free and inexpensive materials. **Science and Children** has a section called "Ad-vailables." Every issue of **Today's Education** carries a column describing free or inexpensive items. **Energy & Education (86)**, a newsletter from the National Science Teachers Association, also incorporates a list of free and inexpensive resources. A compilation of recent publications from federal agencies or federally funded projects is included in each issue of **American Education**. The **NASA Report to Educators (167)** announces "Recent NASA Publications and Films."

The library and teaching professions have been singled out here to provide examples. Journals and newsletters in other professions can be just as productive. The axiom is to search the periodicals in any professional field which your library emphasizes.

Periodicals keyed to special business activities may give access to supplementary resources. **Automotive Industries** is a good illustration. Not only does it offer free single copies of its feature articles, but it also contains columns on technical literature and new products, which can be consulted for vertical file leads.

Attention should be given to periodicals issued by associations to reflect the interests of their members. While some are related to the professional and business realms already mentioned, there are many which tap other interest areas. **Dynamic Years** is an example. This magazine for "working Americans in their middle years" is published by Action for Independent Maturity (AIM), a division of the American Association of Retired Persons. AIM is producing a growing series of pamphlet-sized "guidebooks," which it announces in the pages of **Dynamic Years**. The articles and columns in the magazine also contain frequent referrals to pamphlets available from other sources.

Similarly, government periodicals can touch on many aspects of interest. **American Education** and the **NASA Report to Educators** have already been cited. These citations merely hint at the many federal periodicals which are potential guides to supplementary materials. For example, in each issue of the **Family Economics Review (88)**, there is a sampling of recent U.S. Department of

Agriculture publications, many of which are desirable vertical file items. This quarterly report is distributed free by USDA's Consumer and Food Economics Institute. Readers of **Consumer News (61)**, a semimonthly newsletter from the U.S. Office of Consumer Affairs, will find clues to supplementary resources sprinkled through its pages. These leads include publications from the private sector as well as from government agencies. The U.S. Department of Energy's biweekly **Energy Insider (87)** contains a column of pertinent new publications in the field. Some are highly technical, others of more general interest.

While these examples come from the federal level, don't stop with United States government periodicals in your search for supplementary materials. Remember that state agencies may list useful titles in their newsletters, too.

NEWSPAPERS

Newspapers can report supplementary materials as well as current events.

The prospects for lucky finds are particularly high in the columns and sections of a newspaper that are devoted to special interests. The garden column may list booklets on African violets or poinsettias. Regular columns dedicated to such diverse groups as CB'ers, stamp enthusiasts, and antique collectors can sometimes furnish leads. The daily health feature often includes offers of authoritative leaflets by the physician who conducts the column. Homemaking columns frequently contain pamphlet suggestions. The outdoor page often alerts sportsmen to such helpful items as newly printed fishing and hunting regulations. Financial columnists may suggest guides to investments or income taxes. Travel pages offer a variety of sources of information for the vacationer. Even the advice-to-the-lovelorn column has on occasion produced some useful recommendations.

Currently, there is a great proliferation of direct action columns in newspapers which offer the know-how and influence of the press in answering calls for help from readers. These services carry such names as "Action Line," "Trouble Shooter," or "Ask Us." In replying to requests for information, these columns sometimes suggest such resources as pamphlets or maps.

DIRECTORIES

When librarians consult directories, they usually do so in the course of answering reference questions. Directories can also serve as acquisition devices by helping librarians track down sources of supplementary materials for their collections.

No better example could be found than the **Encyclopedia of Associations (84)**. This reference tool is the "open, sesame" to organizations in every arena of activity from whale preservation to rodeos. Using it, you can contact groups which are the best prospects for publishing or distributing information in select subject areas.

The **United States Government Manual (236)** can be a valuable partner in your search for pertinent federal documents. By studying this guide, you can determine which agencies are likely to be involved in producing the material you need. Sources of information within each agency are suggested. Contact addresses are provided. Frequently, even individual publication titles are listed. The manual is revised annually.

Help can also be obtained from directories which concentrate on narrower spheres of interest. One example is the **Conservation Directory: A List of Organizations, Agencies, and Officials Concerned with Natural Resource Use and Management (187).** This directory is issued annually by the National Wildlife Federation.

No discussion of directories would be complete without a mention of your local telephone directory. If you examine the classified section, you will find lists of organizations, institutions, and governmental units that can provide you with important reinforcements for your files.

BOOKSHELF BROWSING FOR LEADS

While certain titles and certain categories of books have been singled out for recognition in this chapter, don't forget that clues to supplementary resources may be found in the pages of many books in your library collection. You can prove this by leafing through the "catalog" and "yellow pages" volumes which have been so popular recently. The **Parents' Yellow Pages (48)** is an appropriate example. Scattered throughout this compendium of information are a number of profitable leads to pamphlets and posters.

In this chapter, you have been introduced to some of the ways of locating supplementary resources. No matter how numerous or varied the tools are which you choose to use, there is one inescapable truth you must keep in mind. You will never be able to fold your arms and say, "Well, that's done!" A collection of supplementary resources is a dead collection unless it is constantly being replenished. Nourishing such a collection is an eternal undertaking.

CHAPTER 2

TECHNICAL AND MECHANICAL PROCESSES:
GENERAL ASPECTS

Since the supplementary resources described in this book represent a variety of specialized collections and materials, only the technical and mechanical procedures which are widely applicable will be discussed in this chapter. Techniques which are structured to fit a particular type of material such as maps or pictures will be covered in separate chapters.

ORDERING

Postcards are appropriate for most routine requests for free materials. Form postcards can be invaluable time-savers. Below is a sample of one form for soliciting free material:

We would welcome a free copy of the following publication(s) for our information files:

Please add our library to your mailing list for future editions. Thank you for your assistance.

File Librarian
Smith Memorial Library
111 Main Street
Morris, Michigan 49010

Form postcards can be tailored to special needs. For example, if you want to conduct a mass mailing campaign aimed at local chambers of commerce, you might use a form postcard such as the one on page 36. Desired items can be circled or checked if you do not need the full gamut of materials.

Under most circumstances, form letters offer little advantage over form postcards. I have yet to see a form letter that wasn't easily pegged as a form letter even when "disguised" with typed headings and handwritten signatures. Since they are so obviously mass produced, they are unlikely to call forth any warm, personal response.

We would welcome complimentary copies of the following materials for our files:

    Map of your area

    Recreational opportunities in your area

    General information about your community

Thank you.

    Travel Files
    Mitchell Public Library
    215 Michigan Avenue
    Mitchell, Michigan 42020

It should also be kept in mind that most requests for free materials are handled by clerks far down in the ranks who are going to treat form letters with the same degree of nonchalance that they reserve for postcards. In fact, form letters may even spark annoyance because of the extra time required to read what might have been condensed on a postcard.

Since there are exceptions to all generalizations, I must admit that I have seen form letters used effectively on rare occasions. One such instance involved a form letter developed by a brand-new library. In an appealing fashion, the letter explained the status of the library and invited organizations to send complimentary materials to help build a young and growing facility. Another instance occurred at our own library when we designed a special form letter to request information on Christmas observances in various countries. The letters were deliberately made short and succinct. They were sent to the embassies of various nations and drew a generous response. The use of form letters should be reserved for exceptional situations such as those just noted.

Individually written letters are a much more expensive method of solicitation than either form postcards or form letters. Yet there are certain situations that call for such individualized communications:

1.   If special explanations are necessary or personalized attention is being requested, a letter is more appropriate.

2.   When the source is an unusual one—unaccustomed to handling requests for materials—a letter will help to smooth the way.

3.   If the supply of an item is limited, a letter may have a better chance of receiving first attention.

When such letters are sent, they should be on the institution's letterhead.

In making requests for material, indicate that it is to be sent to a particular person, position, or collection. This will save time in sorting mail. While letters customarily call for a signature, you can change this pattern when you use form postcards. Instead of a person's name, you can substitute a position designation such as "File Librarian" or a collection designation such as "Travel Files." By avoiding personal names, you will eliminate the confusion caused by changes in staff.

Money and effort can be saved by asking to be placed on mailing lists for free materials. While some sources have abandoned mailing lists, there are still many organizations, institutions, and agencies that are willing to continue this courtesy.

Take advantage of the readers' service postcards which some magazines include for the convenience of their subscribers.

If you anticipate heavy usage or the need to provide access under more than one subject heading, it would be logical to ask for two copies at the time of the original request or order.

In ordering materials marked with restrictions such as "For teachers only," your library imprint will usually erase all barriers. As a safeguard, you may include a statement to the effect that your library serves the group in question.

Should free material be requested by title? Or is it better to place subject requests? Asking for a specific title is appropriate if you are soliciting a newly published item, a particularly significant or unique publication, or a title mentioned in a recognized list of free materials.

It must be pointed out, however, that there are hazards in requesting specific titles, especially older materials. If the item you are seeking is out of print, you may get nothing at all in response to your communication. If the title you request is still available, a clerk may send it to you while ignoring newer and better materials filed alongside.

Subject requests can sometimes be more productive than title requests. When making them, be careful to precisely define the topics that interest you. If you are serving a particular type of clientele, indicate that also. Avoid vague requests such as "Send all your publications." If you're unsure about the output of a particular source, ask for a list of their publications. You can then order more intelligently and profitably.

When you order a new edition of a publication, retain the old edition in your files until the replacement arrives. But pencil a note on the outside indicating that a revision has been requested. The date of the request should also be recorded. If a reply is received indicating that no new edition is available, you may decide to keep the old edition in the collection. In this case, make a note on the face of the item indicating that no new edition is obtainable.

Check old addresses before using them. Organizations and businesses move frequently these days, and the Postal Service will forward mail for only one year.

To cut postal costs, you may want to investigate the bulk mailing permit which the United States Postal Service makes available to nonprofit organizations. The permit presently costs $40.00 a year. With this permit, organizations can qualify for a postal rate for postcards and envelopes which is currently set at $0.027 per item. Bulk mailing permits offer impressive savings in postage, but they also carry rigid restrictions. Messages must be mass produced. They cannot be individualized by a typewritten or handwritten addition such as the title of a pamphlet. This means that solicitation requests must be written in very generalized terms. To qualify for a bulk mail rate, postcards or envelopes must be mailed in lots of 200. They must be sorted by the mailer.

The requirements accompanying a bulk mailing permit are restrictive, but they are not insurmountable. The public library in Portage, Michigan, employs this technique to request free materials. This library has conducted successful mass mailings for materials from such sources as chambers of commerce and from organizations publishing career material.

If you are interested in the possibility of using a bulk mailing permit, ask for more detailed information at your local post office so that you can carefully weigh the benefits against the disadvantages.

As distribution costs rise, more suppliers will be asking you to send a mailing label or a stamped, self-addressed envelope (s.a.e.) with your request. While there seems to be no good way to minimize the cost and nuisance of s.a.e.s, one library has devised a clever method of dealing with the demands for mailing labels. The Brooklyn (New York) College Library uses a peelable return mailing label on their request postcards **(102)**. The label carries a notation that it is to be used for the return mailing. This system allows the library to retain the economy of a postcard while still providing the required mailing label.

Special techniques are sometimes required in buying federal documents.

If you are ordering publications from the Public Documents Distribution Center in Pueblo, Colorado, or from the Superintendent of Documents in Washington, D.C., you may elect one of two methods of payment:

1. Check or money order

2. A deposit account against which purchases are charged

Foreign libraries are subject to other payment requirements.

Be sure to read instructions carefully when you order from lists such as the **Monthly Catalog, Selected U.S. Government Publications**, the **Consumer Information Catalog**, or the **Subject Bibliographies**. The ordering regulations are complex and stringent. Be sure to follow the requirements spelled out in the list you are using.

While some regulations may be irksome, the turn-around time in delivery of federal documents has been revolutionized. The average delivery time from the Superintendent of Documents is now 12 to 15 days contrasted to the long waits of the past.

Since Congress now requires that the sale of federal publications be on a self-sustaining basis, prices are subject to frequent changes. Librarians who have access to the **GPO Sales Publications Reference File (99)** and its updates can check current prices by using this tool. The PRF is a complete sales catalog of the GPO on microfiche. It is issued bimonthly, and an updating service is also available for the alternate months. A subscription to the PRF is expensive. You may be able to consult it at depository libraries or at larger public or academic libraries.

As well as providing distribution through the mails, the Government Printing Office maintains 25 bookstores across the country.

Some federal units outside the Government Printing Office have been designated as official sales agents of the Superintendent of Documents. For example, publications of the Department of Commerce are available for sale at a number of its district offices as well as from the Superintendent of Documents. New publications of the Bureau of Labor Statistics can be ordered through the Bureau's regional offices as well as through the Superintendent of Documents.

In addition to such joint sales arrangements, there are some governmental publications which are for sale *only* by the issuing agency or its authorized representatives. The most striking examples occur in the area of maps. You will find a discussion of this practice in chapter 8.

When unusual provisions are made for the sale of federal documents, you can expect to find them described in the publications lists or announcements of the agency involved.

For an excellent introduction to the intricacies of ordering U.S. government publications, write to the Superintendent of Documents for a free copy of the **Consumers Guide to Federal Publications (62).**

Should you keep records of the requests you make for vertical file materials? The answer depends upon the nature of the materials and the nature of the requests.

When supplementary materials must be purchased, a record should be kept of outstanding orders. This is necessary to account for expenditures and to avoid unplanned duplications. The pattern this record takes will depend upon the ordering routine practiced in your institution. Whatever the system, there should be an order card or some comparable notation on file for every item ordered.

Do not throw order records away when the materials arrive. With the addition of a sequential number and a notation of the subject heading chosen, you may have the makings of a simple circulation system. More will be said about this later.

What about keeping comprehensive records of requests when free materials are involved?

There are circumstances when it is appropriate to keep some type of record for materials that are available without charge. If you are choosing items from a list of free and inexpensive materials, it is useful to mark any entries which you have decided to pursue. This will give you a quick picture of the status quo if you consult the same list again. It is also important to keep notes of contacts made for free publications destined for local history files. Here a follow-up is necessary if the needed items are not promptly received. In addition, you might want to keep a "tickler" file for certain statistical annuals—both free and priced—which are a critical part of your general files. You may also discover that a combined address and check-in file for college catalogs can expedite the annual chore of updating these resources.

Selective records such as those cited can be helpful without being burdensome.

On the other hand, it would be a wasteful and unnecessary operation to attempt to keep records for all free materials requested.

Not all librarians agree with this stand. In their book, **How to Organize and Maintain the Library Picture/Pamphlet File (113),** Geraldine Gould and Ithmer Wolfe recommend a system of controlling requests for free publications which involves a three-section card file. The first section is devoted to a list of sources which have been approached for free material and from which replies have not yet been received. The date of the request is noted. When a response is received, the record card is transferred to the second section of the file after a description and evaluation of the incoming material is added. The subject heading chosen for the material is also indicated on the card. Notations are made of items which are judged inappropriate for the collection. In the third section of the file are subject cards on which are listed all sources from which free material has been received on a given topic. Records are also kept for "dead" sources. The authors maintain that in actual operation this is a simple system which saves staff time.

Despite their sincere endorsement, I continue to believe that the time used in detailed record keeping might be better spent in canvassing more sources for more free materials. You may infrequently find that you have sent two requests to the same agency. However, this occasional lapse consumes far less time than typing and leafing through lengthy packs of records. If the librarian occasionally suspects that an item has already been received, it's an easy matter to check holdings and circulation records—much easier than maintaining an inventory of every single item requested. The charm of free material is that it does not sap the library's finances. Part of this economy can be dissipated by keeping involved order records.

Attempting to use such records as an evaluative checklist of sources or as a list of contacts on given subjects has its limitations, too. In a rapidly changing world, such a list loses its currency almost at the moment of creation. Company and organization policies are altered frequently. New publications programs are started, others abandoned. Yesterday's "dead" source might be tomorrow's darling.

If you feel the need for checklists on given subjects, turn to the many compilations of free and inexpensive materials which are published periodically. It's much cheaper and just as productive to use them.

Bargain Hunting

It's a delightful and heady experience for a financially pressed librarian to discover that materials which have a price indicated can often be obtained free. This is true even in these days of rising costs.

Many organizations will contribute complimentary copies of their publications to libraries. Be sure that the word, "library," is prominently displayed on your request.

Even when national organizations insist on a fee for their publications, you may be able to obtain free copies by approaching state or local chapters.

In acquiring federal documents, money can be saved by using the right approach. Federal agencies will often provide single free copies of publications which are offered for sale by the Superintendent of Documents. It pays to directly solicit individual offices. The component agencies of the Public Health Service are good examples. In most cases, they will furnish libraries with single complimentary copies of their publications, even when they are GPO sales items.

Another technique for acquiring federal documents free of charge is to cultivate your local congressional representative, who has access to many publications. Election years are particularly opportune times to encourage this relationship.

Pamphlet Jobbers

In an effort to centralize the acquisition of pamphlets, some libraries turn to firms which are variously known as pamphlet jobbers, pamphlet services, or pamphlet agents. While their numbers have diminished, there are still firms performing this function.

The arguments for ordering materials through these middlemen rather than directly are these:

1. It simplifies bookkeeping.

2. It cuts down on correspondence.

3. It facilitates follow-ups on unfilled orders.

The reaction to these jobbers among librarians is mixed.

Some small libraries with staffs that are limited in number or lacking in training welcome these services eagerly.

On the other hand, I have heard complaints about the length of time it takes for orders to be filled. Other complaints have dealt with incomplete orders which dragged on for months and unrequested duplicates which had to be mailed back.

A major drawback is that some agencies will not accept orders for free materials.

Among the established pamphlet jobbers are the following:

1. Bacon Pamphlet Service, Inc. **(27)**
   Will accept orders for any pamphlet or paperbound book published in the U.S. or Canada unless it is free. This includes documents from the U.S. Government Printing Office and the Queen's Printer in Canada. Service charge on orders under $5.00.

2. William-Frederick Press **(253)**
   Will accept orders for free materials as well as for pamphlets and paperbacks that are for sale. Service charge of $0.20 per title (not per copy), plus postage.

My preference is for placing orders directly with publishers or sponsoring organizations because of the quick, uncomplicated contact this establishes. Pamphlets may go out of stock if too much time is consumed in working through an intermediary. Speedy acquisition is particularly important when pamphlets deal with topics of intense and immediate interest. In addition, direct responses from publishers or organizations will frequently furnish leads to other publications.

Still I recognize that in some libraries the use of a pamphlet jobber may spell the difference between having a viable pamphlet file or having one that is moribund.

If you are interested, the pamphlet services will provide you with descriptive literature. It is also helpful to talk with librarians who have used these agencies.

A modified form of pamphlet jobber is the firm which offers sets of vertical file materials on selected subjects of great current interest. Library Reference Service **(144)** is an example. The possibility of acquiring 50 items on child abuse in one fell swoop is certainly an appealing one. However, before making any wholesale commitment to a firm dealing in vertical file sets, it would be wise to sample one subject packet. This will enable you to determine the currency and appropriateness of the publications supplied by that dealer.

INITIAL PROCESSING

When all of your solicitations and orders begin to bear fruit, you must have an efficient routine established to cope with these acquisitions.

As you open envelopes or wrappers, do not discard them until you make sure that the name and address of the issuing body is repeated on the enclosed publication. In a surprisingly large number of cases, identification is incomplete or entirely lacking on the pamphlet, poster, or map. Such omissions must be corrected by adding the information by hand. Why?

1. A source indication is necessary to determine whether the information is authoritative.

2. A source indication will reveal the purpose or thrust of a publication, alerting the user to any slant or bias that may be present.

3. A source indication is important to students who are required to incorporate full bibliographic information in their reports.

4. Identification of the supplier is essential when new editions are needed or when patrons desire to obtain personal copies.

Every newly received item should be stamped immediately with the date of receipt. The need for this step is obvious when the item itself carries no indication of date. In this rapidly changing world, it is imperative to know the currency of the information you're dealing with. While the date the librarian applies does not necessarily equate with the date of publication, it at least gives an indication of the period when the item was being actively distributed.

Do not skip this step even when the item itself carries an indication of its publication date. When your request for the latest edition of a statistical publication produces one that was released two years ago, your date stamp will indicate that this was the newest compilation available at the time of receipt.

Dating a pamphlet or leaflet in a prominent place will also be useful to the inexperienced patron who is not skillful at hunting for the publisher's indication which is often fairly well concealed or disguised with a code.

Even busy librarians welcome a quickly discernible indication of date. Seeing a date for 1976 stamped on the cover of a pamphlet will immediately warn you that you won't find the latest figures on taxation in this particular pamphlet. A readily observable receipt date also speeds the process of weeding.

Dating can be expedited by the use of a band dater on which the month, day, and year can be changed. These daters, which come in various sizes, can be purchased in office supply stores or from library supply houses. Band daters, made to order, are available with the library's name incorporated into the stamp. Check the yellow pages of your phone book for rubber stamp firms which can supply such custom-made daters.

In applying the date stamp or combined name and date stamp, care should be taken that no important printed material is obscured.

If the cover of a pamphlet is too dark or too glossy to accept stamping, apply the date notation to the first inside page.

New material should also be marked with an indication of its cost or free status. This can be useful information to the librarian deciding on replacement or to the patron who wants to obtain a personal copy. It's desirable to place this information in the same spot each time to facilitate location. In pamphlets a good location is at the top inner corner of the first inside page. A small check can be added to show that order records have been cleared. This same location is a good spot to record source information when it is not given in the item itself.

Indication of library ownership should be stamped on each publication. This can be applied with a separate stamp or, as indicated earlier, with a band dater incorporating the library's name.

If your library has more than one department or division which collects supplementary materials, it's wise to include the department or division name in the possession stamp. In this way, vertical file material from the children's room won't be confused with vertical file material from the reference department.

Unless the name of your library clearly indicates its location, it's a good idea to include the address in your possession stamp. Since people move so frequently these days, library materials often turn up in far-distant places.

This is the strategic time for a rough sorting of incoming materials according to their eventual disposition—maps, general pamphlets, vocational monographs, pictorial material, local history, etc. Such an initial sorting helps to make these resources available for emergency reference use even if processing cannot be completed for some time.

Once this division has been accomplished, the materials are ready for incorporation into the library's files.

ORGANIZATION

The usefulness of supplementary resources is determined to a large extent by the way they are organized. The scheme of organization must be simple to use and provide quick, thorough access to the material. The choicest pamphlets, pictures, and maps lose their value if you must depend on flashes of memory, blind intuition, or sheer chance to locate them.

Unfortunately, supplementary resources are so diversified in format and use that it is impossible to wrap them all up in one neat little organizational package. Pictures present different organizational problems than pamphlets. Vocational monographs offer some organizational complications that are not associated with college catalogs. Because these variations are inescapable, the organization of the different types of materials will have to be considered individually in later chapters.

LABELING

Speed in finding and filing supplementary resources is directly related to the manner in which they are marked.

Once again the varied nature of supplementary resources may call for a variety of approaches. This is true of pictures and maps. Their special labeling problems will be discussed in the chapters devoted to these materials.

As you establish your labeling procedures, beware of certain common traps. The first consists of merely underlining words in the cover titles of pamphlets or in the headlines of clippings to serve as guides to placement. The few seconds gained by omitting proper labeling will be lost many times over in the filing process. Headings which are instantly recognizable and uniformly placed do much to reduce filing time.

A second pitfall to avoid is penciled headings. The theory behind this practice is that headings on supplementary resources are subject to change and, therefore, should be in pencil to permit easy alteration. The need for occasional heading revisions does not justify penciling. Penciled headings are not bold enough to begin with. To compound the problem, they quickly become faded and smudged. Not only are they difficult to read, but they are messy looking as well. It is not hard to effect a heading change even when the original is inked or typed. A gummed label or pressure-sensitive label can be applied in no more time than it takes to erase old lettering.

Is it better to hand print headings or make labels on the typewriter? Many librarians prefer typewritten labels because they are always uniform in appearance while printing ability varies from staff member to staff member. The usual procedure is to type the headings on labels which are then applied to the items themselves. Thin leaflets or flyers, however, can be inserted directly into the typewriter. Some libraries use special typewriters which have extra-large type in an effort to increase legibility.

I would cast my vote for handprinted headings. It's a rare staff that cannot produce at least one clerk or student assistant who can letter neatly and legibly. Handprinted headings are much more forceful than typed headings, thereby facilitating quick identification. They usually can be applied directly to the material or folder, saving the cost of adhesive labels as well as the time needed to adhere them.

Choosing a favorite brand of marking pens is a highly individual process, much like selecting shoes. There are many makes of fine-line marking pens available in a variety of colors. You will want a pen that has a bold line but that is fine enough to form clear letters in the space available. Try out prospective choices on difficult letters such as "e."

From time to time, there will be pamphlet covers which are so dark that direct handprinting is impossible. Some libraries cut out a section of the cover and print on the page below. An easier and better solution is to apply an adhesive label and print on that. Adhesive labels will also solve the problem of high gloss covers to which ink will not adhere.

Two basic types of adhesive labels are available. One is the gummed label, which must be moistened before application. The other is the pressure-sensitive label, which needs only to be smoothed into place. Adhesive labels are offered in a variety of sizes and designs. They can also be bought in a wide range of solid colors or with color bands.

The location of subject headings on supplementary resources is important in achieving effective use of these materials. A uniform spot should be selected for the placement of the headings. On pamphlets, leaflets, and mounted clippings, headings should be at the upper left-hand corner as the item will stand in the file or box. Maps, pictures, and unmounted clippings may call for adjustments, which will be covered in later chapters.

The upper left-hand corner is a logical place for subject headings because this is the starting point to which we have been oriented in our reading.

Since smaller items can stand erect in either boxes or file drawers, the heading will always be at the true top of the material. But bigger items may have to be turned to fit into vertical files. Large pamphlets should be turned so that the "spine" or closed edge is at the top. The heading should be applied along the closed edge.

There are two good reasons for electing to keep the closed edge uppermost in the file drawers. First, when cut edges are turned upward, it's very easy for small items to be carelessly slipped between the pages. Second, it is hard to distinguish where one pamphlet ends and the next one begins.

One aspect of the labeling process is making provision for special files.

Color coding can facilitate access to such resources and prevent mistakes in filing. The most effective method of separating materials by color coding is through the use of labels which either are made of colored paper or are color banded.

While some libraries attempt to use color coded dots, they are a poor choice for marking supplementary resources. They are likely to peel off when subjected to friction or handling. The only way to prevent this is by the expensive process of covering each dot with clear tape or adhesive-backed plastic film.

Colored ink also has been used in color coding. However, variations in color are not as obvious as with labels. Furthermore, some inks tend to change color with the passage of time.

Stamps offer an easy and efficient means of differentiating groups of supplementary resources. For example, the word, "Travel," stamped just above or ahead of the subject heading, is a quick and effective way of indicating that certain leaflets belong in a special collection of travel brochures.

Stamps made to individual specifications can be obtained from local firms for a relatively modest fee.

There are rubber stamp kits on the market from which you can construct stamps as the need arises. But the time spent in picking out the letters and inserting them in the holder cancels out any monetary savings.

When color coding or a stamped notation is used to distinguish particular types of resources, the same device must be used on the file folders which house these resources. If you choose to use yellow labels for your vocational collection, the file folders holding these publications should also have yellow labels. Even labels on cases, file boxes, and index trays can be of the same color to provide the maximum in coordination.

Another function of the labeling process is to supply information for the circulation of supplementary materials. If multiple copies of a publication are represented in the collection, they may be labeled with a copy notation such as "c.1" or "c.2." If an accession number is used as part of the circulation system, applying it also becomes part of the labeling process. Conversely, materials meant for reference use only can be stamped, "Not for circulation" or "For use in library only." More will be said about the circulation of supplementary resources later in this chapter.

HOUSING

Don't expect sympathy if your excuse for failing to supply supplementary resources is a lack of elegant equipment. Improvise! Sturdy cardboard boxes will serve as filing cases. So will wooden crates if you're lucky enough to find any. Large laundry soap containers can be cut down to function as pamphlet boxes. These makeshifts can be painted or covered with wallpaper scraps to disguise their humble origins. Roomy mailing envelopes can be sealed at the flap and slit open along the side to substitute for file folders.

Filing Cases

Metal filing cases are the most popular devices for housing supplementary resources. Critical judgment is needed in their selection. They should be made of heavy gauge steel. A full suspension system is essential to allow easy access to the last folder in the drawer. Drawers should glide effortlessly on roller bearings. Following blocks or compressors should be provided to keep file folders erect. These supports should be easy to operate. Thumb latch controls are helpful in keeping drawers safely closed when not in use.

Choice of case size will depend on the projected location, the nature of the materials to be housed, and the available budget. The two most popular sizes in vertical files are letter-sized and legal-sized. Dimensions vary slightly among the various manufacturers. Legal files are more expensive than letter files.

Many libraries prefer legal-sized cases because the extra width will accommodate larger items and also because many pamphlets will stand two to a row. Legal-sized drawers are certainly the logical choice for housing pictures, since these resources are likely to be outsized and it is undesirable to fold them. However, for a collection consisting of pamphlets and clippings, the extra floor space and money consumed by legal files may not be justified. Theoretically, legal files should result in great savings in space because materials can be spread out horizontally. However, I conducted an actual test run, transferring pamphlets and clippings from a letter-sized file with letter-sized folders to a legal-sized file with legal-sized folders. The saving in space averaged only one-half inch for every eight inches of closely compressed material. This saving is offset by the extra floor space required by the wider files. The discrepancy between theory and practice is that the contents of folders in real life are a mixed bag. They do not consist of neatly matched pamphlets that will stand two by two in perfect order. Some are fat, some are lean. Some are wide, some are narrow. Many folders contain uneven numbers of pamphlets so that perfect pairing is impossible.

Because of the special needs presented by pictures, some libraries go one step beyond legal files and invest in oversize files which will house these large-scale resources more comfortably. The housing of pictures is discussed more fully in a later chapter.

As well as drawer size, the choice of filing cases involves a decision as to height. Four-drawer vertical files are less expensive than lower cases in terms of the amount of material which can be stored. They also require less floor space per cubic foot of enclosed material. However, strong arguments can be advanced in favor of three-drawer units. They provide an ideal counter-height top on which to examine material. They will not impede vision. As a result, they offer more flexibility in placement than four-drawer units.

Filing cases differ in type as well as size. Many libraries choose horizontal filing cases for their map collections or for storing charts and posters. The use of horizontal cases in map storage is examined in detail in chapter 8.

Lateral files represent still another variety of storage. Their potential importance lies in their adaptability to areas where conventional files are impractical. They can, for example, nestle against the wall in narrow quarters where a standard file would project too far. Lateral files also present a pleasant appearance since they do not jut sharply into the room. This has tempted some librarians to buy lateral files for aesthetic rather than practical reasons.

Caution should be exercised in buying lateral cases. In their most common form, these cases must be approached from the "side" rather than from the "front." Drawers which house materials at right angles to the user are difficult to consult. As a result, locating and refiling materials involves a great deal of neck twisting. Much more practical for library use are lateral cases with partitioned drawers, which allow materials to be arranged facing the user. Most manufacturers offer this alternative in their lateral files.

Internal Filing Devices

The accessories used within file drawers can be as important as the files themselves. Good quality manila folders are the mainstays of pamphlet files. While envelopes are useful for storing unmounted pictures and unmounted clippings, folders are much more appropriate for filing pamphlets.

Folders must, of course, be selected to match the dimensions of file drawers. Reinforced tabs are a desirable feature to watch for in choosing folders.

Some librarians prefer to have the tab in the same position on all their file folders. They claim that such single-cut file folders make it possible to look straight down the line at subject headings. However, if single-cut file folders are not filled with enough material to make them stand well apart, one tab can completely obscure another.

To make it easy to spot folder headings in the files, it is much better to use staggered tabs. Although some libraries use fifth-cut folders, I prefer third-cut because of the added tab space available for labeling.

It is desirable to have a separate folder for every subject heading in your files. While this procedure is more expensive initially, the costs are balanced by the time saved in locating material and in refiling it. In addition, the folders provide physical protection for your resources. When vertical file materials are inserted without folders, lighter materials tend to slip to the bottom of the drawer, where they are overlooked or are crushed by heavier items.

In using manila folders, take advantage of the scoring at the fold, which permits bending the bottom into box form to cope with increased contents.

When materials overflow the original folder, a second folder can be added. Be sure to label the folders "1" and "2" so that users will be alerted to the existence of two containers. An even better solution for handling swollen resources is to use expanding file pockets. These durable devices will absorb quantities of material without sagging. While expanding wallets are available with flaps that fold over the top, the best choice for library files is the file pocket with its open top and closed sides. The closed sides keep materials from sliding out while the open top allows for easy accessibility.

Choose your brand and style of expanding file pockets with care. There is a great variation in the amount of expansion possible. The best pocket that I have discovered is manufactured by the Alvah Bushnell Company **(41)**.

File guides are used in many libraries to indicate letter divisions, major subject headings, or cross references. They may even carry scope notes. Homemade file guides can be improvised from old manila folders. Pressboard guides are available from library and office supply houses. They may be purchased with regular tabs or with metal tabs into which labels can be inserted. Metal tabs are stronger and facilitate the changing of headings, but they do add to the price of the guides.

Some libraries see no need to employ file guides in the drawers housing their pamphlets and clippings. Instead they record "SEE ALSO" references and scope notes on the file folders themselves. For "SEE" references, the user turns to the index to the files.

Some libraries employ file guides as substitutes for file folders. Pamphlets and clippings are placed behind a file guide bearing the appropriate heading rather than being inserted in a folder. Since file guides are never removed from the drawers, this procedure is supposed to facilitate refiling. However, the practice has serious drawbacks. It is difficult to lift a mass of pamphlets and clippings from a drawer when they are not in a folder. While folders tend to keep subjects separated for refiling, loose pamphlets and clippings become jumbled together. Furthermore, file guides cannot offer any physical protection to small or fragile resources in the drawers. All in all, replacing file folders with file guides is a regrettable substitution.

If funds are obtainable, hanging file folders are a splendid addition to any vertical or lateral file. Frames are available which can be inserted in any standard file drawer. Rugged folders are suspended from the frame. They slide freely back and forth on the rails. You can transfer your manila folders and their contents to the hanging folders or you can file items directly into the hanging folders. Because they do not rest on the bottom of the drawer, hanging folders can accommodate large amounts of material without bulging or sagging. It is easy to remove or replace material because folders are so maneuverable. **Pendaflex®** is the best-known name in the field of suspension files. **Pendaflex** frames and hanging folders are manufactured by the Oxford Pendaflex Corporation **(196)**.

Specialized filing devices for maps, pictures, clippings, and local history materials are discussed in the chapters devoted to these supplementary resources.

File Boxes

When material is stored in pamphlet boxes on book stacks, it consumes less floor space than if it were housed in filing cases. Furthermore, extra space must be allowed in planning library quarters for the opening of file drawers.

Despite these facts, most librarians would be reluctant to part with their floor files. They are convenient. They allow for maximum organization and control. They offer protection from dust and light.

Still, the file box has an important role to play in housing supplementary resources. There is no "either/or" ultimatum in managing these resources. It's perfectly proper to house part of your holdings in filing cases and part in file boxes. The trick is to use both approaches to the best advantage.

To illustrate, if you're proud of your collection of mail-order catalogs, you may decide to arrange them in pamphlet boxes on an open range of shelves. The public will be sure to notice such a special collection and will enjoy browsing through the boxes.

File boxes are also excellent devices for storing back runs of annual reports or statistical series which might otherwise clog file drawers. These boxes can be tucked away in back rooms or basements until the material is needed.

When material is withdrawn from the file drawers for housing elsewhere, there should, of course, be a notice in the file that this shift has been made. This applies not only to back runs of continuations but also to oversized material that is stored away from the filing cases. The notice might be printed on a sturdy sheet of paper. In the case of resources such as federal publications that are free of copyright restrictions, a location note can be placed on a photocopy of the cover. When a run of statistical reports is involved, the issue in the file might carry a stamped note saying, "Earlier editions in storage."

Boxes should be selected to fit their station in life. If they are to be used for long-term storage in secluded areas, inexpensive closed boxes are suitable. Hinged pamphlet files also provide good protection from dust and light, but they cost considerably more. Acid-free boxes for local history storage are discussed in chapter 7.

When boxes are to be used on open shelves in the public service areas, sturdy construction is essential. Visibility, accessibility, and security become major considerations, too.

In using ordinary pamphlet boxes, which are closed except for the back, it is difficult to examine or pull out individual items without removing the entire contents of the containers. Back openings are always hazardous, too, since it is very easy for stored materials to fall out. This danger applies to Princeton files as well as to ordinary pamphlet boxes.

Open-top, cut-corner boxes are a vast improvement. Since they are enclosed on four sides, they prevent spillage. Yet the diagonal cut of the boxes allows easy access to materials.

The staff in our library improvised another solution which works very well. Open-back boxboard files are turned so that the front panel rests on the shelf. This provides a four-sided container open at the top. A book pocket pasted on the new "front" of the container allows the insertion of a card identifying the contents. The card can be easily replaced if the contents change.

Serial Shelving

In an all-out effort to conserve space, a few libraries place pamphlets on shelves in the order in which they are received. A serial number or a combination letter and number is assigned to each pamphlet. Access to individual pamphlets or to subjects covered is achieved through a card index or card catalog.

As a refinement of this type of housing, Dale E. Shaffer developed his Sha-Frame® system, which is described in chapter 3.

Microfiche

An unusual method of housing has been adopted by the McKinley Memorial Library in Niles, Ohio. This library maintains a vertical file on microfiche (VFOM).

The pivotal factor in the decision to employ microfiche was lack of space. The McKinley Memorial Library is part of a landmark structure and cannot expand its physical quarters. The director, Dr. Chester B. Stout, is convinced of the vital role which an adequate vertical file can play in good library service. Converting vertical file materials to microfiche offered an opportunity to provide an extensive collection within the spatial limitations of the library.

Dr. Stout hastens to point out that he and his staff find other advantages to the VFOM besides space saving. They are convinced that it is more convenient and efficient to handle a vertical file in this manner than in the traditional manner. Dr. Stout reports acceptance of the changed format by the public also.

When material is requested for the VFOM, a form letter is used which asks for copyright clearance to make microfilm reproductions and/or copies for users. The letter indicates willingness to pay a reasonable rate (not to exceed $0.25 per article) for the privilege. If copyright clearance is not available, the letter instructs the supplier not to send the requested material. This procedure is followed in acquiring free material as well as in ordering priced items.

The McKinley Memorial Library does its own in-house filming with its own equipment. Microfiche master jackets are prepared, which then constitute a security file. Diazo duplicates are made for the file used by the public. The microfiche is arranged using an alphanumeric Cutter code.

The vertical file on microfiche now contains some 65,000 items on approximately 26,000 microfiche. Using a key punch machine and computer, an extensive index has been prepared to provide access to the file. The index has grown to a 1,094-page computer print-out, recording approximately 27,350 entries for subject headings and cross references.

The library has sixteen readers for use in working with the microfiche. Machines are available which allow increased magnification for patrons with poor eyesight.

Prints can be produced from the microfiche by using a reader-printer. A charge of $0.15 is made for each print. Any copyright clearance fee would be additional. Dr. Stout reports that there is surprisingly little call for prints. In eight years, the library hasn't made over 300 prints.

Although its solicitation letter indicates that the McKinley Memorial Library has completely abandoned the traditional vertical file in favor of microforms, this is not entirely true. For example, certain items are retained in hard copy which will not reproduce well. This is true of materials with important colored detail. Some local history items are also on file, at least temporarily, in hard copy form. There is no doubt, however, that microfiche is the main vehicle for vertical file materials in this library.

Among the advantages that Dr. Stout claims for his innovative VFOM are:

1. Saving of needed space.

2. Elimination of problems created by dealing with materials of varying sizes and shapes.

3. Elimination of the need for making repairs to hard copy materials.

4. Efficient retrieval through the computer-produced index.

5. Ability to turn any item into a "large-print" resource by use of increased magnification.

6. Complete security control. Conventional files experience depletion through theft and failure to return circulated items. Any attempts at replacement consume time and money. The VFOM stays in the building. The only "take-home" items are notes made by the patron or prints made from the microfiche. In case of some mishap to diazo duplicates, the security file is available as a backup for the production of more duplicates.

7. Capacity for reproduction of files for other library facilities. Dr. Stout suggests that a duplicate file could be made for branch libraries or, in a multi-storied library, for each floor of the library.

8. Production of duplicate resources for patron use. If a diazo copy is being used, another diazo duplicate can be quickly made from the master jacket for a second patron.

Librarians who want to learn more about the development and statistical evaluation of the VFOM may obtain a copy of Dr. Stout's dissertation (225).

The McKinley Memorial Library is to be commended for its commitment to the value of vertical files and for its ingenuity in overcoming physical limitations. Its solution is one that might be carefully studied by libraries facing a space shortage, although part of the space saved may be consumed by the equipment necessary to prepare and operate a vertical file on microfiche. The potential for duplicating all or part of a VFOM in other library locations might interest a major public or academic library.

As far as other libraries are concerned, the VFOM has characteristics which make it a more questionable choice:

1. Initiating a VFOM calls for a major investment of money in equipment, materials, and manpower. Dr. Stout's dissertation gives some insight into the extent of this investment.

2. The necessity for working with copyright clearances creates a bottleneck that can be frustrating, time-consuming, and costly.

3. Problems with copyright clearance can prevent the inclusion of titles in a VFOM. Publications in which color or fine pictorial detail are of prime importance do not qualify as suitable candidates for a VFOM.

4. Many people—even those with healthy, young eyes—find it difficult to do extensive reading using a microfiche reader. (After studying Dr. Stout's dissertation on microfiche, I can solemnly attest to this fact.)

5.   When resources are available only on microfiche, vertical file materials can never be used for displays within the library or at events such as garden shows outside the library.

There certainly is good reason to consider preparing security copies on film of irreplaceable or historically important pamphlets. The advantages of converting an entire vertical file to microfiche are less clear-cut.

WEEDING

Subtraction is as crucial a process as addition in maintaining a healthy collection of supplementary resources. Some librarians obtain a deep-seated comfort from seeing file folders jammed full of material even if it is dated and inappropriate. In reality, they are doing themselves and their patrons a disservice. They mislead their public with these bloated folders by promising something they can't really deliver. They risk misinforming their patrons through the presence of invalid material. They waste the time required to leaf through useless items. They squander space that might be put to more profitable use.

Weeding should not be a "sometime" thing. There is little justification for postponing action until the situation gets desperate and then indulging in a crash project. Weeding of supplementary resources must be done regularly, consistently, and constantly.

In a well-controlled collection, the processes of adding and discarding materials are inseparable. For weeding properly begins when the librarian leafs through the daily pile of mail or examines a stack of leaflets presented by a patron. Hopefully, the librarian will avoid thinking, "Oh, well, I might as well keep this since it's free." If critical standards of currency, authority, need, and format are applied at this point, there will be less deadwood to deal with later on.

The conjunction between acquisition and weeding can be carried even further. As new materials such as maps or pamphlets are prepared for addition to the collection, the librarian can check them against the holdings already there. This offers an opportunity to assess the older material against the potential contribution of the new. This would be the time to ask questions such as these:

1.   Will the new addition supersede older publications on the same subject? Or do the older materials contain historical or background information which is omitted in recent works?

2.   Does the new item add a different dimension or merely restate what is found in other materials on the subject? If it does not offer a fresh approach, is it needed anyway because of the popularity of the topic?

3.   If a new item is found to be the duplicate of a supplementary resource already in the collection, is there enough demand to justify keeping both copies? (If the answer is "Yes," the original copy must be pulled to allow for adding a distinguishing copy number.)

4.   If the new item is an annual report, statistical compilation, or serial bulletin, should only the latest edition be kept? If a backfile is

considered desirable, how long should it be? (In the case of statistical publications, the decision may hinge on whether statistics for past years are repeated or summarized in the newer issues.)

As this process of checking new resources against the old is conducted, the librarian can simultaneously go through the steps of the weeding process, watching for:

1. Material that has outlived its usefulness or its authority.

2. Material that needs repair or replacement because of physical condition.

3. Continuations such as annual reports or catalogs for which newer editions need to be ordered.

4. Subject headings which need modernizing or which should be split into finer groupings.

5. Overcrowded folders, boxes, or drawers.

Another type of spot weeding used in some libraries consists of checking the contents of folders which are awaiting refiling after being used. To indicate that a group of materials has been evaluated, an inconspicuous date notation may be penciled on the folder.

While the forms of spot weeding just described are helpful, they provide a random approach at best. There must also be opportunity for an orderly, overall assessment of the collection—from the first drawer to the last. This progressive weeding should be carried out on a steady, continuing basis. It will enable you to review *all* subject areas. It will help you discover interest fields which are dormant because they need an infusion of fresh, new material. It will alert you to headings which are no longer needed and which may be profitably eliminated. (But remember to pull the index cards when you delete those headings!)

Weeding doesn't arbitrarily mean immediate disposal of an item selected for discarding. You may choose, instead, to leave it in the files with a prominent note on the cover indicating that replacement material has been requested. The note should be dated. This procedure will alert the staff and the public to the fact that newer information is on the way.

In an attempt to expedite weeding and to shift part of the burden to clerks and student helpers, some libraries have experimented with symbols which predict the prospective life span of supplementary resources. For example, subject headings written in red might indicate items of permanent value, while those in green signify ephemeral materials. A "P" stamped on a supplementary resource might represent a permanent addition, while a "T" stands for "temporary." Some libraries have even marked materials with a weeding date indicating the probable length of time they would be of value.

When a weeding date is supplied, pages can pull any "expired" items as they refile materials. When color or letter coding is used, clerks or pages can withdraw "temporary" materials from drawers or shelves when weeding time rolls around. Both of these schemes call for the librarian to review the material that has been pulled.

I do not recommend either of these plans. A librarian would have to be equipped with a crystal ball to make the required predictions. Furthermore, these schemes discourage the librarian from assessing all the material under a given heading as weeding occurs.

In libraries where statistics are critical in the fight for funds, it may be desirable to keep a tally of the number of supplementary resources discarded as well as of those added so that some estimate can be made of the total holdings.

Local history materials call for an entirely different concept of weeding, since long-term preservation is the goal. The treatment of local history resources will be discussed later in this book.

CIRCULATION

Should supplementary resources be restricted to use in the library since they have a high potential reference value? Or should they be allowed to circulate so that the public can use them at home, at work, or in the classroom?

In trying to reconcile these opposite pulls, one major library established two comprehensive collections of supplementary resources, one for reference use and the second for circulation. This approach is too demanding of time and space for most libraries.

The best solution is a compromise, allowing circulation but selectively restricting certain items. Even the effect of this restriction can be softened.

If there are choice statistical items in your files which you find invaluable for reference use, try to get an extra copy so that you can circulate one and still have a backup copy in the library. The second copy can be marked "Not for circulation" or "For use in library only" or "Reference copy." If you are unable to obtain a duplicate of the latest in a series of statistical publications, restrict only the newest edition and allow the remainder to circulate.

Because of their diverse nature, the circulation of supplementary resources is a complex process. It has the potential for more misunderstandings and conflicts than the circulation of more standardized materials.

Circulation control of supplementary resources ranges from one extreme to the other. There are libraries in which a card and pocket is affixed to every pamphlet. There are others where circulation control is so minimal that pamphlets and clippings are recorded only as miscellaneous materials, no overdue notices are sent, and no follow-up is ever made on unreturned items.

The libraries which use cards and pockets argue that these pamphlets represent an important information resource, accumulated with effort and sometimes with a respectable expenditure of money. They also claim that the time and money spent in providing cards and pockets is balanced by the time saved when pamphlets are circulated.

This system is most workable in a library with a limited collection of pamphlets or in a library which can take advantage of volunteer labor to cut production costs. Some school libraries resort to cards and pockets because they want to unitize all resources by assigning Dewey numbers to pamphlets and shelving them with books on the same subject.

Libraries which exercise only a token jurisdiction over the circulation of pamphlets and clippings operate on the theory that these items are entirely expendable. The suspicion arises that libraries which subscribe to this philosophy either have very poor collections which do not justify greater control or else they are blind to the value of these resources to staff and public alike.

Are supplementary resources really expendable? Yes, if being expendable means that they should be used freely and fully until they wear out or outlive their usefulness. No, if being expendable means that they should be treated as giveaways.

When you have laboriously accumulated pamphlets and clippings on a subject such as adoption, it can be a painful experience to have them lost in circulation. It's hard to casually write off such resources as being "expendable" when their loss drastically diminishes the information you can offer your public.

Most libraries try to steer a precarious middle road between the two extremes of circulation control. The most common circulation record maintained is a very simple designation of type of material, subject, and number of items borrowed. The patron's identification and the due date complete the record.

Depending upon the library, the circulation of these special resources may be done entirely by hand or it may involve some kind of mechanical record.

Hand charging is practiced in many public libraries, school libraries, and special libraries.

In public libraries, a separate card or slip is normally used for each transaction. Some libraries make do with old scratch cards on which they pencil a record of the loan. Others convert book cards for hand charging, reserving a special color of card stock for supplementary resources. Such cards are used over and over again until the card is filled up. Still other libraries have special forms printed.

In designing a special form for hand charging, the grouping of items depends on what is considered prime information for filing the records. Some libraries prefer to approach charge slips by subject, filing them in a single alphabetical arrangement or placing them by subject under the due date. In such arrangements, the subject of the borrowed items should have a prominent location on the charge form. This is a sample of a specially printed form for the loan of pamphlets and clippings.

DATE DUE_____

SUBJECT _____

ITEMS BORROWED _____

_____

_____

NAME _____

ADDRESS _____ ZIP CODE _____

Other libraries prefer to use the name of the borrower as a filing guide, since a patron may borrow material on several subjects at the same time. In this case, the borrower's name should be given a conspicuous spot on the form. Under this setup, the patron's name must be repeated on the circulation envelope.

Special libraries which allow users to charge out materials themselves may employ a dated sheet of paper fastened to a clipboard as their circulation record. The borrower enters the required information on the paper. Shown below is the sheet used in one special library which allows "honor system" borrowing. To simplify circulation, it encourages its patrons to take the complete folder on a subject. A library that chooses to give patrons the option of taking only one or two items from a folder would have to add an entry for the number of items taken.

VERTICAL FILE SIGN-OUT SHEET					
Date Signed Out	Folder Title	Signed Out By	Daytime Telephone	Date Due (Use Stamper)	Date Returned

An "honor system" circulation scheme must be kept simple or users may bypass it entirely.

Instead of individual transaction slips or cards, school libraries may turn to large master cards or notebooks, with one transaction being listed below another. When a loan packet is returned, the transaction is crossed off. A refinement of this system is to maintain an individual card for each subject represented in the library's files. The cards are kept in a separate arrangement. All loans involving a particular topic are entered line after line on the appropriate subject card. One argument for employing this system is that it measures the relative demand for each subject area.

Most libraries feel a need to provide some kind of carrier for the pamphlets and clippings they circulate. The purpose of the carrier is to isolate each loan group, protect the materials, and offer a place for recording pertinent circulation information. By far the most popular type of carrier is a large paper envelope.

Old mailing envelopes can be utilized for circulation. Envelopes especially constructed for the purpose are sold by library supply houses. They are made of sturdy kraft paper with reinforced edges. Office supply firms offer envelopes with string ties for added security.

When old mailing envelopes are used, circulation data can be placed directly on the surface of the envelopes since they are readily discarded. Libraries which purchase special envelopes usually apply a date due slip or printed form to the front of the envelope.

The date on which the material is due is the most crucial bit of information to add to the outside of the envelope. In addition, a notation of the number of items taken will assist the borrower to collate his material, and it will enable the librarian to make a quick check when the envelope is returned. Besides this information, some libraries indicate the type of material taken and the subject heading. A full notation of this sort would look like this:

> Feb. 17, 1979   Conservation—3 pamphlets
> 4 clippings

The name of the borrower is not essential on the envelope unless the charge slip is filed alphabetically by this information.

Instead of writing circulation information on the envelope, some libraries provide the patron with a carbon copy of the charge slip. This duplicate is returned with the envelope.

If supplementary resources are directly circulated from several departments in a library, envelopes should carry departmental designations.

There are libraries which choose to circulate pamphlets without benefit of an envelope. In such cases, the due date is frequently stamped on the back cover or on the inside of the back cover. Librarians following this pattern point out that the accumulation of dates indicates the demand for a pamphlet which is useful knowledge in weeding or reordering.

Some school libraries have developed carrying devices which serve as circulation controls as well. One example is the subject envelope. A subject envelope is used to house a group of clippings and pamphlets on a single subject, such as milk. Each subject envelope carries a card and pocket. The card and pocket bear a record of the subject and the number of items housed in the envelope. The envelope is circulated as a unit.

In school libraries where teachers borrow large groups of supplementary resources for classroom use, numbered pamphlet boxes may function as both carrying devices and circulation controls. A card and pocket affixed to each pamphlet box carries the box number. When a box is filled and sent to a classroom, the card is marked with the subject and number of items taken, as well as an indication of the teacher borrowing the material. The card is filed in the circulation records. For this system it is practical to use a box which is closed on four sides and open at the top, or else to tip an open-back box so that the opening is at the top. This will prevent spillage and will allow headroom for tall items.

While hand charging is widely used for supplementary resources, many libraries employ a mechanical charging system for all library materials. This calls for adjustments to accommodate special resources.

Libraries which have Gaylord or Demco charging machines may imprint the borrower's identification and the date due on a regular book card and then fill in the descriptive information by hand. To avoid confusion, a card of a different color may be used for charging out these special materials.

When photocharging is employed, a form such as that shown below can be used. Once a photographic record is made, the form and the transaction slip can be placed in a pocket on the loan envelope. If loan envelopes are of the expendable type, the form and transaction slip may be stapled to the envelope itself.

SPECIAL MATERIALS		
Type	Subject	Number

When only one item such as a single pamphlet is involved, libraries using photographic charging may put the pamphlet itself under the camera and take a picture of the subject heading section. In such instances, the transaction slip is sometimes clipped to the pamphlet itself, eliminating the use of an envelope.

With an automated circulation system that uses a light pen or other scanning device, provision can also be made for special materials. A solution reached by one library is to circulate pamphlets using a set of numbered envelopes. As well as its number in the set, each envelope carries a unique "zebra" number, which is scanned as part of the loan transaction.

All circulation systems—whether hand charging or mechanical—that limit description of loaned material to type, subject, and number have a common basic weakness. They cannot provide identification of individual items.

With a small, closely-knit clientele in a special library, further identification may not be important. In libraries serving a larger, mixed clientele, lack of identification has greater impact.

Does it really matter? It does if you want to make sure that you aren't sending overdue notices for material that has already been returned. It does if a patron can find only part of his loan and asks, "Exactly what is it that's still missing?" A little more effort on circulation records might pay off in better public relations. An added argument for better circulation control arises from the increased cost of some supplementary resources.

One way of aiding the identification of circulated items is to jot down a few words from the pamphlet title or from the headline of a clipping on the charge record. A clipping might also be pegged by jotting down the initials or abbreviated form of the newspaper's name and a numerical notation of the date.

Another method of pinpointing materials and speeding the circulation process is to use accession numbers, which can be recorded on the charge record. Libraries may maintain an accession notebook in which they place a simple record of each pamphlet added to their files. The accession number is duplicated on the pamphlet itself. Since numbers are not repeated, they constitute a foolproof device for charging out material and checking on its return.

As indicated earlier, order cards may be converted into accession cards with the addition of a sequential number and a subject heading. If you want to extend this control to free pamphlets, a "bare-bones" accession card may be typed for each of these items. Good sense should be the guide. For example, it's wasteful to type accession cards for serials, catalogs, or annual reports since it's so easy to describe these publications. "Red Cross 1978 Annual Report" is almost as easy to write as "Red Cross 78397." Clippings do not need accession cards. As pointed out in a previous paragraph, they can be readily identified by a notation such as "Chic Trib 1-9-78."

A variant use of accessioning is to stamp or print a sequential number on each item without maintaining a notebook or file to indicate the assignment of numbers. Since no records are kept, it is impossible under this system to determine the title of an individual pamphlet from its number. However, the scheme does simplify the charging out of material and the checking of files for returned items.

A numbering machine may be used to speed up the mechanics of accessioning. These machines usually number from 1 to 999,999. The Bates Manufacturing Co. (29) produces on individual order a numbering machine which features a year band as well as consecutive numbers, e.g., 78 1130. At the beginning of a new year, the year band is reset and the accession number returns to one. This type of accessioning immediately reveals the age of a pamphlet.

If separate accession numbers are not provided in the case of duplicated titles, the copy number becomes an important part of the charging record.

The idea of providing cards and pockets for pamphlets should not be dismissed too lightly as a practical means of achieving closer circulation control.

While libraries with substantial collections cannot afford cards and pockets for all of their holdings, it might be feasible to provide them for the most expensive or critical items in the files. If cards are used which resemble book cards, they should be of a different color stock to avoid any possible confusion.

Since many libraries treat picture resources as a separate collection, the circulation of these supplementary materials is discussed in detail in a later chapter.

CHAPTER 3

PAMPHLETS AND CLIPPINGS:
THEIR VALUE AND THEIR ORGANIZATION

Pamphlets and clippings under most circumstances are organized jointly, housed jointly, and used jointly. The mixture of these two resources is what most librarians mean when they refer to "vertical files."

Despite this marriage of convenience, clippings and pamphlets spring from different origins and demand separate processing.

Any study of these resources must reflect this blend of similarities and differences. In the pages that follow, the elements common to both clippings and pamphlets will be discussed together. Considerations that are peculiar to one or the other will be treated separately.

THEIR VALUE

Why bother with clippings and pamphlets? You're busy enough coping with the ordering and cataloging of books. Why take on another chore?

The answer is simple. For your investment of time and money, you will get a return great enough to turn a Wall Street speculator green with envy.

The contributions which these supplementary resources can make are many.

1. *Compactness and Retrievability.* Vertical file materials are likely to be written in a way that offers a compact, highly organized approach to a subject. They can serve as a type of abstracting service, presenting the essence of a subject in capsule form. Many people who would shy away from a thick book feel perfectly comfortable with pamphlets and clippings. Even avid readers sometimes want only a quick overview of a subject.

Another attractive feature of vertical files is the ease of retrievability. The process is simple. You think of a subject. You go to the files. There you find a variety of materials from a variety of sources which have been pulled together for instant use. When time is at a premium, this rapid accessibility can be a blessing to both patrons and staff.

Students discovered years ago how easy it is to find information in vertical files and how easy the information is to use once you've found it. That explains why they are such enthusiastic fans of vertical files. Many of them turn hopefully to the vertical files for any and all subjects before consulting other resources. I remember the boy who wistfully inquired about pamphlets on the Peloponnesian War.

2. *Focus.* Some vertical file materials are helpful because they zero in on a small segment of knowledge. They function much like an electronic microscope, focusing on a minute portion of a specimen. A good illustration of this contribution is a pamphlet from the National Easter Seal Society titled **Toothbrushing and Flossing: A Manual of Home Dental Care for Persons Who Are Handicapped.**

3. *Uniqueness.* Veterans of the reference corps know that many times pamphlets and clippings will supply information which is impossible or at least excruciatingly difficult to locate elsewhere. A rock music fan might ask you, for example, how many electric guitars were sold in the United States last year. After an initial moment of panic, you would turn to your trusty vertical files and find the answer in the American Music Conference's **Music USA (13)**.

Even when some coverage is available in book form on certain difficult subjects, it may be very sparse. Here again the vertical file may help to fill the gaps with unique material. In our library we know that the fine points of flag etiquette are better represented in our vertical files than in any book we own. We have laboriously collected clippings, pamphlets, and even letters of response from national authorities which go far beyond any book coverage.

4. *Authority.* Vertical file materials often possess an authority which matches or even surpasses that of books.

The carefully researched pamphlets issued by state historical commissions or state historical societies are good evidence of this quality. It is also apparent in the confidence with which users consult U.S. Department of Agriculture bulletins on lightning protection or on selecting and operating beekeeping equipment. This same feeling of reliability is associated with the publications of the Cystic Fibrosis Foundation, which deal competently with the many ramifications of CF from diagnostic techniques to vocational guidance.

5. *Currency.* Despite technological advances and crash publishing projects, there still is a time lapse in the production of books. Vertical file publications can help you to fill this gap. Because these supplementary materials are quick and inexpensive to produce, new ideas and the latest statistics often appear in this form long before they laboriously work their way into book format. Because of these very same virtues, vertical file materials are frequently revised. Since you can obtain them free or for a relatively small fee, you can afford to keep up to date by adding the new editions to your files.

Typical of this flow of current information is the annual **Survey on Sports Attendance**, issued free by the Daily Racing Form, Inc. **(70)**.

A dramatic demonstration of the up-to-the-minute quality of vertical file materials occurred when the State of Michigan first announced restrictions on the sale of DDT. Cooperative extension service bulletins on household, garden, and agricultural insects were quickly revised to substitute alternate methods of control. Our book collection could not duplicate this rapid and complete realignment.

6. *Multiplication of Sources.* No library, however large, has the book resources to satisfactorily cope with mass demands. What do you do when several classes are assigned to study air pollution? How do you handle the heavy seasonal demands that occur at Mother's Day or Christmas? Clippings and pamphlets offer a way to bolster your book collection with a variety of supplementary offerings on popular topics. Because they are free or relatively inexpensive, you can enjoy the luxury of adding them abundantly to your collection without making great inroads into your budget.

7. *Breadth.* The vertical file offers an opportunity to provide information in areas where there is occasional or sporadic demand. When budgets are limited, each book must be weighed for the contribution it makes to the library week after week.

Since vertical file material does not involve the same financial drain, it is possible to be much more liberal in selection. While you may not feel justified in investing in a book on catfish, pamphlets on the subject may satisfy your patrons.

8. *Referral.* Vertical file materials can help you to reach beyond your own walls.

Librarians in small- and medium-sized libraries often shudder at the word, "bibliography," but we gladly add bibliographies to our files. Not only do these bibliographies point out resources that our library owns, but they also open broader horizons to our patrons. We can arrange interlibrary loans or obtain photocopies of items suggested in these lists.

Libraries at the national, state, and local levels are active in producing bibliographies. Representative of these publications is a series of literature guides called **LC Science Tracer Bullets (138)**, which are available free from the Library of Congress. Recent titles in the series have covered tidal energy, dryland agriculture, and cryobiology.

Governmental agencies other than libraries publish bibliographies geared to their individual spheres of activity. This is particularly true at the federal level. The National Institute of Law Enforcement and Criminal Justice is an example. Bibliographies in special interest areas are also available from private institutes and associations.

The vertical file can also point to resources beyond the walls of your library through the use of ordering lists. Plans for handicraft projects furnish a good example. Lists of project plans can be obtained from associations such as the American Plywood Association and the Western Wood Products Association. They are also available from commercial publishers such as **Popular Mechanics**, Craft Patterns Studio, and Directions Simplified, Inc. Your library may not be able to buy widely among the plans included in these lists, but the lists themselves will serve as guides for your patrons so they can order personal copies of the projects that answer their needs.

Another type of outreach made possible by the vertical file is through the use of directories which indicate where to turn for further information. Considering the present interest in genealogy, there could be no better illustration than the guides published by the National Center for Health Statistics **(172)**, which tell where to write for birth, death, marriage, and divorce records.

THEIR ORGANIZATION

By Sequence or Size?

As indicated in chapter 2, some libraries do not attempt to physically group their pamphlets by subject. They simply arrange the pamphlets by order of receipt. The pamphlets are marked with a sequential code consisting of numbers or a combination of letters and numbers. Access is achieved through a card index or card catalog. The code number of each pamphlet is recorded under the appropriate subject or subjects. If author and title cards are used, the code number is recorded there also.

Dale E. Shaffer has incorporated a modified form of serial arrangement in his **Sha-Frame**® system for organizing pamphlets. His plan calls for arranging pamphlets by size as well as by acquisition order. The system revolves around use of the **Sha-Frame** pamphlet rack, which Shaffer sells. The **Sha-Frame** consists of seven sloping rows of open bins. The bins are of two different sizes. The smaller bins are used for small pamphlets. Medium-sized pamphlets are housed in the larger bins, with one bin being reserved for large pamphlets. As pamphlets are processed for the **Sha-Frame**, they are sorted by width size. Each pamphlet is assigned a unique call number which reflects both its order of arrival and its size—i.e., 1-S, 2-S, etc.; 1-M, 2-M, etc.; 1-L, 2-L, etc. The pamphlets are then filed in appropriately sized bins by call number from left to right.

Shaffer's plan calls for an alphabetical card catalog with a main entry card under title for each pamphlet. There are also subject cards. The subject headings are key-word headings chosen without guidance from any formal list. Series and author cards may be added, if desired. A shelf list is maintained. The system is described in Shaffer's booklet, **The Pamphlet Library (217).**

Among the claims which Shaffer makes for his system are speed of processing, flexibility, effective use of space, visibility of materials, and ease of retrievability.

The crucial flaw in organizing pamphlets by an accession code or by the **Sha-Frame** system is that pamphlets cannot be retrieved directly. The librarian or patron must first determine the proper code designations from a card catalog or card index and then search out each pamphlet one by one. When hunting for a number of pamphlets on a particular subject, the search can become both time-consuming and aggravating. Unless the searcher is highly motivated, that person may abandon the hunt before it is completed.

Furthermore, when pamphlets are accessible for casual browsing, as they are under the **Sha-Frame** system, they are not likely to remain in the precise order necessary for retrieval by a serial code.

Despite his promise of simplified processing, Shaffer's proposals for a shelf list and catalog are, in reality, quite elaborate. These procedures could be pared down. What cannot be remedied is the awkwardness of retrieval.

By Dewey or LC?

It should come as no surprise that some librarians propose classifying pamphlets and even clippings by the Dewey Decimal or Library of Congress classification systems. In theory, employing Dewey or LC for all library resources would simplify and correlate their use.

This is not a new concept. It appears in the early literature of the profession, when the few pamphlets permitted inside a library were given legitimacy by being classified and placed on the shelves with their more respectable cousins. Sometimes single pamphlets were allowed this distinction. Oftentimes related pamphlets were bound together into what were called pamphlet volumes, or groups of associated pamphlets might stand in boxes alongside their book counterparts.

The classification of pamphlets is still an active practice today. Some librarians shelve their pamphlets with related books in the traditional manner.

Others have set aside small rooms or corners where boxes of pamphlets stand in class order. Classified pamphlets and clippings are even housed in vertical files.

While a few stabs have been made at constructing special classification codes, most classification schemes for pamphlets and clippings center around Dewey or LC. The arguments marshalled for using Dewey or LC classification are these:

1. It is easier to organize pamphlets and clippings if a ready-made scheme like Dewey or LC is used.

2. It is logical to apply the same finding code to all library resources on the same subject. If a library uses Dewey, the numerical guide, 636.7, should lead you to everything the library owns on dogs—whether it be books, pamphlets, or clippings. The concept of unifying all library resources is particularly appealing to school librarians. They are eager to be able to present a quick overview of all library holdings on a given subject to teachers and pupils.

3. It is helpful to have related subjects standing in close physical proximity. The patron who is interested in sports will find it useful to have all sports pamphlets within easy eye range at once rather than having them dispersed alphabetically under such widely separated headings as "Baseball," "Volleyball," and "Golf." Physical closeness also makes it more convenient to work one's way back to broader classes if the answer can't be found under a specific topic. If the Dewey number, 553.82 (Diamonds), doesn't produce the needed information, there are pamphlets nearby under the general number, 553.8 (Gems), which may help.

4. It is easy to survey the library's holdings in the basic areas of knowledge because of the classified arrangement. Strengths and weaknesses in relation to the collection as a whole are readily apparent.

Unhappily, the classification of pamphlets and clippings by Dewey or LC is neither as simple nor as appropriate in actual practice as it seems in theory. One of the special characteristics of pamphlets and clippings is that they can concentrate on small areas of emphasis. The Dewey Decimal and LC classification systems were designed for use with books. They simply are not constructed to cope with the minutiae of information presented in vertical file materials. How do you apply such classification schemes to bring out the exact nature of a pamphlet on candlelighting ceremonies or a leaflet on scavenger hunts? The potential choices in dealing with a highly specialized subject are to concoct an astonishingly long and complex classification number or to bury the item under a general class number that will not give a precise clue to its contents.

Shelving pamphlets with related books only serves to guarantee that the fineness of identification possible in an alphabetical subject arrangement will be lost. The tendency will be to simplify shelving by assigning the generalized Dewey or LC numbers used for books. To compound the problem, it will be physically and economically impossible in most libraries to provide for dispersal of pamphlets and clippings in exact position among the books. If you own just two pamphlets on a particular subject, are you going to put them in binders or provide a separate pamphlet box so that they can stand in precise order on the shelves? The answer is usually "No," with the pamphlets being lumped in a box at the end of a major classification group.

Generalized classification and generalized shelving blur the emphasis on specifics which is the prime contribution of so many pamphlets and clippings. Perhaps this is not such a grim prospect in a very small library where resources are so limited that they can be quickly screened. But the larger the collection, the more frustrating a generalized approach becomes because of the sheer number of items that must be handled to find a specific fact.

Currency is another problem in applying Dewey or LC. Since new ideas or developments often are represented in clippings and pamphlets long before any book appears on the subject, what is the librarian to do until catalogers get around to making a pontifical judgment about the proper Dewey or LC designation? If you guess, you may find yourself completely out of line when the "official" decision is finally made. If you put the materials aside to wait until the book publishers catch up with the subject, you will have lost an opportunity to be of immediate help to your patrons.

Nor are Dewey or LC the most flexible of arrangements. A major breakthrough in science that might be easily handled in an alphabetical arrangement can cause a real crisis in a numerical or alphanumerical system where one division is balanced precariously on another.

There is good reason for challenging the benefits that supposedly derive from placing pamphlets and clippings in schematic order so that related subjects rub shoulders. These claims simply do not jibe with the usage that is most commonly made of pamphlets and clippings. Laymen and librarians alike usually have a very precisely defined subject in mind when they approach these resources. The patron who wants to get rid of the bats in an attic couldn't care less that the pamphlets on bats, Dewey 599.4, stand in neighborly order with the pamphlets on whales, Dewey 599.5. That person is not interested in whales.

It's true that in school libraries teachers may request blanket loans of materials in terms of broad units, such as transportation or energy. But the students preparing reports for those same units will approach the library for information on such isolated topics as air cushion vehicles or solar cells.

Rather than simplifying access to pamphlets and clippings, Dewey or LC classification creates an extra barrier. An artificial symbol stands between the user and the material. Instead of turning directly to the files for a pamphlet on fences, it becomes necessary first to determine what numerical code has been assigned to pamphlets on that subject.

Because of these many drawbacks, Dewey or LC classification are poor choices for dealing with pamphlets and clippings.

These supplementary resources should be organized instead by an alphabetical arrangement of subject headings. This method, which is sometimes called a dictionary arrangement, has much to recommend it.

1. *It is direct.* There is no need to translate verbal ideas into an artificial number code.

2. *It is simple.* Alphabetical arrangement is easy to understand and manipulate. In libraries where patrons are encouraged to help

themselves, this simplicity will be particularly appreciated by the young, the inexperienced, and the undereducated.

3. *It is detailed.* A dictionary approach allows for the use of individualized and definitive terms, which speeds access to materials and enables them to make their fullest contribution.

4. *It is adjustable.* New subjects are easily added to a dictionary arrangement. Refinements of old subjects are also easy to incorporate.

All in all, alphabetical arrangement is the most efficient, economical, and productive scheme currently available for coping with pamphlets and clippings.

Full Cataloging or the Subject Approach?

Cataloging of pamphlets is an unnecessary luxury for the average school or public library. An author or title approach to pamphlets is rarely required, as pamphlet requests are almost exclusively subject-oriented. It is true that a school or public library may occasionally treat an exceptional pamphlet as a mini-book, providing both classification and cataloging so that it can take its place on the regular shelves. This happens most frequently with pamphlets which depict facets of local history. Aside from such rare exceptions, school and public libraries should hold entirely to alphabetical arrangement and a subject retrieval system.

In university or special libraries, there may be pressure for more ambitious treatment of the pamphlets in the vertical files. But even here, benefits of full cataloging should be carefully weighed against the substantial costs involved. A compromise plan has been developed in some special libraries. They hold to a simple subject approach for the bulk of their pamphlets. For a small number of pamphlets which are of special significance or which are likely to be requested by author, title, or sponsoring agency, they insert a full set of catalog cards in their general catalog. The cards indicate the location of these select pamphlets in the vertical files. A notation is made on each pamphlet indicating that it is represented in the card catalog. Such a compromise permits the library to retain the economy and ease of a subject index, while still providing more elaborate access to a limited group of pamphlets.

Librarians are sometimes tempted to single out well-known series such as the **Public Affairs Pamphlets** for full cataloging. A pamphlet series is usually housed as a unit after such processing. The need for this cataloged information simply is not great enough to justify the expense. Nor is separate housing desirable. If access by series name is considered absolutely essential, a more practical plan would be to file the pamphlets by subject while retaining a series list indicating where each pamphlet has been placed.

If you find it difficult to settle for a subject approach alone, remember that the **Business Periodicals Index** and the **Applied Science & Technology Index** are subject indexes. Even the **Readers' Guide to Periodical Literature** omits title entries, while the **Vertical File Index** makes no provision for author indexing. The subject approach is the one feature which all these tools consider indispensable.

When pamphlets and clippings are entirely arranged by subject and entirely retrieved by subject, the job of assigning headings takes on a sobering importance.

In fact, choosing subject headings for vertical file materials becomes an even more exacting task than classifying and cataloging books. It's true that a single classification number must be selected for a given book, but many alternate approaches can be arranged through multiple subject entries in the card catalog. On the other hand, the one subject heading assigned to each pamphlet or clipping provides the only access to that item.

Where does a librarian turn for help in carrying out this crucial operation?

Through eight editions that spanned 39 years, many libraries consulted **Subject Headings for the Information File (28)**, a list that was based on headings used in the Public Library of Newark, New Jersey. This old standby has long been out of print.

For a time, the Toronto Public Library published a compilation titled **Subject Headings for Vertical Files (229)**. Its purpose was to provide uniform headings for the branches of the Toronto Public Library system. Since it was heavily weighted with entries that were purely Canadian in application, its use elsewhere was as a sample of a working system. This list, too, is now out of print, and there are no immediate plans for updating.

While it is still being sold, Norma O. Ireland's **Pamphlet File in School, College, and Public Libraries (136)** is completely outmoded.

To my knowledge, there are no other comprehensive lists of subject headings on the market which are especially designed for vertical files.

What other possibilities exist for finding appropriate subject headings?

Some libraries attempt to use book headings for their vertical files as well. The rationale behind this practice is that common headings will coordinate all the resources of the library, making it easier to find everything the library has in a particular subject area. Furthermore, patrons and staff need to become familiar with only one set of subject headings. This sounds utopian. However, serious problems can arise when it is applied.

What's wrong with using a compilation like **Sears List of Subject Headings (214)** as the master authority for vertical files? A great deal! Sears was designed for use with books, not pamphlets and clippings. Furthermore, it was planned for the needs of a relatively small collection. Its headings are too generalized and too sparse to cope with the intricate diversities of pamphlets and clippings. Using its headings for vertical file materials is like giving directions for finding Philadelphia by saying only that it's in the state of Pennsylvania. The long time lapse between editions of Sears presents another difficulty. Because of this lag, it cannot supply headings for the many new developments picked up in pamphlets and clippings. Nor can it stay abreast of shifts in terminology that occur during the interim period. The final caution in using Sears is that, despite sincere efforts to streamline and modernize headings in the latest edition, some unwieldy or clumsy entries still linger on.

Since Library of Congress headings are much more extensive in number and represent a continuing stream of cataloging, do they offer a better solution than Sears? The answer is a resounding "No!" Once again, there is the problem of applying book headings to resources which are much more finely focused. Once again, there is the problem of locating headings for new topics that haven't yet appeared in book format or which haven't yet cleared LC.

There are other substantial problems as well. Library of Congress subject headings were developed for use in a massive library dedicated to scholarly research and to the preservation of materials for posterity. They are not in tune with the speech patterns or thought processes of most people who use school, public, or even academic libraries. The present assortment of LC subject headings is honeycombed with awkward, archaic, and arcane terms.

The standard explanation offered for continuation of objectionable headings has been that the task of changing the LC card catalog constitutes too massive an endeavor. In 1981, the Library of Congress will close that catalog. Will this event initiate a flow of clear, practical headings from LC? It would be nice to think so, but there is no assurance. Even when the Library of Congress has had unrestricted opportunities to create new headings, its track record has been dismal. The results have been such classic headings as "Conflict of generations."

Even after its card catalog is closed and a new automated system is activated, the Library of Congress will still remain a monolithic scholarly repository, producing subject headings geared to the needs of such an institution.

It's no wonder that the Hennepin County Library (124) decided to abandon strict adherence to LC headings in favor of relevant terminology and a wide assortment of useful cross references. Under the direction of Sanford Berman, a refreshingly down-to-earth scheme of subject headings has been developed. The authority file of the Hennepin County Library is for sale to other libraries on microfiche. A bimonthly publication, the **HCL Cataloging Bulletin**, keeps its subscribers up to date on new developments. In its attempts to be sensitive to ethnic groups, Hennepin County created some subject headings which have been criticized for their obscurity. Despite such reservations, this user-oriented library is to be applauded for a giant step in the right direction.

The quandary over using book headings for vertical file materials can be easily resolved by observing a few basic principles. It's perfectly proper to use book headings for pamphlets and clippings when they do the job as well as it can be done. Never try to make do. It would be a tragic mistake to attempt to force a vertical file collection to conform to a given set of book headings. The odds for finding suitable choices among book subject headings are much greater with the Hennepin County Library program than with either Sears or LC.

Even if you fail to use book headings for your vertical files, you do not have to forgo referrals from the card catalog. Although your headings for pamphlets and clippings may differ from those for book entries, there are still methods for creating a referral system in the card catalog. They will be discussed later in this chapter.

The librarian in search of headings may find that the **Vertical File Index** (240) can be of some assistance. When you order from this buying guide, mark your order record with the subject heading under which the pamphlet is entered. The notation will be a handy check when you are deciding on terminology. An overview of the subject headings used in the **Vertical File Index** can be obtained from its quarterly subject compilations.

Don't expect the impossible from the **Vertical File Index**. It can be tapped for helpful hints, but it won't solve all of your heading problems. In the first place, it incorporates a fairly small list of subject headings. Furthermore, the range of subject headings is spotty, since it reflects only the pamphlets which happen to be selected for inclusion.

Most headings in the **Vertical File Index** are specific and contemporary, but occasionally, subject choices are included which are cumbersome, generalized, or overly traditional. This means that selectivity should be your motto in using subject designations from this tool.

Periodical indexes are excellent aids in establishing vertical file headings. A periodical index must be current to survive. As a result, it's likely to offer headings for new areas of interest simply because it has to deal with them and deal with them immediately. In addition, periodical articles are likely to focus upon very specific subject areas. This means that subject headings in periodical indexes are likely to be direct and explicit.

For general all-around use, the best ally that a librarian can have in developing vertical file headings is the most famous periodical index of all, the **Readers' Guide to Periodical Literature**. Its coverage is extensive. Its headings are detailed. There is a continuing effort to modernize and refine subject designations.

The **Readers' Guide** is not without flaws. You will find some terms in the index which are oblique, outmoded, or unnecessarily formal. As of this moment, it is still using:

"Biology—Periodicity" for biorhythms

"Deformities" for birth defects

"Right to labor" for right to work

"Support (domestic relations)" for child support

Nor are all of the headings in the **Readers' Guide** consistent in form. For example, it employs an inverted order for "Children, Handicapped" while using regular word sequence for "Mentally handicapped children."

Nevertheless, its merits as a subject heading source far outweigh its failings.

The wisest use of the **Readers' Guide** in selecting subject headings is as a guide and not as a commitment. It is a mistake to adopt any or all **Readers' Guide** headings without adjusting them to your concepts of clarity and to the peculiar needs of your resources and clients. Unfortunately, many libraries rely so heavily on **Readers' Guide** that they don't even bother to create a subject heading index of their own. They simply use a duplicate volume of **Readers' Guide** as an index, checking the headings which they have activated. Headings chosen from later issues of the guide are penciled in this master book. One large library I have visited doesn't attempt to maintain even this type of record. Since all of its subject headings are copied from **Readers' Guide**, it assumes that staff and patrons can consult any issue for leads to its vertical files. The fact that many headings in the guide have changed drastically doesn't seem to have struck home.

While the **Readers' Guide** can be the first line of resort in most instances, you may want to look for valid headings in more specialized sources when you find yourself dealing with highly specialized subjects. For example, the **Business Periodicals Index** is a good introduction to the vocabulary which is employed in commerce and industry. A few of the other specialized indexes which may be helpful are:

Applied Science & Technology Index

Art Index

Education Index

Public Affairs Information Service Bulletin

In coping with specialized topics, don't forget the basic reference books in these areas. Encyclopedias, handbooks, and dictionaries can often supply the background information or authoritative terminology you need to make a proper decision.

Despite all the professional aids you can muster, in the end you will be thrown on your own good judgment and ingenuity in choosing subject headings. There will be many times when you will have to deal with pamphlets and clippings long before the **Readers' Guide** gets around to admitting that such subjects even exist. Some of your choicest finds may be on topics which are too minor or too localized to win the notice of the standard indexing tools. In addition, there will always be the need to personalize subject headings to fit the contents of your files, the personality of your community, and even the phrasing of the requests you receive.

While the preceding paragraphs have dealt primarily with the location of subject headings for general collections, similar patterns and cautions apply to special libraries. Such libraries will want to center their subject heading search on the tools specifically designed for their areas of concentration.

Libraries in the health care field, for example, can turn to **Medical Subject Headings (181)**, the thesaurus generated by the National Library of Medicine. The headings in this list are precise and authoritative. They are revised regularly to reflect changes in terminology and to incorporate new subjects. Subscribers to **Index Medicus** receive an updated copy of **Medical Subject Headings** in January each year as part of their subscription. The list can also be purchased separately.

Another useful source for subject headings in the medical area is the **Cumulative Index to Nursing & Allied Health Literature (67)**. Each year the annual cumulation contains a list of the subject headings used in the index. The list is also offered for sale separately.

A special library serving educators or students in education courses can consult the **Education Index** for possible leads to subject headings. It should also investigate the rich assortment of headings offered in the **Thesaurus of ERIC Descriptors (227)**. This authority file is a gold mine of specific terminology that can be adapted for direct headings and cross references as well. Be sure that you understand the ground rules by which it is organized. Inverted headings, for example, are never employed. The **Thesaurus** is supplemented between editions by a listing of new subject headings which appears in each issue of **Resources in Education** and the **Current Index to Journals in Education**.

These two areas of specialization—health care and education—have been used to demonstrate what other types of special libraries might be watching for in the way of subject heading aids.

Assigning Subject Headings

A few easy principles and procedures can help you with this challenging operation.

The first rule is to concentrate responsibility for subject heading assignment in one person if possible. This is not a job which can be doled out to any staff member or volunteer who happens to have a few minutes of free time. In order to establish an integrated gridwork of subject headings, there must be one person who has an overall view of the system and can provide for the intermeshing of its many parts.

At a certification workshop sponsored by our state library, I asked one group of participants to organize a local history file. In their report to the full workshop, they took pains to stress their discovery that a committee is not a good medium for assigning subject headings.

While subject heading selection is essentially a one-person job, this does not mean that the advice of other staff members should be ignored. They should be encouraged to suggest pertinent cross references for which a need arises as they work with the files. They should be solicited for help when you encounter materials that defy categorizing. For unless you consider what others use as access points in running down information, you may actually be hiding it from them.

Subject headings should be specific. This quality reflects the nature of most questions we receive. Libraries rarely encounter a request for general materials on berries. Instead we're asked how to cut back raspberry canes or how to make a strawberry barrel.

This natural emphasis on the specific has been magnified by the increasing sophistication and complexity of the world in which we live. While students several years ago were asking for material on drug addiction, today they have narrowed their requests to LSD, cocaine, or "angel dust."

Specific headings are great time savers in locating information. Lumping everything from measles to syphillis under a general topic like "Diseases" may make subject heading a breeze, but it certainly slows up the retrieval process. Having to search through fat folders filled with irrelevant materials to get the actual subject matter you want is a slow and frustrating procedure.

Specific headings are especially appealing to patrons and inexperienced staff members who use the files. They can't always make the mental jump between the information they seek and generalized subject headings. Not everyone will think to look for bookcase plans under "Storage."

What about the embryonic collection of pamphlets and clippings that is just getting under way? What about the vertical files in a very small library? Aren't broad headings more logical in these circumstances? Admittedly, broad headings require less time for subject assignment and the preparation of index cards. They save supply money because fewer folders are used. When resources are skimpy, it's possible to quickly leaf through general folders to find what is needed.

But a collection that is a living collection is also a growing collection. Sooner than you think, the time will arrive when your folders are literally bursting with riches. To make them manageable, you will have to divide the contents. Wouldn't it be better to avoid as much of this disruption as possible by assigning specific headings in the beginning?

Good subject headings should always be simple and direct. Don't try to be elegant or scholarly. You'll just create intellectual smog. If you have a pamphlet on stump removal, it belongs under that stark, simple heading rather than an artificial euphemism.

Even library terms hallowed by tradition should be reexamined in the interests of simplicity and directness. "Architecture, Domestic" has very little meaning to the general public. Why not replace it with "House plans"? No one asks for material on "International correspondence"; "Pen pals" is the phrase used by the public, and that should be the phrase used in your collection. Such colloquialisms are a legitimate choice for subject headings if they help to provide easier access to the facts in your files.

In the pursuit of simplicity and clarity, inverted subject headings should always be judged critically before they are employed. They were originally intended to emphasize key words and to bring affiliated subjects together. In this capacity, they have a useful role to play. But when used indiscriminately, they hinder more than they help. Awkward inversions such as "Education, Bilingual" and "Mothers, Unmarried" are prime examples. My pet aversion is "Buildings, Prefabricated." The artificiality of this inverted form is demonstrated by the fact that most people refer to these structures as "prefabs."

Extreme reliance on subdivisions can also interfere with a direct approach to pamphlets and clippings. There are many instances where subdivisions are useful or necessary devices. For example, they provide a way of neatly separating the materials that accumulate on a particular country. But where subdivisions can be gracefully and sensibly changed to independent entries, this should be done. Why pyramid "Pets" into "Pets—Cats" and "Pets—Dogs," when these animals could be placed under direct headings? Now and then you may find it necessary to turn to a general pamphlet about pets to find the answer to a question on cats or dogs, but this is a fragile excuse for building a hierarchy of headings under "Pets."

Subdivisions tend to become lengthy and convoluted. Let's suppose that your material on dogs is so extensive that it needs to be separated. If you use the hierarchical approach, you may now find yourself with such overgrown headings as "Pets—Dogs—Breeds."

It is necessary to maintain currency in subject headings. As new nations emerge, as government agencies are renamed, as scientific terminology changes, and as women like Jacqueline Kennedy remarry, your subject headings should reflect these shifts.

To save time, some librarians leave pamphlets and clippings under the outdated heading and rely upon a cross reference to lead the user to the material. This is an ill-advised shortcut. If a political area splits into several independent states, why should material on these states continue to be lumped under an obsolete heading? As well as creating confusion for the user, it makes the library look very foolish. There is the matter of fierce national pride to consider, too. Foreign students and immigrants may be offended by the use of old political terms that represent bondage to them. While this example deals with political units, the same urgent need for updated headings exists in other contexts. For instance, parents of afflicted children may object to having "Mongolism" as the active subject heading with only a cross reference from "Down's syndrome."

Subject headings should honestly reflect the contents of pamphlets and clippings. This means that the librarian must venture beyond the title or headline to determine what the text really covers. A little investigation before assigning a heading not only insures access to information but may save you embarrassment as well. A booklet bearing the cover title, **Making Elderly Housing Livable**, might deal with the remodeling of old houses or with the provision of suitable places for older people to reside.

Inevitably you will find yourself faced with the problem of deciding what to do with a pamphlet that covers two subjects—both of which constitute important areas in your files. You can, of course, arbitrarily decide on one heading and ignore the other. Or you might toss the pamphlet into a very general heading where there is a good likelihood that it will be overlooked completely. A happier solution is to obtain a second copy and cover both approaches. Or you might photocopy portions to place under the second heading if copyright infringement is not an issue. Isn't this an expensive solution? No more costly than using staff time to agonize over the dilemma.

One word of caution, however! If you duplicate material under two headings, be sure to note on each item the location of the other copy. When you chance upon one of these resources at some distant date, you won't have to wonder if you assigned the right heading to convey its dual nature. You will immediately be reminded that you covered all possibilities. The simple notation becomes a great time-saver.

When a new edition of these bifurcated pamphlets is issued, you can make do with a single copy. Place the latest edition under the more popular heading. Leave the older issue under the alternate subject but add a note referring the user to the new edition.

Another method of handling a multi-faceted item is to place a referral note under the alternate subject heading, alerting the user to the material and its location. Referral notes should be large enough to avoid being lost among the pamphlets and clippings in the file folder. When photocopying is permissible, as with federal publications, a photocopy of the pamphlet cover can be used as a referral device under the alternate heading.

A great deal of time and mental anguish can be saved by developing scope notes which record decisions and directions about subject headings that are troublesome or confusing. Memories are short. Staffs change. A scope note can serve both as a quick refresher for an established librarian and a helpful orientation for a newcomer. With the help of these notes, you can define once and for all what will go under "Food" and what will go under "Nutrition" in your collection.

Cross references are an integral part of the subject heading process. They are like the cross strands that hold a spider's web together. Be generous in their use.

Cross references can help you compensate for the fact that people's minds are as varied as their fingerprints. What seems perfectly obvious to you may be obscure to your co-worker. Try to provide for all possible roads that others might travel in getting to the heading you've selected. This may even mean stretching logic a bit. A referral from "Fish" to "Shellfish" is technically incorrect. But it's wise to make this referral anyway. In common parlance, the difference between fish and shellfish becomes blurred.

Cross references can help to lead your users from obsolete headings to current headings.

They will enable you to show family relationships between subjects that are separated in your files.

In creating cross references, some librarians fall into the trap of basing referrals on the contents of individual pamphlets or clippings rather than on the logical relationship between subject headings. A booklet on awnings has been published which contains an unexpected but useful section on cabanas. These librarians would make a cross reference from "Cabanas" to "Awnings" on the basis of these few pages in a single pamphlet. This is a dangerous practice. If you use cross references to lead to isolated pamphlets or clippings rather than to normally allied subjects, you are destroying the integrity of the subject headings. When the items you've singled out for special treatment are lost or discarded, the artificial references become meaningless gibberish because they have no intrinsic validity.

Solutions are available which do not threaten the long-term reliability of the subject heading network. For example, a referral note might be placed inside the folder on cabanas suggesting that the awning booklet be consulted. If legally permissible, photocopies might be made of the pages on cabanas.

The job of assigning subject headings and creating cross references is an awesome one, but it can be fun, too, as you watch an orderly gridwork emerge.

For the novice setting up a brand-new file or reorganizing a tired old file, the best procedure is to start with the easy and obvious subject headings. As you gather confidence and experience, you will be able to venture into more precarious areas.

Novice and veteran alike must avoid becoming so possessed by a subject heading system that it turns into a master and not a servant. A good subject heading system is not static. It changes and grows. Don't be afraid to employ innovations and adjustments if these deviations will better represent your resources and provide easier access to them.

Indexes

An index to the subject headings employed in pamphlet and clipping files is essential. Some librarians who are seeking shortcuts insist that an alphabetical file is self-indexing and needs no separate record. They point out that even cross references can be self-contained by recording them on the file folders or on separate guide cards. These claims are not sound. An alphabetical file is self-indexing only until one folder is removed or one folder is misfiled. Then it loses its authority as an index.

Using the file itself as an index is also physically tiring and emotionally frustrating for the librarian processing new materials. It means trotting to the files and opening drawers to verify headings.

Locating information becomes more cumbersome, too, when you must track down the material by opening and closing file cases rather than by consulting a separate index.

A separate index usually takes one of two forms.

It may consist of a list of headings typed on sheets of paper. The sheets may be compiled in a binder. This type of index is compact. If a binder is used, the index is very portable. It is also easy to flick one's eyes down the pages to see the relationships between subjects.

However, an index of this sort does not adjust well to change or expansion. Altered headings or new headings must be squeezed in wherever you can find room for them, making the index more difficult to interpret. If your vertical file is growing as vigorously as it should, you will find yourself faced with the need to retype the list of headings frequently. This is a costly process.

The other basic form of index is a card index. It is an open-ended structure. It can be added to indefinitely. Corrections are easy to make. Tracings can be hidden on the back sides of cards.

The traditional card index is made up of 3x5-inch cards housed in card catalog trays. Preferably, the cards should be punched so that they can be held in place by a guide rod.

It is also possible to use rotary card files or "v" files to hold index cards.

Normally, each subject heading is represented by a separate card.

While subject headings in a card catalog are usually recorded in red letters or capital letters, this technique is not necessary in a card index. It's better to reserve the use of red letters and capital letters for cross reference notations, as will be demonstrated later in this chapter.

Below is a typical index card in this modified format. It is typed in black:

Federal Bureau of Investigation

Cross references employing the common directions, "SEE" and "SEE ALSO," will be a prominent feature of your card index.

These sample cards indicate cross references:

Blizzards   SEE   Snowstorms

(Sample card for "SEE ALSO" reference is shown on page 76)

Signs

    SEE ALSO   Billboards
                    Road signs

◯

As you can see, the samples do not follow the indentations or spacing traditionally used for cross references in card catalogs. Nor is the traditional pattern of capitalization observed. This revised format is suggested because of its clarity. For added impact, "SEE" and "SEE ALSO" can be typed in *red* capital letters.

Good sense must be used in recording cross references. They may sometimes be entirely too numerous to list. In this event, use a blanket referral, as in this sample:

Diseases

    SEE ALSO   Names of individual diseases

◯

To prevent blind leads when headings are eliminated, tracings should be recorded on the back of each subject card, indicating the references from other headings to this particular entry. The tracings should be entered so that they can be read while the cards are in place in the file drawer. In effect, they will be upside down in relation to the printing on the front of the card. Making tracings on the back of an index card frees the front for more effective use with "SEE ALSO" references.

If it is at all possible, "SEE ALSO" references should be added to the fronts of the folders in your files. This will eliminate trips back to the index to check on supplementary headings. If desired, "SEE" references can also be inserted in the files on separate guide cards.

Ideally, the scope notes for your holdings should be incorporated into the index for your holdings. This would create a single master facility for use in assigning headings and tracking down resources. It is possible to give hints on the index cards themselves about policy decisions. For example, the index card for "Motels" might carry this note: "For material covering both motels and hotels SEE Hotels." However, authority explanations are often too lengthy to squeeze on index cards. For this reason, it would be much better to record your scope notes on cards of a different color, which would stand directly behind the corresponding index entries.

Scope notes may be added to the fronts of vertical file folders when such notations will facilitate use of the material.

To round out the picture of library resources offered by the card catalog, some libraries insert cards calling attention to subject headings for which there is vertical file material. Usually these catalog cards are provided in addition to the special index to pamphlets and clippings. Occasionally they replace the separate index entirely.

In most libraries, the referral entries in the card catalog are interfiled alphabetically with the book cards.

This common alphabetizing calls for some way of distinguishing between the resources and their locations. The subject entries for vertical file materials may be typed on colored cards or cards which are color-banded at the top. The words, "Vertical file" or "Information file," may be typed or stamped at the top left side of the card. On the other hand, the referral card might read like this:

GREENHOUSES

    For additional information on this subject, consult the vertical files.

                                 O

It has been suggested that a form card be used on which various types of resources are listed (248). The card for a given subject would have only those categories checked where information was available. A form card of this type might look like this:

FARMS

    For additional information on this subject, consult the special collections checked below:

☐   Vertical files

☐   Map collection

☐   Picture files

☐   Travel files

O

It must be recognized that some patrons will not notice or understand the check marks on such a card. They will assume that there is information in any collection listed.

Differences in the headings chosen for books and supplementary resources do not present insurmountable difficulties if you want to use the card catalog to publicize your vertical files. You can simply adjust the wording of the referral cards to make up for the discrepancies. If books on résumés are entered under "Applications for positions" and you are using the direct heading in your vertical files, the referral card might take the form shown below:

APPLICATIONS FOR POSITIONS

    For more material on this subject, SEE the folder on "Résumés" in the vertical files.

O

Another solution might be to evade any mention of the vertical file headings and use this general instruction instead:

APPLICATIONS FOR POSITIONS

For pamphlets and clippings on this subject, SEE the reference librarian.

O

In libraries which have substituted a book catalog for a card catalog, referral notes for vertical file resources can still be incorporated. The general guidelines would be similar to those for the traditional card format.

The inclusion of vertical file referrals in the general catalog is a common practice in school libraries where a "unit" catalog melding all media is desired. It is also useful in public libraries where the card catalog is in a room separate from that housing pamphlets and clippings. Since catalogs in book form are usually distributed to branches and affiliated libraries, the incorporation of vertical file entries into these catalogs will alert outlying agencies to additional resources.

However, serious questions can be raised about the need for referral entries in the card catalog of a small public library where the vertical files are very obvious and where the same librarian services both books and supplementary resources. Under such circumstances, some librarians suggest that a large placard or poster calling attention to the vertical files is a more economical solution.

CHAPTER 4

PAMPHLETS:
THE BROAD VIEW

WHAT IS A PAMPHLET?

It's anything you want to think of as a pamphlet. There is no agreement even among authorities as to the definition. **The Random House Dictionary of the English Language** describes a pamphlet as "a complete, unbound publication of generally less than 80 pages stitched or stapled together." On the other hand, Unesco says, "A pamphlet is a non-periodical printed publication of at least 5 but not more than 48 pages, exclusive of the cover pages . . . ." **Webster's Third New International Dictionary** carefully straddles the issue by defining a pamphlet as "an unbound publication other than a periodical having fewer than a fixed number (as 50, 80, 100) of pages . . . ." Acknowledging its diverse nature, the **American Heritage Dictionary of the English Language** depicts a pamphlet simply as "An unbound printed work, usually with a paper cover."

In practical terms, treatment seems to count more than format. If you treat a publication like a pamphlet, it becomes a pamphlet to all intents and purposes. And the decision as to treatment should be based on the type of handling that will make the publication most useful.

Despite emphasis on number of pages as a distinguishing feature, this criterion is ignored in most libraries. A one-page flyer may get pamphlet treatment. At the other extreme, our vertical files contain several husky paperback books that deal with elusive subjects.

It's equally important to be flexible in determining the classes of materials that can be described as pamphlets. In actual operation, a pamphlet collection can include an astonishing assortment of resources.

If you were to sample such a collection, you might find glossaries such as the U.S. Environmental Protection Agency's **Common Environmental Terms.** You might discover directories like the **List of U.S. Air Carriers** from the Civil Aeronautics Board. News releases might be a part of a pamphlet collection since they often contain detailed information not available elsewhere in a library's holdings. The news releases which the U.S. Department of Transportation distributes are good examples. To meet the needs of local churches, clubs, and schools, there could be copies of Thanksgiving Day or Arbor Day proclamations. The collection might include scripts for short plays or skits such as that perennial favorite, the **Lighthouse Keeper's Daughter.** Some pamphlets might consist of laws of intense public interest, such as landlord-tenant laws or firearms control legislation. You could come upon publicity announcements. Typical examples are announcements from national lecture bureaus or publicity about greeting cards which charitable organizations sell. You might even find that some pamphlets are really sheet music. A farsighted librarian, for example, might have tucked a copy of **Rudolph the Red-Nosed Reindeer** into the files to meet the inevitable Christmas demand.

The ultimate test as to what qualifies as part of a pamphlet collection is potential usefulness.

The guides to supplementary resources discussed in chapter 1 will be of great assistance in locating conventional pamphlets as well as the more unusual items that masquerade as pamphlets. But even more essential than having good finding guides is having a librarian who is prepared to search out and welcome useful material, no matter how or where it makes its appearance.

The paragraphs that follow will delineate some of the special resources that can be treated as pamphlets.

TRADE CATALOGS

Trade catalogs can be an integral part of a library's pamphlet service. In our library we have a sizable collection of garden catalogs from leading nurseries and seed firms. We attempt to include choice items such as catalogs of wild flowers, rock plants, and water lilies. We make a point of trying to represent firms headquartered in our part of the country. This collection serves a twofold purpose. It keeps our green-thumb set happy, and it functions as a reference tool for the library staff in identifying trees, shrubs, and flowers. Most of these catalogs can be obtained free, although a few special publications such as Wayside Gardens' famous catalog require a fee.

Mail-order catalogs of the "wishbook" variety can be rewarding additions. When it comes to the giant catalogs such as Sears', most libraries process them as books and house them with their book collections. But the smaller catalogs can best be treated as pamphlet materials. They are particularly popular at Christmas time. They also have other uses besides holiday gift giving. We have used the Abbey Press catalog (1) to track down the wording of mottoes or prayers which patrons have seen displayed as decorations in offices or homes.

Because collections of garden and mail-order catalogs are quite distinctive in nature and oftentimes quite great in number, some libraries choose to house them in pamphlet boxes. Patrons delight in browsing through catalogs displayed in this manner.

Specialized trade catalogs should not be overlooked. You'll find them sprinkled throughout our vertical files. Many varieties are represented—for example, school supplies, electronics, automotive parts and accessories, and agricultural paraphernalia. Nor are hobby interests ignored. We have catalogs that concentrate on model trains, china painting, jewelry making, and needlework. These catalogs are filed by subject among the other "pamphlets" in the vertical files.

Most libraries, big and small, collect publishers' catalogs. These are usually kept in the department or closed area devoted to book ordering. I would urge, however, that catalogs for skits and plays be housed in a more accessible place since they are in demand by schools, clubs, and amateur theaters. Catalogs for large-print books should also be readily available since they will be consulted by patrons who want to choose gifts for friends or relatives.

Your involvement with trade catalogs can be as modest or as extensive as your needs warrant. Special libraries often scour the field for all available catalogs in their interest areas. Large libraries with business and technology sections sometimes build up collections of thousands of trade catalogs. Where such extensive concentrations of catalogs are involved, they are usually housed separately in files or on shelves. Arrangement can be by company name or by subject. Indexes are often developed to cover all angles of approach.

SCHOOL CATALOGS

No public or secondary school library is living up to its obligations if it doesn't have a collection of college and vocational school catalogs that is both up to date and widely representative. Academic libraries also have a responsibility to acquire catalogs, particularly at the graduate level.

With production costs soaring, colleges and universities do not distribute their catalogs to individuals as generously as they once did. This restriction makes the library collection all the more important. Although there are some exceptions, institutions of higher learning usually furnish catalogs to libraries free of charge.

While the primary use for college catalogs is to help prospective students, they can perform other reference functions as well. For example, we've employed our collection of college catalogs to determine commencement dates, track down faculty members, and pinpoint special facilities, such as a reading disability center.

Collections of college catalogs can now be purchased on microfiche. Arguments for purchasing such sets center on ease of acquisition and savings in shelf space. Microfiche collections do, however, have some drawbacks:

1. The annual subscription rate is substantial.

2. Many people find it difficult to study material in this format.

3. Microfiche sheets are easily misfiled or lost.

4. Microfiche eliminates the possibility of circulating catalogs for home or classroom use.

5. The number of patrons who can consult the collection at any one time is restricted to the number of microfiche readers the library can afford.

6. Some libraries which subscribe to microfiche services have experienced gaps in updating and inconsistencies in index headings.

Catalogs, bulletins, and announcements from vocational and correspondence schools can be as important to your patrons as those from the most prestigious universities. Locating such schools and discriminating among them is a challenging job. The first and best course of action to follow is to contact your state department of education for a list of trade, technical, business, and correspondence schools approved to operate in the state.

Educational associations in these fields which have been recognized as accrediting agencies by the U.S. Office of Education will provide lists of their approved schools. Among these are the National Association of Trade and Technical Schools (169), the National Home Study Council (180), and the Association of Independent Colleges and Schools (23).

Publishers have released directories of vocational schools from time to time, and these can be helpful in ordering descriptive literature. There is a problem in updating these directories frequently enough to keep pace with this ever-changing field. Even the **College Blue Book's** special volume, **Occupational Education (57)**, suffers from this time lag although it is revised every few years. To attempt to cope with this dilemma, Croner Publications, Inc. provides a looseleaf service, the **American Trade Schools Directory (16)**, which is updated by monthly supplement sheets.

If you are completely stumped in locating training schools for a particular trade, write to a labor union or trade association in the field. Methods of discovering such organizations are discussed in the chapter on vocational materials.

If there are well-known military or boarding schools in your region, you may need to represent these schools, too, among your catalogs.

In collecting information about educational institutions, your first obligation is to achieve blanket coverage of your own area. Next make a concentrated canvass of your state. Finally, spread your nets for important schools across the nation and even in foreign countries. Community interest is the key factor in deciding how thorough your inclusion of distant schools should be.

Because their numbers will be large, school catalogs should be housed separately from other supplementary resources. College catalogs are usually arranged alphabetically. Ignore the generic term, "university," in alphabetizing them. Special types of educational institutions such as military and preparatory schools should be kept together for easy consultation. Trade and technical school information is most usable if grouped by the kind of instruction offered.

A card file that is a combination of source list, shelf list, and index will expedite maintenance and use of the school catalog collection. This device is particularly essential if catalogs are allowed to circulate. Cards are arranged alphabetically by name of the school. Addresses should be indicated to facilitate future orders. Any unusual ordering procedures should be noted. Information essential to proper labeling and housing should be specified. Finally, a record of the catalogs, bulletins, and announcements currently in the collection should be added in concise form.

There is no need to keep older issues of catalogs unless they represent local schools. In this case, you may choose to establish a long run as part of your community history collection.

ANNUAL REPORTS

Annual reports are available from such diverse entities as the American National Red Cross, the FBI, and General Motors. As sources of information about organizations, businesses, and government agencies, annual reports possess a potential for usefulness in two directions. The current report provides a contemporary picture of the body and its activities. On the other hand, a series of reports spanning a period of years reflects the evolution of the body.

How many years you choose to represent should be determined by the character of the requests you receive. In many cases, only the latest issue will be required to give sufficient insight into the nature of the issuing body. A one-year limit is especially easy to enforce if the current report summarizes statistics from several previous years. A longer run of annual reports may be desirable if each edition presents important and unique material that is not repeated elsewhere.

Certainly, annual reports originating from local sources should be considered for long-term preservation.

While annual reports are useful for the information they furnish about their sponsors, they have another role to play in public libraries which should not be overlooked. They can serve as patterns for institutions, organizations, or firms that want samples to follow in planning their own reports.

Larger public libraries often become involved in extensive collections of annual reports from businesses and industries. The theory behind such collections is that they will be studied by investors and job hunters. A small public library should exercise caution before plunging into such a project. It's true that the reports are free, but they do require time to solicit and maintain. Unless you're willing to go all-out in soliciting these reports, your collection will prove more frustrating than helpful. Nine times out of ten, the company that you're asked about will be one you don't have represented.

Small libraries might well limit themselves to collecting a representative group of annual reports to serve as models for local businesses and industries. It's another matter as far as the reports of firms in your community are concerned. These should be collected intensively.

Secondary school libraries may want to acquire annual reports from some of the corporate giants to assist classes that make mock investments in the stock market as part of their study of economics.

In college or university libraries which serve business students, a large collection of corporate reports is essential both for class assignments and for job hunting.

REPRINTS AND TRANSCRIPTS

Reprints (also called offprints) have assumed a more important role with the advent of the new copyright law. They can be utilized in two ways.

They may reproduce sections of resources that the library already owns. Reprints of this type may be acquired to help meet the demand for material on popular subjects. Another reason for adding such reprints is to make circulation of the information possible.

On the other hand, reprints may represent resources which the library does *not* own. In this case, reprints permit the library to make a discriminating selection of items from a tool which could not otherwise be easily consulted.

Reprints are available from a variety of periodicals, ranging from highly specialized publications such as **Teacher** and the **Journal of Studies on Alcohol** to more popular magazines such as **Consumer Reports** and **Boys' Life**. Occasionally, reprints are even available from books.

Unfortunately, there is no universal magic formula for locating reprints.

Some periodicals which provide reprints contain notices to that effect. If a periodical originates with an organization or institution, reprint information may be included in the publications catalog of the parent body. Sometimes the publisher or issuing agency will distribute a special reprint order form listing the titles available. Reprints may be picked up in serial indexes or bibliographies such as the **Vertical File Index (240)**.

The only solution is to be on the alert for leads wherever they occur.

Special librarians may obtain access to reprints from periodicals they do not own by consulting the particular edition of **Current Contents (69)** appropriate to their area of concentration. The various editions of **Current Contents** list the tables of contents of journals in specific fields. They also contain directories providing the mailing address of the senior author of almost every article listed. Since many scholarly journals offer a generous number of reprints to contributors, some special librarians find it profitable to write to the authors of articles which sound promising. Subscriptions to **Current Contents** are expensive. If you cannot afford the investment, you may be able to find a nearby university which subscribes to the service.

Since reprints represent a complex and growing resource, all that can be done here is to mention a few examples of what is available.

Periodicals may offer separate copies of all the major articles they contain. This is true of **Science** and **Scientific American**. Reprints from **Science** may be ordered from the reprint service of the American Association for the Advancement of Science **(6)**. Offprints from **Scientific American** are for sale by W. H. Freeman and Company **(97)**.

On the other hand, periodicals may select only certain articles to appear as reprints. This is the case with reprints from **Nation's Business, Boys' Life, Rehabilitation Literature**, and **Consumer Reports**.

Periodicals issued by the federal government may be a source for reprints. The Food and Drug Administration **(93)**, for example, will provide free reprints of articles selected from the **FDA Consumer**. Send for a copy of the FDA publications catalog for titles and instructions. Reprints of some key articles in the **Monthly Labor Review** are available free of charge from the Bureau of Labor Statistics of the U.S. Department of Labor. Check the **United States Government Manual (236)** for the address of your regional BLS office, and ask to be put on the mailing list for **New BLS Publications**, which will announce the reprints as they are released. While certain reprints from the **Department of State Bulletin** are for sale by the Superintendent of Documents, libraries may obtain single copies of any **Bulletin** reprint without charge by contacting the U.S. Department of State **(234)**.

The number of encyclopedia publishers furnishing reprints of articles from their sets has dwindled. **World Book Encyclopedia** and **Compton's Encyclopedia** still offer interesting assortments of reprints. Price lists are available from both publishers. While there is a charge for multiple copies, single copies of these reprints are provided free to libraries.

Some reprint series are not based on one publication alone. For example, the Aluminum Association, Inc. **(4)** offers an extensive collection of free reprints culled from a variety of periodicals as well as from other sources. Resources for the Future, Inc. **(207)** furnishes free reprints of papers by staff members and funded researchers which have previously appeared in journals and books.

Reprints available in the area of vocations are discussed in the special chapter on that subject.

Transcripts of radio and television programs have a contribution to make if they are selected judiciously. Be particularly cautious with interview programs. This format with its broken continuity can be disconcerting to some patrons. Center your choice on subjects that are of great interest or that are lacking in adequate coverage.

Meet the Press (152) is an old-timer among transcripts of the interview type. **Mental Health Matters (154)** is a newcomer. It consists of transcripts of community service radio programs prepared by the Alcohol, Drug Abuse, and Mental Health Administration.

New developments in the field of science are well-covered by the transcripts from two radio programs. One is **Man and Molecules (147)**, sponsored by the American Chemical Society. The other program is **Science Editor (210)**, which originates at the University of California.

In discussing transcripts and their role in libraries, it should be pointed out that transcripts made from oral history tapes are appropriate additions to local history files.

NEWSLETTERS, BULLETINS, AND MAGAZINES

Despite the fact that some definitions eliminate periodicals from consideration as pamphlets, there is a place for these alien resources in the vertical files.

When a library cannot afford to subscribe to specialized periodicals, sample issues in the vertical files will serve a double purpose. They can be examined by patrons who want to subscribe to magazines in special interest fields. These trial copies also function as reference sources, since the ads, feature columns, and terminology represented in even a single issue can be instructive. Typical of sample magazines which might be included in public library files are the **Model Railroader** and the **American Horseman**. Sometimes sample copies of magazines will be furnished free by publishers. They may also be contributed by staff and patrons. They should be filed by subject.

Newsletters or regularly released bulletins may also be absorbed into the vertical files when a library desires to preserve a limited number of recent issues rather than maintain a longer run. When a new issue arrives, the oldest copy in the files is discarded. Among the publications which a given library might choose to house in this short-term, revolving fashion are the **SFI Bulletin** from the Sport Fishing Institute, the **MS Messenger** from the National Multiple Sclerosis Society, and the **Status Report** from the Insurance Institute for Highway Safety.

Similar treatment may be given the newsletters and bulletins which are available for the asking from the information services and embassies representing various foreign countries. Typical of these publications are **Qatar News**, from the Qatar Embassy; **Austrian Information**, from the Austrian Information Service; **News of Norway**, from the Norwegian Information Service; **Venezuela Up-to-Date**, from the Venezuelan Embassy; and **France**, from the Press and Information Division of the French Embassy.

Some newsletters and bulletins originating with governmental or private sources are indistinguishable from conventional pamphlets. Each issue is an integrated composition completely devoted to a single, specific subject. Such newsletters and bulletins are more like pamphlet series. They should be treated accordingly. One example is **Canada Today/D'Aujourd'hui (45)**, a beautifully illustrated and substantial newsletter available from the Canadian Embassy. Each issue concentrates on some aspect of Canadian geography, politics, economy, or culture. Another example is the **Royal Bank of Canada Monthly Letter (209)**. Each **Monthly Letter** is an essay on such topics as futurists, employee morale, or family life. In dealing with newsletters or bulletins of this sort, each individual issue should be considered as an independent item and should be placed under the appropriate subject heading.

TRAVEL LEAFLETS

Travel leaflets do more than merely entice the vacationer to distant spots. They can also help to answer reference questions. Every public librarian knows the tourist who was busy taking photographs but neglected to jot down any identification of the scenes. Travel leaflets may help to solve this dilemma. They can also assist with many other types of information such as ferry schedules, opening dates of tourist attractions, admission fees, and insert maps of parks or recreation areas. My favorite example of travel reference concerns a local family that was hosting a foreign student. They wanted to take her with them on a short trip to Canada but didn't know if she would be allowed to cross the border and return. We found the necessary procedures in travel literature from the Canadian Government Office of Tourism.

Since current travel material will be needed both by the public and the staff, accumulate it generously and update it frequently.

As well as the customary leaflets, try to acquire schedules for the airlines, bus lines, and railroads that serve your area. Collect material on summer study programs abroad and on student travel arrangements. Watch for information on travel opportunities and arrangements for the handicapped. In addition to covering established attractions, be alert for special travel developments such as world fairs or Olympic games, which call for a crash effort to acquire literature. Remember that road maps are helpful supplements to the travel collection. They are discussed in chapter 8.

Fortunately, many groups and agencies are eager to furnish information on travel attractions.

On the national level, a great deal of material useful to travelers is generated by the National Park Service in the form of booklets, folders, and maps. The information covers national parks, monuments, recreation areas, historic sites, seashores, riverways, and lakeshores.

Mini-folders can be obtained free by writing to the superintendents of individual units in the National Park System. The other publications of the National Park Service are for sale by the Superintendent of Documents.

The NPS has no complete catalog of its materials. It does distribute a price list, **National Park Service Sales Publications (183)**, which includes some of its diverse output. It also publishes an **Index of the National Park System and Affiliated Areas (183)**, which gives the mailing address of each unit in the system so that you can write to those which interest you.

The Forest Service of the U.S. Department of Agriculture is responsible for a wealth of information about recreational use of the national forests. While publications of a general nature originate with the national headquarters, the regional offices and the individual forest supervisors carry on their own publishing programs as well, turning out excellent maps and descriptive textual material. While most of these publications are distributed free, there is now a $0.50 charge for the larger maps. The Forest Service (95) will provide you with a list of field offices so that you can request information directly from a particular region or forest.

An unusual set of travel guides has been prepared by the Department of the Interior's Bureau of Mines. They present interesting highlights about mines and mineral operations you can see from the highways as well as some mines you can visit. Historical sites and even ghost towns are included. The set contains six booklets, each describing a different part of the country. **Mining and Mineral Operations: Visitor Guides (37)** are for sale by the Superintendent of Documents.

The operations of the United States Travel Service were formerly directed at visitors from foreign countries. Now it is making its services and publications available to residents of the United States. The results are impressive. Among its many releases are a series of **Traveler's Guides to Special Attractions** and a packet of **Consumer's Guides to Travel Information.** Send to the United States Travel Service (237) for a list of the publications you can obtain free of charge.

The U.S. Department of the Navy has developed a series of **Port Guides** designed to assist Navy personnel on liberty in foreign countries. The store of explicit information they contain will make them invaluable to civilian travelers as well. Maps are included. Write to the Human Resource Management Division of the Bureau of Naval Personnel (203) for a listing of titles and prices. Orders are filled by the Naval Publications and Forms Center (203).

This rundown by no means exhausts the possible sources of travel literature at the federal level. For example, the Bureau of Reclamation, the U.S. Fish and Wildlife Service, and the U.S. Army Corps of Engineers have produced materials about recreational opportunities on the public land and water areas that they supervise.

At the state level, state chambers of commerce make good contacts for travel literature. State governmental agencies are also productive sources. Titles and jurisdictions vary from state to state. The responsibility for encouraging travel may rest with such diverse bodies as a tourist development agency, the state department of commerce, or the highway department. Parks departments or departments of conservation and natural resources often have excellent material to distribute on park areas, picnic grounds, and campgrounds. State units which supervise water resources may have printed information on water access sites or canoe trails. Game and fish agencies will furnish guides to hunting and fishing possibilities and regulations. State arts councils may publish guides to cultural attractions.

As well as statewide groups, there often are regional organizations that can be tapped for literature. For example, in Michigan we have such groups as the West Michigan Tourist Association, the East Michigan Tourist Association, the Southeast Michigan Travel and Tourist Association, and the Upper Peninsula Travel and Recreation Association.

Travel material about individual cities can be obtained from local chambers of commerce. Convention and visitors bureaus are also promising sources. Some city governments are publishing brochures and maps of interest to visitors.

A rich flow of information about foreign countries is available through their travel offices in the United States. Embassies and consulates may also be approached.

Your patrons and your staff can be cultivated as sources of travel literature, too. The descriptive material they acquire on their journeys can be choice additions to your collection, since many booklets or leaflets are distributed or sold only at the site of a tourist attraction.

There are a number of printed aids which will make it easier for the librarian to take advantage of the many organizations and agencies distributing travel material.

Leads to some of the travel resources issued by federal agencies will be found in **Selected U.S. Government Publications (216)**. Several of the **Subject Bibliographies (226)** distributed by the Superintendent of Documents are especially related to travel interests. They are:

SB 016—**Historical Handbook Series**

SB 017—**Recreational and Outdoor Activities**

SB 089—**Visitor Activities in the National Parks**

SB 140—**Public Buildings, Landmarks and Historic Sites of the United States**

SB 170—**National Park Service Folders**

In the free brochure, **Helpful Information Sources**, the United States Travel Service **(237)** offers a number of suggestions for acquiring travel information from federal agencies.

On the state level, clues to travel material can be obtained from the **Monthly Checklist of State Publications (163)**. In addition, a handy list of contacts is provided in **State & Territorial Tourism Offices**, a free directory issued by the United States Travel Service **(237)**. Another convenient place to locate state tourism agencies is in **State Administrative Officials Classified by Functions (223)**.

For collecting material about individual communities, an invaluable aid is the **World Wide Chamber of Commerce Directory (255)**, published annually by the Johnson Publishing Company, Inc. While its most important feature is the access it offers to local chambers of commerce, the directory includes references to state chambers of commerce as well. It also provides coverage of an international nature.

Another tool which cuts across several levels—national, regional, and state—is the **Catalog of Guides to Outdoor Recreation Areas and Facilities (38)**, published by the Bureau of Outdoor Recreation of the U.S. Department of the Interior. This 60-page publication will alert you to recreation guides produced by private, state, and federal sources. It even includes a few Canadian entries. You can obtain a free copy from the Bureau.

Also offering a multi-level approach is the **Festivals Sourcebook**, edited by Paul Wasserman and Esther Herman **(244)**. It is a compilation of recurring fairs, festivals, and community celebrations in the United States and Canada. Since it lists the names and addresses of contacts to approach for additional information, this guide will enable librarians to write for travel literature about any desired activity.

On the international scene, the Office of Public Information of the United Nations issues a free directory of **Information Services and Embassies in the United States of Members of the United Nations (232)**. Its title is a bit misleading. The directory has only one entry for each country. That one entry may be an information service, embassy, consulate, or permanent mission to the UN.

A source which includes the addresses of all foreign embassies and consulates in the United States as well as those of all permanent missions to the UN is the

National Directory of Addresses and Telephone Numbers, prepared by Stanley Greenfield **(114)**.

Of course, any library that owns a copy of the **Congressional Directory (59)** has at hand a full listing of foreign embassies in the United States.

The yellow pages of phone books for major metropolitan areas, especially for Manhattan and the District of Columbia, will also provide addresses for agencies representing foreign countries.

Our neighbor to the north is particularly outstanding among foreign governments for the quantity and quality of its travel publications. If you send for a free copy of **Canada Travel Information** from the Canadian Government Office of Tourism **(47)**, you will find many addresses that will be useful in obtaining travel brochures and maps.

In the search for travel literature, the ads in travel-oriented magazines can provide productive leads. Periodicals such as **Travel/Holiday** and **Sunset** are especially rich in possibilities. The travel sections in newspapers also are sprinkled with ads for free materials.

Frequently, travel articles in both magazines and newspapers will specify sources of literature or will single out booklets of special merit.

Some libraries with miniscule travel holdings do not attempt to separate this special category of materials in any manner. Travel brochures on Mexico rub shoulders in a single folder with studies of economic conditions in Mexico. Other libraries with limited travel materials treat "Travel" as just another subject heading in the general files, with a breakdown provided by subdivisions representing geographic regions. However, travel resources of any significance will soon outgrow these arrangements and make separate housing desirable.

Vertical files do not represent the only suitable homes for travel materials. A library may choose, instead, to house its travel collection on shelves in pamphlet boxes that are open at the top for easy visibility and accessibility.

PRINCIPLES OF SELECTION

Much of the material that we lump under the heading of "pamphlets" originates as advertising or publicity. This fact makes some librarians uneasy.

The trick is to guard against the crass sales pitch but also to be quick to salvage anything of potential value, no matter how "commercial" its origins. The test that any pamphlet must meet before achieving acceptance is how much it will contribute to the collection.

It is perfectly proper for a vertical file to contain generously illustrated booklets of home decorating ideas from manufacturers of paneling and floor coverings. It is acceptable to have information on planning a luau from a nationally known food processor. It's true that brand names appear in these publications, but the American public has learned to pick the diamonds from among the pebbles when it comes to this type of advertising material. And they are much too sophisticated to conclude that the library is in any way endorsing these products.

In urging liberal guidelines, my conviction is reinforced by the realization that most printed material contains some element of salesmanship. A booklet issued by a government agency to describe its activities and goals will be carefully edited to present a favorable image. Publications designed to attract new industry to a state are going to concentrate on the more attractive aspects. Pamphlets issued by professional groups to encourage career recruitment among young people are sure to present a complimentary picture of the profession.

The apprehension which librarians once felt about pamphlets on "controversial" subjects has diminished. In an era when junior high school students are writing papers on abortion and tenth-graders are studying homosexuality, there is less need for trepidation in most communities.

The one cautionary principle that has survived the years intact is to present a variety of viewpoints on touchy subjects. If you have a good collection in favor of fluoridation, try to obtain some material from those who oppose it. Despite the library cliches, it is literally impossible to represent *all* points of view about every controversial issue. But you can attempt to represent the major ones.

Years ago it was quite common to mark pamphlets with a warning to the patron when they were considered to be "propaganda" for a particular cause. That practice has declined as a result of the American Library Association's strong stand against labeling.

The librarian's best defense against charges of conveying propaganda is the variety of interpretations included in the files. I am, however, a complete realist. I know that in some communities this technique will not furnish adequate protection. If labeling must be used, the least harmful method is to apply a note to the folder using words to this effect:

> There are differing points of view about this subject. The
> library has attempted to represent some of them in the material
> in this folder.

Despite a personal dedication to the freedom to read, the librarian must never abandon the need to critically assess material on controversial subjects. Is the issuing source clearly identified? Anonymous material of this nature should never be added to the files. The patron has a right to know what individual or group is presenting these opinions. In the body of the pamphlet, does the writer identify the stand taken openly and honestly so that the reader can judge comments and information sources accordingly? Does the pamphlet attempt an intellectual approach rather than a purely emotional one?

Assessing community needs is important in choosing pamphlets just as it is in choosing books, but it is essential not to interpret these needs too narrowly when building pamphlet resources. The small expenditure of money and space involved will allow you to venture into areas that are impossible to represent in your book holdings. It is a mistake to devote your entire pamphlet collection to what is immediately and constantly popular. The vertical file offers a golden opportunity to explore the back roads of information. A pamphlet that tells how to estimate the board-foot volume of trees in a woodlot may not be called for every day. But when a patron does ask for this information, the need is real and immediate. The patron will go away marveling at the crackerjack librarian who was able to produce the necessary facts at a moment's notice.

School librarians are particularly prone to fall into the trap of restricting pamphlet acquisition to narrow limits. Certain school libraries acquire only material that is curriculum related. This rigid delineation may help to cut the time and money invested in the vertical files. Unfortunately, it will also help to convince students that libraries are agencies useful only with school assignments and not with their needs as complete and independent human beings.

As they build their pamphlet collections, librarians should be sensitive to the needs of special groups within their communities. Luckily, there is now a rich assortment of materials which can be used with Spanish-speaking residents. The federal government is a major source of such pamphlets. **Subject Bibliography 130, Publicaciones en Español (226)** lists Spanish-language publications for sale by the Superintendent of Documents. The Consumer Information Center's **Lista de Publicaciones Federales en Español para el Consumidor (60)** is a compilation of free and inexpensive materials from federal agencies on such subjects as child care, food, and employment. This list is revised annually and is distributed free of charge. In fact, you can order it in quantity to share with your Spanish-speaking patrons.

State governments have also been cognizant of the need for Spanish-language literature. Many states now issue publications in such crucial areas as driver licensing, public welfare, health, civil rights, vocational guidance, and consumer education. Some of them appear in the **Monthly Checklist of State Publications (163)**.

Even private organizations are producing useful pamphlets in the Spanish language. Examples are the American Heart Association, the Mental Health Association, the National Foundation/March of Dimes, and the Public Affairs Committee, which sponsors **Public Affairs Pamphlets**. So great is the flow of Spanish-language materials that Frances Press, Publishers has just released a 19-page compilation, **Gratis en Español!–Guide to Free Informational Materials in Spanish (96)**.

The situation is not so favorable for adults with minimal reading ability who need pamphlets with carefully controlled vocabularies. At present there is very little available from either governmental or private agencies to meet their requirements. A few publishers have developed simple reading materials for use in adult education courses. Although most of these items are designed for a classroom setting, some of them are suitable for library use. For example, you may want to investigate the pamphlets produced by the New Readers Press **(190)**, a division of Laubach Literacy International.

The physically handicapped constitute another special clientele whose concerns should be kept in mind when choosing pamphlets.

Keeping pace with new interests requires the librarian to be something of a fortune teller. For in order to be prepared with materials when the demand strikes, you must be able to predict trends. When the first inklings reached us of the burgeoning interest in solar energy and wind power, we started to watch for pamphlets on these subjects. When we began to suspect that macrame was going to be the next craft craze, we set out to collect materials in anticipation of this demand.

Librarians must do some careful guesswork for another reason. Regrettably, publishers sometimes try to disguise or ignore the advancing age of their releases. The passage of the years does little to affect the value of a pamphlet on the first Thanksgiving, but time erodes the usefulness of materials about such changing topics as industrial development. Watch for evidence of copyright dates.

In selecting materials for the pamphlet files, librarians need to be aware of the regional flavor of much printed information. For example, cooperative extension services issue helpful booklets on flower gardening, but the librarian must remember that rose growing in California is not the same as rose growing in Minnesota. Career booklets published by the employment services of the various states will reflect conditions peculiar to the area. Yet it's a mistake to be too rigidly bound by geographical boundaries. A library in a northern city may find that many of its residents winter in Florida. This dual residency may generate questions which require pamphlets beyond the usual acquisition pattern.

Decisions about ordering extra copies of pamphlets must be based on the popularity of the subject, the value of the publications, and the type of library involved.

School libraries have the greatest need for multiple copies, yet they are often fainthearted about duplicating pamphlets even in areas where crushing demands exist. If mass assignments are regularly given on narcotics, the school library should be prepared with masses of pamphlets to meet the onslaught. If it is impossible to house heavily duplicated items in the vertical files, extra copies can be kept in reserve in storage areas. A note on the file folder will indicate that multiple copies are available.

PAMPHLET SERIES

In library circles the term, "pamphlet series," immediately calls to mind such well-established subscription services as **Public Affairs Pamphlets** or **Editorial Research Reports**. Actually, these subscription services constitute only a portion of the output. There are many commercial publishers, associations, government agencies, and business interests engaged in producing pamphlets which are homogeneous enough in approach, subject matter, and format to be called pamphlet series.

The League of Women Voters **(141)** is an example of a national organization that sponsors pamphlet series. Its emphasis is on domestic problems, international relations, and citizen participation.

As far as organizations at the state level are concerned, California furnishes an outstanding example. The members of the California Medical Association have prepared an excellent series of two-page **Health Tips (122)** for laymen. Almost 400 have been released, covering everything from pacemakers to pinworms. Some Spanish-language materials are included. At least for the present, libraries have been placed on the mailing list to receive free copies of new titles in the series. However, there is a charge for back issues, which can be ordered from the **Health Tips Index (122)**.

Some pamphlet series have been initiated by institutions such as museums. The **Booklet Series** from Old Sturbridge Village **(195)** is typical. These pamphlets focus on life in the early days of New England.

Among the many pamphlet series produced by commercial publishers, one of my favorites is the **Handicrafts for Fun Library**, issued by Craft Course Publishers, Inc. **(65)**. This extensive series of pamphlets will help you meet craft requests ranging from bread dough artistry to decorative quilling.

Business establishments which are not part of the publishing world may develop pamphlet series as spin-offs from their regular activities. This is the case with the **Money Management Booklets (161)**, available from the Household Finance Corporation's Money Management Institute.

The federal government is the matrix for numerous pamphlet series, including such famous ones as the Department of Agriculture's **Home and Garden Bulletins** and the Small Business Administration's **Small Marketers Aids** and **Management Aids for Small Manufacturers**.

State governments can also foster pamphlet series. For example, the Missouri Department of Natural Resources distributes a group of **Bright Idea** pamphlets on various energy-saving devices and techniques.

This rapid overview can do no more than hint at the hundreds of useful series available in addition to the traditional subscription services.

When it comes to subscription services, most of them need no introduction to librarians. Among the established favorites are:

Background Notes (26). U.S. Department of State. Approximately 77 revised or new **Notes** each year.
> Basic facts about the countries of the world written by Department of State specialists. The **Notes** offer a succinct but amazingly thorough overview of each country.

Editorial Research Reports (81). Congressional Quarterly, Inc. 48 reports each year. Semiannual bound compilations.
> Concise, balanced surveys of timely topics. Especially good for historical and statistical coverage. A trusted series in existence since 1923.

Fieldstaff Reports (91). American Universities Field Staff, Inc. 50 reports each year.
> Scholarly studies of political, social, and economic trends in countries and regions of the world. The studies often deal with problems and developments of a more specialized nature.

Public Affairs Pamphlets (205). Public Affairs Committee, Inc. About 15 titles each year.
> A popular series of long standing. Covers a wide range of social and personal concerns. Very readable.

Pamphlets offered as part of subscription services are usually sold individually as well. Is it better to order such pamphlets separately or to subscribe to an entire series? There's a calculated risk in placing a subscription. You may find yourself acquiring items in subject areas where your files are already well-stocked. Topics may be covered that have no pertinence at all for the clientele you serve. Quality may vary from release to release.

On the credit side, it's normally cheaper to subscribe to a pamphlet series than to buy the publications separately. In addition, a subscription is a guarantee that you won't overlook important titles and that you will receive them promptly.

Nevertheless, even the better-known series need to be reassessed carefully and constantly to make sure that they continue to fill your needs.

More attention will be given to specialized pamphlet series in later chapters.

When a library subscribes to a pamphlet series, some means should be provided for checking on their arrival. The schemes used for recording the receipt of magazines can usually be adapted for pamphlets.

As indicated in chapter 3, there is no special virtue in housing a pamphlet series separately in splendid isolation. The pamphlets should be distributed by subject, since most requests for pamphlets are subject requests.

CHAPTER 5

CLIPPINGS

SOURCES OF CLIPPINGS

Armed with no more than a keen eye, a lively imagination, and a sharp pair of scissors, any librarian can garner clippings that will add both breadth and detail to the library's collection.

Clipping Newspapers

Where does one turn first for clippings? To newspapers, of course. It's obvious that the local newspaper will be fertile ground for clippings about community events and personalities. To stop with local affairs would be a great mistake, though, for newspapers can be harvested for articles on all categories of knowledge.

A distinguishing aspect of newspaper coverage is that it often provides a degree of elaboration lacking in periodicals and yearbooks. A good example is the painstakingly detailed coverage that precedes a presidential inauguration.

And, of course, newspapers beat magazines to the punch with current news. If a librarian suspects that questions will come in about new developments such as awards or appointments, that person would do well to clip the newspaper articles, at least for temporary consultation, since magazine coverage will lag behind and indexing in **Readers' Guide** will be even slower.

Newspapers are also noted for highlighting informational oddities. For example, we prize a clipping about an alleged "fur-bearing trout," which helps to settle arguments that crop up periodically.

Special columns or sections devoted to finance, homemaking, health, travel, and gardening should receive particular attention since they often produce helpful clippings. A home hints column, for example, may describe a quick way to remove stubborn bumper stickers. While most of these special columns will contribute occasional gems, some are regularly productive. Sylvia Porter's syndicated column furnishes authoritative, fact-filled clippings week after week.

The "action" columns to which readers write for intervention or information are often clippable, too. They give detailed replies to such questions as these: Is there a service for "sending" cakes by wire just as flowers are sent by wire? Who designs the United States pavilions that are built at world's fairs and expositions? Facts of this sort are hard to come by!

The rotogravure sections that are part of many Sunday editions are worth screening also. It was a clipping from a rotogravure section which provided the information our patron needed about Navajo-style rugs being made in Mexico.

In evaluating newspapers for clipping, avoid being stereotyped in your thinking. Potentially useful material can occur in unexpected places. In self-defense we've learned to clip the special prayers, credos, and poems which appear in Ann

Landers' column, because we know that months or years later we're sure to get a request from someone who recalls a particular inclusion.

Periodicals—Indexed or Unindexed?

When the first edition of this book was written, it was possible to make a neat distinction between indexed and unindexed periodicals. The dramatic proliferation of periodical indexes within the past few years has complicated the problem of dividing the oranges from the apples. It is obvious that not all of the new periodical indexes will survive. What is an indexed periodical today may be an unindexed periodical tomorrow as the result of the death of a particular index.

Furthermore, access to indexes differs from library to library because of budgetary and policy variations. It may even vary from one time period to another in the same library because of money crises.

For the down-to-earth realities of library service, an indexed periodical can be defined as a periodical for which the library has a continuing index to consult.

As far as periodical indexes are concerned, the most common denominator in libraries is ownership of the **Readers' Guide to Periodical Literature**. Therefore, for the purposes of this book, an indexed periodical will be arbitrarily designated as one being indexed in the **Readers' Guide to Periodical Literature** at the time this chapter is being written.

Clipping Unindexed Periodicals

The wealth of information incorporated in unindexed periodicals can be tapped only through a program of regular and generous clipping. Leafing through an issue of **Woman's Day** or **Family Circle** will demonstrate how much helpful material escapes the net of the **Readers' Guide**.

Possibilities are everywhere if you are receptive to them. For example, instead of tossing away old issues of **TV Guide**, consider clipping them for hard-to-find information on entertainment personalities and new TV shows.

"House organs" published by various businesses, industries, agencies, and associations offer a rich potential for clipping. If the car dealers in your area distribute customer magazines such as the **Ford Times**, **Dodge Adventurer**, or Chevrolet's **Friends Magazine**, ask to have the library put on the mailing list.

If staff members or loyal patrons go on airplane trips, have them bring back copies of the company magazines which are available on board.

House publications of the petrochemical industry may produce clippings for your collection. For example, from recent issues of **Panhandle Magazine (198)**, you might have gleaned articles on solar heating and on the development of the Red Delicious apple. A recent copy of **Aramco World Magazine (17)** would have yielded clippings on Arab flags, the ancient kingdom of Ebla, and the history of dates.

Ward's Natural Science Establishment, Inc. and the Carolina Biological Supply Company distribute newsletters about their products that also incorporate short articles on topics of scientific interest. A recent **Ward's Bulletin (242)** featured an article on cloning, while a recent issue of **Carolina Tips (50)** gave instructions for setting up science experiments for science fairs.

Financial institutions can help to enrich library files with house publications that focus on economic conditions and the many factors which influence them. **First Chicago World Report (92)**, Chase Manhattan Bank's **Business in Brief (42)**, and the Citibank's **Monthly Economic Letter (164)** are among the surveys which can provide timely clippings.

Don't forget that "house organs" originating with nonprofit organizations are worth checking, too. The **Humane Society News**, issued by the Humane Society of the United States, is representative of these periodicals.

Fraternal and club publications such as the **Kiwanis**, the **Rotarian**, and the **Elks Magazine** should be screened as clipping sources, since they frequently include articles on topics of general public interest.

Also keep in mind that government agencies may issue "house organs" that are good for clipping. An example is **Agenda (2)**, published by the Agency for International Development.

For an annotated sampling of "house organs," consult the section on free magazines in **Magazines for Libraries**, by Bill Katz and Berry G. Richards **(137)**.

Ken Haycock's **Free Magazines for Teachers and Libraries (119)** is another useful source for locating "house organs" suitable for clipping. Haycock chose periodicals which would both support the curriculum in junior and senior high schools and serve as a resource for teachers and teacher-librarians. Annotations are given. While the list was compiled in Canada, it includes many U.S. publications.

A listing of over 3,400 house magazines is provided in the **Internal Publications Directory (134)**, which is volume 5 of the **Working Press of the Nation**. Despite its title, it covers both internal and external publications. While it is expensive, this directory can function as a reference tool for freelance writers, photographers, and artists, as well as guiding the library to useful "house organs."

In appraising unindexed periodicals, it's important to note that clipping opportunities aren't limited to publications directed at adults or young adults. Children's librarians and elementary school librarians will want to assess the clipping possibilities of periodicals published for people at these age levels. **National Geographic World (178)** is an example. Another is **Daisy (71)**, a magazine published by the Girl Scouts of the U.S.A.

Clipping Indexed Periodicals

Some librarians will shake their heads at the thought of clipping indexed magazines, but there are good practical reasons for doing so. Despite the priceless assistance furnished by the **Readers' Guide to Periodical Literature**, it is only fair to point out that there are omissions in our beloved RG. Many years ago it stopped indexing poetry. It will not help you to keep tabs on those once-in-a-lifetime poems that can be converted into toasts for mother-and-daughter banquets. It's true that now there is an **Index of American Periodical Verse (256)**, but the coverage offered is very spotty. Its emphasis is on scholarly literary magazines. It omits most of the sources which print the "homespun" poems we need for holidays, school programs, and club presentations.

Another indexing gap in **Readers' Guide** involves the contents of the special columns which are an outstanding feature of so many magazines. Question-and-answer columns or those which touch on a variety of topics are not analyzed.

The little treasures of information they contain are literally lost unless you transfer them to your files.

Another factor threatening the universality of coverage in **Readers' Guide** is the widespread existence of variant magazine editions. Elin B. Christianson **(55)** wrote with alarm about this problem in the **ALA Bulletin** for February 1968. The problem still exists. The use of diversified materials for different parts of the country and, to a lesser extent, for special interest editions means that the particular magazine you hold in your hand may not be the edition chosen for indexing in **Readers' Guide**. Public libraries are more likely to encounter regional deviations. School libraries may also face problems with special school editions.

The variation from one part of the country to another may be so great that each regional edition is almost an entirely new magazine. On the other hand, only a section or filler may be inserted for different parts of the country. You can often detect these inserts by the strange pagination they carry. The features in these special inserts are rarely noted in the table of contents, let alone in **Readers' Guide**.

The implications are clear: librarians cannot blissfully assume that **Readers' Guide** is going to provide total access to indexed magazines. They are going to have to clip or do supplementary indexing if they want to make use of information that is bypassed by **Readers' Guide**.

There are occasions when clipping is desirable even for magazine articles that are fully indexed in **Readers' Guide**. When the brown recluse spider first made its appearance in our part of the country, we experienced a rash of calls from frantic parents. Information on the spider was sparse and scattered. We clipped duplicate copies of all magazine articles we could find so that they would be immediately available in our files.

Clipping extra copies of indexed magazines is a good way to cope with those subjects on which high demand for information strains a library's collection. Current examples are child abuse and battered spouses. If you have extra copies of key articles in your files, you will be better able to face the onslaught of mass assignments on these subjects. For libraries that do not circulate magazines, there is an extra bonus. These clippings can be charged out for home use.

In clipping magazines—whether indexed or not—don't be bound by rigid tradition. Ads, for example, are perfectly acceptable additions to library files if they can solve a patron's problem. Watch for advertisements which give instructions for making gaily decorated cakes or centerpieces for holiday celebrations. If General Foods pays for a full-page advertisement featuring an Easter egg cake, you should have no qualms about clipping it for your collection.

When libraries face a space squeeze that forces them to discard back runs of magazines, clipping provides one way to salvage some of the more important material for continued use. In most libraries, the librarian makes the decision as to what to save. In a small special library, users may be encouraged to mark articles which they want preserved when the periodical is discarded.

Sources of clippings for picture files will be discussed in chapter 9.

PHYSICAL TREATMENT OF CLIPPINGS

Supplying Copies

If you are going to do a thorough job of clipping magazines and newspapers, you will frequently find yourself faced with the need for multiple copies. This can occur because important articles are printed back to back. Particularly in the case of local history clippings, it can occur when you find it necessary to place an article under more than one subject heading. There are three solutions.

1. *Provide extra copies of the newspapers or magazines.* In the case of your local newspaper, staff members can be recruited to donate their back papers. In the case of magazines such as **Family Circle** or **Woman's Day**, which are filled with desirable articles, buy two copies right away or watch for extras among old magazines donated to the library.

2. *Photocopy articles when legally permissible.* Periodicals published by the federal government are exempt from copyright restrictions. Some periodicals published by nongovernmental sources carry a notation that the contents may be freely copied. Aside from such obviously safe zones, librarians must study the copyright law and its interpretations as a guide to their procedures.

3. *Use referral notes.* If you cannot solve the problem with extra copies or photoduplication, you might consider placing a referral note in the file folder under the alternate heading.

Marking

While the selection of articles to be clipped should be done by the person in charge of the files, the actual clipping may be carried out by someone else, such as a student assistant or clerical helper.

With a second person involved, the marking of the newspaper or magazine for clipping becomes a pivotal process. It must be done clearly and carefully so that the clipper can proceed quickly and confidently with the job.

In the case of newspapers, slash marks or brackets can be placed with a fine-line marking pen at the top and bottom of the article to be clipped. Red is a good marking color.

If only an occasional article in a newspaper is marked, the page numbers can be listed on the front page to speed the clipper's work. However, in the case of local newspapers most pages carry some article of interest. Under such circumstances, it would be wasteful to bother listing page numbers.

When scanning magazines for clipping, a slip of paper can be stapled to the front cover for recording pages to be saved, as well as any other necessary instructions.

If subject headings can be jotted down during the marking process, the clipped articles can be sorted immediately to make them accessible for quick reference even before their processing is completed.

Clipping

Good equipment is essential to establishing speed and efficiency in your clipping operation. Invest in a really good pair of scissors. This is one case where false economy can be truly disastrous. Nine-inch editor's shears are the best choice for clipping purposes.

There are other clipping devices on the market in addition to scissors. One type is widely distributed through retail stores under the tradename, **Clipit®**. It has a piercing point that permits a column to be removed from the center of a page without cutting in from the edge. The manufacturer's claim that it cuts the top sheet only is quite true, since the sheet must be raised slightly to operate the gadget. In my experiments with the **Clipit**, I find that it leaves a slightly ragged edge and is more difficult to guide than a pair of nine-inch editor's shears.

Razor blades mounted in special holders or knives with razor-sharp tips may also be used in clipping. The **Lewis Safety Knife®** (213) is a particularly good tool. It can be used with a steel-edged ruler to insure straight lines. In working with knives or razor blades, be sure to put a protective mat under the sheet being cut.

When dealing with newspapers, the clipping process can be expedited by slitting the joined pages apart before you begin.

Ragged, uneven edges should be avoided in clipping since they are more likely to catch on other items. Because of this problem, some libraries even try to eliminate right angles when doing their newspaper clipping. They use a slanting cut and block out the extraneous matter with pencil marks.

It is important to allow generous margins on newspaper clippings whenever possible, unless they are to be mounted at an early date. These clippings are extremely fragile. The extra margin area will provide some protection from wear and tear.

When a newspaper article involves more than one piece of paper, care is necessary to prevent loss of the separate parts. Sections of an article may be held together with a tiny bit of transparent tape. Choose the non-yellowing variety. If the tape is applied to margin areas, the taped portion can be cut away without harm when the clipping is mounted. I prefer this method to using paper clips. Paper clips can work loose, especially if they have been slightly bent. They add considerable bulk. Over a long period of time, metal clips may discolor clippings.

In clipping magazines, I find it profitable to remove the staples along the spines of some periodicals that make it impossible to open them fully. Trying to cut or tear pages from a magazine stapled in this manner is hazardous and frustrating. If you are clipping just a small portion of a page, it may be possible to do this satisfactorily without pulling staples. If you are attempting more ambitious clipping, you will find that the project becomes very cumbersome because the magazine will not lie flat. Nor will it open wide enough to allow the cutting of adequate inner margins.

Specially designed staple pullers can be purchased at small cost. You can also use a small screwdriver to straighten the staple ends and act as a lever for removing the staples.

While staples can be a nuisance when clipping magazines, they can be very helpful in dealing with the detached articles. Stapling magazine clippings that extend to two pages or more will prevent accidental separation.

Because magazine articles often are continued for several pages, care must be taken to make sure that all sections of an article have been clipped.

Some librarians scrupulously trim off every bit of advertising from clipped magazine articles. Unfortunately, this operation results in odd-shaped little pieces which are particularly susceptible to wear and tear. It's much better to leave magazine sheets intact unless you plan to mount them. The extraneous material will protect the vital portions and it will not disturb the patron any more than it does when reading the complete magazine.

Saving the entire page is also a good idea when the portion you want to highlight consists of only one or two paragraphs in a full page of text devoted to other subjects. You can use a brightly colored pen to make bracket marks or a circle around the pertinent portion. The remainder of the page will offer physical protection and eliminate the need for mounting.

Sourcing and Dating

A clipping which does not bear any indication of its source and date has no right to be in your files.

If you do not know the source of a clipping, how can you testify to its authenticity? If the clipping does not carry a date, how can you be sure that facts in it are current enough to still have validity?

When you record this important information on clippings, do not use a pencil. Record the information in ink.

For clipping your local newspaper, it's possible to have a rubber stamp made bearing the name of the paper. A revolving band dater might be used to mark the date.

If space for identification is limited on newspaper clippings, use abbreviations. Just be sure that they can be interpreted. KG 9-15-78 is an acceptable shorthand in our files for the **Kalamazoo Gazette**, Sept. 15, 1978.

When sourcing and dating magazine clippings, the information should be recorded on the first page of the article.

Preservation of Magazine Clippings

It is customary in certain libraries to cope with magazine clippings by fastening them into paper folders slightly larger than the clippings. The folders are often homemade from materials such as kraft paper, although commercially prepared manila folders may be used. The magazine clippings are usually stapled in place, although they may be secured by paper fasteners or even stitched on the sewing machine. The subject heading is indicated on the outside of the folder.

Such protective measures—or the alternate choice of mounting—may be justified if the magazine clippings are delicate, worn, or subject to very heavy usage. I have found, however, that when magazine clippings consist of entire pages, they stand up quite well without further treatment. Folding the pages in half will add to their bulk and reduce the possibility of tearing. The folding should be done so that the title of the article appears on the outside. Different procedures are essential, of course, if you clip just a small portion of a magazine page. Such small clippings are subject to damage unless they are mounted.

Preservation of Newspaper Clippings

It is possible for full-page newspaper articles to be housed in the vertical files without extra strengthening. The lengthy features that appear in the rotogravure sections are an example.

As far as smaller newspaper clippings are concerned, I am strongly in favor of mounting all of them. Why? There are many reasons:

1. Small clippings are easily crushed under the weight of heavier objects.

2. Subject headings have to be squeezed into odd spaces or superimposed on print. As a result, they are difficult to read.

3. Packs of loose clippings are difficult to leaf through when speed is important.

4. Unmounted clippings are easily lost because of their small size and unassuming appearance.

If a newspaper article is valuable enough to warrant marking, clipping, and sorting, it's worth the extra step of mounting.

Librarians have tried to substitute all sorts of procedures in place of mounting, but none of them are quite satisfactory. Some libraries just insert the clippings, sorted by subject, into manila folders. Others put them into old mailing envelopes or commercially made clipping envelopes. One library handles its local history clippings by first putting them into small envelopes or small folders labeled with subtopics. They are then placed in a standard-sized manila folder headed with the main topic.

Folders and envelopes are perfectly satisfactory means of housing newspaper clippings TEMPORARILY. But they will not provide the protection which delicate clippings need to withstand handling by staff and patrons. Nor will they prevent the wear and tear which occurs when many clippings are housed together in packs in the vertical files.

In past decades, a good many librarians relied on a device called the **U-File-M Binder Strip**® **(230)**. It is still being manufactured. The **U-File-M** is a narrow piece of strong paper edged with small tabs. Both the binder strip and the tabs are adhesive backed. The binder strip can be attached to a backing sheet or placed along the inside crease of a manila folder. The tabs are used to hold newspaper clippings in place along the strip. In this way, a sizable group of clippings can be joined together. While **U-File-M Binder Strips** are sold separately, you can also buy them already mounted in folders.

U-File-Ms are successful in keeping related newspaper clippings together, but even with the use of manila folders, they cannot hope to match mounting for the protection offered to these fragile bits of paper.

Mounting newspaper clippings does cost money, but I feel that this investment is more than justified because it puts needed information into a format that will protect the material and make it easy to use.

Mounted material does consume more space than unmounted material. But what virtue is there in saving space if in doing so you are creating barriers to your service to the public?

I am well aware of the financial facts of life in libraries. But there are ways of achieving mounting which will not break the budget.

Newspaper clippings selected for your general files can be mounted on a standard grade of typing bond. I experimented with this technique for many years and found it workable. The light backing provided by this paper will support clippings over a period of years under normal wear. This should cover the typical life span of usefulness enjoyed by general newspaper clippings.

If you cannot absorb the labor costs involved in mounting, enlist the efforts of volunteer groups. Girl Scouts, 4-H Clubs, retirees, and school service organizations can be approached to take on this project.

Preservation of Local History Clippings

The term, "local history," is used here in its broadest sense. For a public library or high school library, it might mean clippings about the community as a whole. For a special library, it might mean clippings about the institution or business that the library serves. Whatever their range, clippings which have historical value deserve particularly careful treatment because their value increases with time.

The villain accused of much of the blame for paper deterioration is acidity. As well as being intrinsically weak, newsprint is high in acid-producing ingredients. At present, there is no way of deacidifying and buffering large numbers of clippings that is both physically safe and economically feasible for the average library.

While newsprint itself poses a dilemma, libraries often aggravate the problem by mounting local history clippings on high-acid paper and placing them in folders of paper with high-acid content.

For a long time it was believed that the rapid deterioration of modern papers was entirely due to the substitution of wood pulp for rag fibers. It was assumed that modern all-rag paper was as stable as its counterpart of centuries ago. But the W. J. Barrow Research Laboratory, working under the sponsorship of the Council on Library Resources, proved that the solution wasn't that simple. Their experiments seem to demonstrate that the alum-rosin sizing introduced in the nineteenth century is the major agent in boosting the acid content of modern paper. It appears to wreak havoc on both rag and wood-pulp paper. This means that a quick switch to all-rag paper for mounts and folders will not automatically solve a library's preservation problems.

Fortunately, the research in paper longevity has resulted in the development of a "permanent/durable" paper, which is said to have a life span of centuries because it is acid-free and is made of long fibers which give added strength to the paper.

If you are making a real pledge to the future with your local history collection, investigate the advantages which permanent/durable paper would offer.

Some suppliers of acid-free or permanent/durable materials are listed in the annual buyers' guide which **Library Journal** incorporates in one of its summer issues.

Whatever type of paper you finally choose for your local history clippings, insist on a good quality stock free of groundwood. Papers that contain groundwood are unstable. They quickly discolor and become brittle when exposed to light and air. Two additional characteristics which paper experts check are the paper's resistance to tearing and its endurance in folding. It would be profitable for you to check these points, too.

In choosing mounts, always keep in mind that thickness or weight are not the final determinants of a paper's longevity. Some libraries have had unfortunate experiences with mounting on construction paper which is bulky but short-lived. Weight and thickness are important, but the ingredients that have gone into making the paper are even more so.

At one time scrapbooks enjoyed great popularity among librarians as a means of preserving local history clippings. Scrapbooks are not unmixed blessings. In the first place, much of the paper used in making scrapbooks deteriorates rapidly. In the second place, it is usually necessary to provide a detailed index to a scrapbook in order to unlock the treasures it contains.

As well as being concerned about the proper mounts and folders for local history clippings, librarians should keep in mind that newsprint is particularly vulnerable to light, high temperatures, and atmospheric pollutants. Efforts should be made to protect local history clippings from these environmental hazards.

Trimming and Placement of Clippings

In preparing newspaper clippings for the mounting process, they should be trimmed closely.

If the subject heading is indicated on the clipping, it should be jotted on the back of the mount before it is cut away. This will facilitate labeling later on.

If the date and source notes on the clipping are jeopardized by trimming, they should be transferred to the mount immediately.

Clippings must be fitted to the shape of the mounting paper. This often necessitates cutting columns into sections. A large group of clippings can be prepared ahead of time for pasting by cutting them to fit the mounting paper and then paper clipping them to the mounts. If an article is broken up into several sections, some libraries number the sections lightly before paper clipping them to the mount so that mix-ups in pasting can be avoided.

Precutting does save time since the paster can concentrate on pasting without having to pick up scissors repeatedly.

In placing clippings on mounting paper, always be sure to leave room at the top of the page for the subject heading. Allow room also for the library's identification stamp.

Theoretically speaking, it is economical to mount more than one article on a sheet if they relate to the same subject. In actual practice, however, this isn't as easy as it sounds. In order to achieve this maximum use of each mount, you will have to:

1. Be lucky enough to stumble on related articles as you clip.

2. Stockpile your clippings until you acquire articles which can be mounted together.

3. Check the files each time to see if there are any partially filled mounts.

As far as general clippings mounted on inexpensive paper are concerned, it is more wasteful to expend staff time hunting for unfilled mounts than to use a fresh piece of paper. If the mounted clippings circulate, the problem is magnified still more.

In a local history file where clippings are mounted on more costly paper and do not circulate, the practice of filling pages with multiple clippings becomes a more practical goal. Making full use of each mount will help to conserve storage space as well as paper. Hopefully, historical clippings will be mounted in chronological order on the pages so that they will present a sequential record of each subject. Pasting clippings haphazardly in empty spaces will give a very distorted view of the progression of events.

There is another way to economize on space and materials in preparing clippings for the general files. You can cut standard-sized mounts in half to accommodate small clippings. I like to use these smaller sheets with the longer sides placed vertically. In this way, the mounts can stand tall in their folders and display their subject headings on a level with the full-sized mounts. They can also be placed two abreast in the folders, thus saving space.

Adhesives

When it comes to actually attaching clippings to their mounts, there are a variety of products which invite consideration.

Pastes and Glues

The best all-around liquid adhesive that has come to my attention for mounting purposes is a "white glue" manufactured by Gane Brothers & Lane, Inc. **(101)**. It is called **"Yes"®**. Unfortunately, it is more expensive than many library pastes or glues.

For other possibilities, consult the catalogs of the various library supply houses. They will list products which may be used for mounting.

The best way to find the most desirable paste or glue for your particular needs is to buy various brands in the smallest size offered. Actually working with these adhesives will enable you to test them for economy, lasting quality, ease of use, and physical effect on the materials to be mounted.

To do a satisfactory job of mounting clippings, paste and glue should be smooth and thin enough to flow easily over the paper. They must not, however, be so "watery" as to soak the clippings.

Most pastes and glues will need thinning to the proper consistency unless the distributor specifically indicates otherwise. There is no magic recipe for determining the proper amount of water to add. You will have to experiment until you achieve the proportions exactly right for your purposes.

Rubber Cement

Rubber cement is an appealing adhesive to many librarians because any excesses can be easily rubbed off a paper surface with fingers or an eraser. Furthermore, rubber cement does not wrinkle or curl even thin paper.

There are two methods of using rubber cement.

Applying cement only to the back of the material to be mounted creates a "temporary" bond. While the material will stick to the backing, it can usually be removed without damage at a later time. There are limits to this maneuverability as far as clippings are concerned. It is true that clippings of better quality paper can be easily peeled from their mounts. But once thin newspaper clippings have dried, they can be pulled only partially free before they tear.

Some librarians welcome the flexibility allowed by "temporary" mounting. They like being able to reposition items. They speak favorably of the possibility of reusing mounts once clippings or pictures have lost their currency.

Most libraries, however, are more interested in having a clipping stay put than they are in easy methods of removing it. For the rough and tumble life that most library resources lead, temporary mounting with cement is a risky business.

To obtain a "permanent" bond using rubber cement it is necessary to apply the cement both to the mount and the back of the item to be mounted. With this method, you lose the option of moving a clipping or picture once the cement has set. While this two-coat application provides a firm seal for the present, a number of librarians have raised questions about the long-term permanence of rubber cement as a mounting agent. The judgment is that it will hold for some time but not indefinitely.

As a matter of fact, the label on one bottle which I have indicates that for "maximum permanence" it is necessary not only to apply coats to both surfaces, but also to add still another coat to one of the surfaces. This seems to indicate some doubt even in the mind of the manufacturer about the durability of rubber cement.

Rubber cement costs more by the gallon than most library pastes. It is used undiluted unless it thickens when exposed to the air. Then a special thinner must be bought. The need for multiple coats should also be counted in as a cost factor. When all these considerations are taken into account, rubber cement must be rated as a relatively expensive mounting agent.

The Library of Congress has stated that rubber cement "speeds paper deterioration and makes clippings darken and become brittle much more rapidly than they would under normal conditions." This comment was made in **Preservation Leaflet Number 5: Preserving Newspapers and Newspaper-Type Materials (204)**.

A final alert must be sounded concerning rubber cement. As this chapter was being written, there was concern about possible health hazards caused by the benzene used in the manufacture of rubber cement.

Spray Adhesives

There are adhesive products on the market which are sold in cans and which are meant to be sprayed on the backs of materials to be mounted.

One type creates a temporary bond which permits repositioning. Its primary use is for art and display work. It would not be appropriate for vertical file materials since the bond will not hold up under stress.

The second type of spray adhesive establishes a permanent bond. It is a fast method of mounting. Clippings dry quickly without wrinkling. However, permanent spray adhesives have many drawbacks which outweigh their attractive features. They are expensive. They are extremely flammable. They can be hazardous to health. They can also be a physical nuisance. Although the label on a leading spray indicated that the adhesive could be washed off with soap and water, the only thing that I could find to remove it from my fingers was nail polish remover vigorously and repeatedly applied.

Pasting Techniques

When a liquid adhesive is to be applied to clippings, place them face down on a protective underlay. Sheets of old newspapers are good for this purpose. If the newspapers are slit open, soiled sheets can be easily thrown away—leaving fresh pages below.

A paste cloth can be used to smooth the clipping and make sure that the adhesion is complete. Soft paper towels make fine substitutes for paste cloths. As an added advantage, they do not have to be laundered as paste cloths do. They can just be thrown away.

Mounted clippings should be separated by sheets of waxed paper until they are completely dry.

Clippings should be placed in a press or under weights while they are drying to prevent curling or wrinkling. This is not necessary if rubber cement or a spray adhesive is used.

All the outer edges of a clipping should be firmly fastened to the mount. Applying spots of adhesive only to the four corners leaves free edges that can easily catch on other materials and tear. Furthermore, a loosely mounted clipping will not draw full supportive strength from the heavier backing paper. These warnings apply to other shortcuts such as stapling clippings to mounts or taping only the corners of clippings.

Adhesive Tapes

Cellophane tape becomes yellowed and brittle with age. In time it discolors the clippings and mounts on which it is used. Avoid this type of tape like the plague.

Some manufacturers claim to have solved these problems with a newer type of transparent tape that has an acetate base. The most widely distributed acetate tape is the 3M Company's **Scotch Brand Magic Transparent Tape®**.

While acetate tape is slightly opaque, it does not interfere significantly with vision and it will allow photocopying.

Applying this tape to the outer edges of a clipping is a quick process, but the finished product looks a little untidy. This may not be a significant point where news articles are concerned, but it would be a factor to consider in mounting pictures.

The cost of non-yellowing transparent tape should be carefully weighed against other adhesives before employing it on a large scale as a mounting agent. Since it is essential to secure the entire outer edge of each clipping, a roll of tape disappears in a hurry.

Mounting tapes are available which have adhesive on both sides. They produce neater results than ordinary tape because they remain hidden under the mounted material. However, my efforts to use double-faced tape have been frustrating. It takes considerable dexterity to apply the tape accurately to the edges of a clipping or picture. If you don't come close enough to the edge, a loose flap is left. If you overlap, the surplus must be trimmed away. To further complicate matters, materials secured with double-faced tape have a tendency to pull free from their mounts with hard usage. It should also be noted that double-coated tape is much more expensive than regular varieties.

Dry Mounting

If money is available, the finest method of mounting is a technique called dry mounting. The conventional form of dry mounting is achieved by means of a thin paper coated on both sides with a thermosetting adhesive. It looks something like waxed paper. It is available in sheets or rolls.

The instructions call for first tacking a sheet of dry mounting tissue to the back of a clipping, picture, or map. The tacking is accomplished by means of a quick application of heat. Both pieces of paper are then trimmed together. In working with small newspaper clippings, you can often cut several units from a single sheet of tissue. Scraps can be pieced together to fit a clipping, but each separate section of tissue must be tacked in place.

The printed material and its underlay of tissue are next tacked to the mount. The "sandwich" thus created is sealed permanently through a combination of heat and pressure.

Tacking can be done by means of a special tacking iron or with an ordinary laundry iron. The final "baking" can also be done with a household iron. But if you are planning to do more than an occasional piece of dry mounting, you will want to consider investing in more efficient equipment.

It is possible to use a thermal copier for dry mounting, but keep certain reservations in mind. In the first place, the thermal copiers in common use are limited as to the size of materials they can accommodate. Stiff, heavy backings cannot be employed. Furthermore, many people in the field are convinced that a superior job of dry mounting can be achieved only by means of specially designed dry mounting presses.

These presses are available in several sizes. If the items to be mounted are larger than the press, they can be baked a section at a time.

While the dry mounting I recommend for library clippings is the conventional type done with a permanent dry mounting tissue such as **Seal MT5®**, I must hasten to point out that alternatives exist. There are dry mounting tissues on the market which have been designed to meet special requirements such as easy removability, low processing temperature, or adaptability to textured materials. There is even a type of dry mounting adhesive which has a neutral pH balance for archival use.

Dry mounting tissue and presses are available from library supply houses, from school supply houses, and from firms which serve photographers.

For descriptive literature on dry mounting, send to Seal, Incorporated **(212)**. The textbooks used in college audiovisual courses will also provide information about dry mounting.

Dry mounting can involve a significant investment of money in equipment and materials. It also can require a considerable investment of staff time in cutting tissue to proper size and baking the mounted items. But if properly done, the results are beautiful to behold—offering a smooth, neat, and lasting bond.

If you would like to discover what dry mounting is like by experimenting with a laundry iron, these are the steps to follow:

1. Set the iron at "silk" or "rayon."

2. Put clipping or picture face down on a surface protected against heat.

3. Place dry mounting tissue on back of item to be mounted.

4. Tack the tissue in place by applying the iron lightly to the center of the area to be used.

5. Trim tissue and attached paper to desired size.

6. Place the clipping or picture face up on a sheet of mounting paper.

7. Tack two opposite corners to the mount. This can be done by carefully lifting a corner of the top layer and touching the iron to the tissue underneath.

8. Cover with a clean sheet of paper.

9. Iron with a slow, firm, circular movement over the entire area to be attached.

While experiments with electric irons may give you an introduction to dry mounting, remember that the results can't compare with those produced by a dry mounting press, which provides even heat and steady pressure over the entire surface at once.

Adhesives for Local History Clippings

For newspaper clippings with historical value, the Library of Congress advises using a neutral or slightly alkaline paste. This suggestion is made in **Preservation Leaflet Number 5: Preserving Newspapers and Newspaper-Type Materials (204)**.

The leaflet indicates that a homemade cornstarch paste can be employed. My own experience with homemade pastes is less than satisfactory. They tend to become lumpy. They soak through clippings. Clippings must dry under weights for long periods of time. The adhesive quality of homemade pastes is unreliable and short-lived. They can mold or attract insects unless treated with preventatives.

There really is no good solution to the problem of supplying nondestructive pastes for historical clippings. Homemade pastes are time consuming, difficult to use, and of questionable durability. Commercially prepared vegetable pastes are little better. Depending upon the composition of the paste, they can present the same problems as homemade adhesives. They usually come in the form of powder. They may have to have a buffering agent added to eliminate acidity or a fungicide added to prevent mold.

I suspect that the Library of Congress's endorsement of pastes of the cornstarch variety is based on the archival principle that nothing shall be done which can't be undone. Therefore, reversible adhesives such as cornstarch paste, which can be removed with water, are considered desirable.

In most libraries, reversibility is not a key consideration in mounting local history clippings. What is wanted is a secure, trustworthy bonding that will survive indefinitely. Good quality mounting sheets are likely to hold up better than the newspaper clippings they carry, so there is ordinarily no need to consider removal.

If you decide to use pastes or glues to mount your local history clippings, my suggestion is to be realistic about the situation. I have worked with local history files containing mounted clippings which are 40 years old and still in usable condition even though ordinary commercial pastes or glues were employed. If you provide acid-free mounting paper, the potential life span could conceivably be lengthened despite the use of these conventional pastes or glues.

Where funds can be arranged, I would heartily recommend dry mounting for local history clippings. I would suggest using a permanent form of dry mounting tissue such as **Seal MT5**.

Another Seal product, **Fusion 4000®**, has received a great deal of attention because it meets certain archival tests. It has a neutral pH balance; it can be bonded at lower temperatures; and mounted items can be unmounted by reapplying heat.

The neutral pH balance and lower temperature requirements are favorable factors. However, as indicated earlier, easy removability is of little importance as far as local history clippings are concerned.

I have talked with users who have some reservations about **Fusion 4000**. Rather than being a paper coated with adhesives, it is a plastic adhesive in film form. This, my contacts say, makes it tricky to use. They also indicate that the adhesive does not always offer a secure bond. Before making a wholesale commitment to this type of dry mounting material, I would suggest that you experiment with small quantities or talk to local photographers who are experienced in dry mounting.

It's only realistic to recognize that newspaper clippings will not last forever, no matter what type of adhesive is used. Some libraries which have clippings of a historical nature may want to consider recording their older clippings on microfiche when they ultimately reach the fragile stage.

Another possibility for coping with delicate clippings is to make photocopies of them on permanent/durable paper. Any photocopying should, of course, be within the limitations of the copyright law.

Lamination

In a world without budget burdens, the crowning treatment for clippings would be lamination. Unfortunately, wholesale lamination of clippings is beyond the means of the average library. If it is done at all, it should be reserved for the most precious of your holdings. This process is discussed in more detail in the chapter dealing with the preservation of maps.

Encapsulation

As a substitute for lamination, a new process called encapsulation has been developed. It provides airtight plastic protection without requiring the use of heat and without effecting any physical change in the processed material. This procedure is more fully described in chapter 7. Because of the cost factor, it would have to be reserved for highly significant clippings.

Labeling

The final step in processing clippings is to record the subject heading and apply the identification stamp of the library. The subject heading should be placed at the top, left-hand side of the mount so that it can be read easily as the mount stands in its place in the file. Naturally, all subject headings should be printed in ink or typed on adhesive labels. Never use pencil!

If the source and date are difficult to decipher on the clipping itself, they should be repeated on the mount.

CHAPTER 6

VOCATIONAL MATERIAL

Interest in the ways of earning a living is a preoccupation that spans the generations. It ranges from the six-year-old who wants to be a fireman when he grows up to the 45-year-old who decides to change jobs in midstream. Added to this spontaneous interest is a demand created by career units in the school curriculum.

Any library—public or school—can make a big contribution to its users by maintaining up-to-date, well-organized files of career material.

GUIDES TO VOCATIONAL MATERIAL

The tools which are useful in selecting general vertical file materials can also be utilized to enrich vocational files. Sections on career aids are included in such composite lists as Ruth Aubrey's **Selected Free Materials for Classroom Teachers (24)** and **Free and Inexpensive Learning Materials (106)**, from George Peabody College for Teachers. The **Vertical File Index (240)** will alert you to many important new publications.

In addition to such general guides, there are specialized listings which concentrate entirely on career and guidance materials. Some are compiled lists which are revised annually, biennially, or at longer intervals.

An impressive example is **Current Career and Occupational Literature: 1973-1977 (110)**, by Leonard H. Goodman. Dr. Goodman is career development coordinator at the Counseling Center of the University of North Carolina. This volume brings together approximately 2,400 selected references for levels from kindergarten through adult. The first part of the book is composed of information about various vocational series. The second part of the book consists of an annotated bibliography of career publications arranged alphabetically under 450 occupational titles. A third section is devoted to a variety of supplementary materials on such subjects as financing an education and job hunting techniques.

The volume has a two-fold usefulness. It provides helpful descriptions and ordering information to aid in the selection of career materials. In addition, the subject headings and cross references used to organize the bibliography in part 2 can serve as leads to the librarian who is establishing a filing system for a vocational collection. The H. W. Wilson Company plans to issue a new edition of this guide at two-year intervals.

The predecessor to Leonard H. Goodman's book was Gertrude Forrester's **Occupational Literature: An Annotated Bibliography**, which librarians consulted in various editions over a span of 30 years.

Another useful tool is the **Chronicle Career Index (56)**, which originates with Chronicle Guidance Publications, Inc. This compilation of vocational and guidance materials is updated annually. The body of the book consists of an alphabetical list of over 700 sources of publications and audiovisual materials. A short descriptive note is provided for most of the titles listed under each source. To help in isolating career material there is a separate section titled "Occupational Information," which is arranged by job titles. This section furnishes cross references to the sources in the main part of the book.

Also revised annually is the **Educators Guide to Free Guidance Materials (82),** produced by Educators Progress Service, Inc. While it shows a strong emphasis on audiovisual resources, this multimedia guide does include a section of printed materials on career planning. The entries are annotated.

Every item listed in the **NVGA Bibliography of Current Career Information (186)** has been evaluated according to the standards of the National Vocational Guidance Association. While books and films are included, most entries are for free and inexpensive materials of the vertical file type. The bibliography is a compilation of the "Current Career Literature" and "Current Career Films" sections in the **Vocational Guidance Quarterly.** The seventh edition of the bibliography was published in 1978. Because five years have elapsed since the last edition, the materials have been divided into two portions, with the more current being listed at the front of the volume. Returning to a shorter interval between editions would increase the usefulness of this guide.

In **Career Education Pamphlets (217),** Dale E. Shaffer presents a list of 217 career fields and related topics. Under these headings, there are over 1,200 entries for booklets, paperbacks, and information sources. The catalog was published in 1976. Plans for revision are indefinite.

For the initial plunge into a career collection, Leonard H. Goodman and Anne E. Garrett selected **A "Starter" File of Free Occupational Literature (111).** This guide lists 117 carefully screened pamphlets which give an introduction to approximately 1,000 careers. The emphasis is on non-rural, middle-class career goals. The current edition was issued in 1975, which diminishes its usefulness. The B'nai B'rith Career and Counseling Services hopes to update this helpful list in the future.

Keys to Careers in Science and Technology (185) is a publication of the National Science Teachers Association. This bibliography presents free and "reasonably" inexpensive materials on a variety of career fields, plus information on affiliated topics such as scholarships and summer programs. Unfortunately, the latest edition available at this time dates from 1973. The Association would like to revise the list but has no facilities to do so at the moment. My reason for still including this once useful guide here is a hope that it will be rejuvenated in the near future.

In addition to compiled lists, there are serial indexes or bibliographies of career materials which are issued at regular intervals throughout the year.

Mention has already been made of "Current Career Literature," a survey found in every issue of the **Vocational Guidance Quarterly (186).** These lists, which are prepared by the National Vocational Guidance Association, include a number of free and inexpensive publications on occupations. Entries are rated according to NVGA standards.

The B'nai B'rith Career and Counseling Services issues a quarterly bibliography called the **Counselor's Information Service (31),** which offers annotated listings of current books and pamphlets concerned with occupations and guidance.

Career Guidance Index (49) records sources of free and inexpensive vocational materials. It is published eight times a year by Careers, Inc.

Before investing in serial indexes or bibliographies, librarians will want to investigate them carefully. Publishers will sometimes furnish sample copies.

It is possible for a library to do an adequate job in the vocational field without subscribing to a specialized serial index.

School librarians may find themselves in a favored position as far as these tools are concerned. Frequently, school counselors subscribe to such professional aids as the **Vocational Guidance Quarterly** or the **Counselor's Information Service.** Under such circumstances, the school librarian can arrange to consult these guidance publications for ordering purposes.

Since it appears irregularly and is limited in coverage, the column, "Counseling Aids," in the **Occupational Outlook Quarterly (35)** does not qualify as a full-fledged serial bibliography. But it does furnish some leads to career material. The **Quarterly** is issued by the Bureau of Labor Statistics of the U.S. Department of Labor. More will be said about it in the pages which follow.

SOURCES OF VOCATIONAL MATERIAL

United States Government

As part of their procedure for locating qualified employees, many federal units prepare pamphlets and leaflets about the career opportunities they offer.

The extent of this publishing program is demonstrated in the **Guide to Federal Career Literature (233),** which is a directory aimed at the college graduate or those with equivalent experience. It describes the principal publications used by various federal departments and agencies in nationwide recruiting for college entry-level positions. The directory indicates where the pamphlets can be obtained.

The **Guide to Federal Career Literature** contains a warning that even though the list is revised periodically, the coverage can never be totally complete or up to date. This means that librarians must maintain frequent contact with personnel offices of key agencies in which their patrons express particular interest.

Individual agencies should also be approached for information about the many federal jobs which do not require a college degree. For example, the U.S. Forest Service publishes a booklet describing nonprofessional employment within that agency.

Copies of recruitment literature can usually be obtained free from federal departments and agencies themselves, even when the titles are listed for sale by the Superintendent of Documents.

You may be able to collect the most famous of all the governmental recruiting materials right in your own home town. These are the publications of the armed forces of the United States. If there are recruiting offices in your community, a quick tour of them will stock your files generously. Otherwise, write directly to the headquarters of each service.

Since so many federal jobs fall under civil service supervision, it is important for public libraries, high school libraries, and academic libraries to provide access to the announcements of the agency formerly known as the U.S. Civil Service Commission **(233).** In January 1979, this agency became the Office of Personnel Management. Its quarterly publication, **Current Federal Examination Announcements,** lists in chart form the competitive examination announcements which are being publicized nationwide. The chart gives only the barest essentials and can be discarded as soon as an updated list arrives. The announcements themselves offer more detailed information. They will have a longer span of usefulness, since they will serve the library patron who is trying to choose a future occupation or who is planning to try for a government job at a later date.

In addition to announcement information, the Office of Personnel Management publishes a variety of other literature about federal jobs and how to get them. One example is the booklet, **Working for the USA (233)**, which gives a succinct overview of federal employment. Another important aid from this agency is a **Directory of Federal Job Information Centers (233)**, providing addresses and phone numbers. Also representative of its publications is the **Federal Career Directory: A Guide for College Students (233)**. It presents concise information about federal careers open to college graduates and about the agencies which employ them.

Some of the publications issued by the Office of Personnel Management are distributed free and can be obtained directly from the agency or the Federal Job Information Centers. Other publications of this office are sold by the Superintendent of Documents. **Subject Bibliography 240 (226)** was devoted to Civil Service Commission materials for sale through the GPO. Librarians will want to watch for the release of a **Subject Bibliography** reflecting the recent reorganization.

Some of the regional offices of the Office of Personnel Management issue publications which focus on federal careers in their geographic areas. Contact your regional office to see whether it has prepared localized materials. A list of these offices can be found in the **United States Government Manual (236)**.

Not all of the vocational material produced by federal agencies is concerned with employment opportunities in the United States government. Many excellent publications are offered which deal with a wider spectrum of occupational information.

For example, the Small Business Administration concentrates on the prospects and problems of individuals who want to go into business for themselves. The Women's Bureau is vitally involved with all aspects of employment for women. The Federal Aviation Administration has issued a number of free pamphlets dealing with careers in aviation, as well as a directory of colleges and universities where such training can be obtained. The Interstate Commerce Commission has just published a series of public advisories on the trucking industry. While part of the series is directed at the consumer, the remaining titles are designed for the trucker entering the business.

One of the most unusual career aids is a monthly summary titled **Occupations in Demand at Job Service Offices (193)**. This bulletin identifies occupations for which large numbers of job openings were listed during the previous month and indicates in which areas of the country these openings occurred. The publication is the work of the U.S. Employment Service.

The Bureau of Labor Statistics is well-known to every librarian for its invaluable publication, the **Occupational Outlook Handbook (35)**. The current edition covers several hundred occupations and 35 industries. This handbook should be the cornerstone of vocational service in all libraries. It is comprehensive; it is reliable; and, since it is revised biennially, it is current. While multiple copies are purchased by many libraries, only one patron can make use of each copy at a time. Luckily, it is a policy of the Bureau of Labor Statistics to publish reprints **(35)** of sections of the handbook. Libraries with heavy career demands can obtain these reprints for their files and thus assure wide access to the information. Reprints are for sale by the Superintendent of Documents or any regional office of the Bureau of Labor Statistics. A list of the reprints available is included in the **Occupational Outlook Handbook** itself. Reprints are also listed in **Subject Bibliography 270 (226)**.

To supplement and update the **Occupational Outlook Handbook** between editions, a companion periodical is issued. It is called the **Occupational Outlook Quarterly (35)**. The **Quarterly** frequently features articles on careers which are so new or specialized that it is difficult to locate information on them elsewhere. Because the subscription price is so modest, it is economically feasible to obtain a second copy to clip for your vocational files. You might want to consider photocopying selected items instead, since the **Quarterly** is not covered by copyright restrictions.

Free reprints **(35)** of some articles in the **Occupational Outlook Quarterly** are distributed by the Bureau of Labor Statistics. As they are issued, reprints are listed in the announcements of new BLS publications. You can be added to the mailing list to receive these announcements by contacting your regional BLS office. The locations of BLS regional offices are given in the **United States Government Manual (236)**.

The Bureau of Labor Statistics publishes many other materials which are vocationally significant. Typical of these publications are the **Education and Job Leaflets (35)**. This series of five brochures lists jobs that require specified levels of education.

Librarians searching for career items from federal sources will want to check **Subject Bibliography 44, Manpower, Employment, Occupations, and Retirement (226)**. While it represents a rather mixed bag, it will furnish some leads.

Because it is easy to become geographically isolated in our thinking, this might be a good place to remind readers that the Canadian national government also is involved in the publication of literature on career opportunities.

State Governmental Units

The importance of vocational materials which reflect conditions in a particular state cannot be overemphasized. In these days of super mobility, it might be argued that occupational literature keyed to the national picture is more significant than localized information. But conditions still vary sharply from one state to another and even from one locality to another. Statistics show that even in this move-happy civilization, many people spend their working lives in one state—yes, even in one community. Furthermore, regional differences become very important to the temporary resident who is part of the local working force.

These facts make it urgent for the librarian to collect as much information as possible on the job picture in the state and the area.

The state employment service is a prime source to consult for such information. The coverage provided differs drastically from one state to another. Some state employment agencies publish booklets which give a composite picture of job opportunities in the state, particularly entry jobs for new young workers. Some compile detailed surveys of the employment outlook in various metropolitan areas, as well as the state as a whole. Training opportunities, wages paid, skills available, and unfilled jobs are all subjects of state publications.

A number of state employment services prepare series of career briefs reflecting regional factors. While some of these series are modest in size, certain states maintain very extensive sets. For example, the Employment Development Department of the State of California publishes a series of occupational guides which currently includes over 260 titles. The Ohio Bureau of Employment Services will issue a series of 300 annually revised briefs beginning in the fall of 1978.

Listed below are some of the states which produce career briefs:

Arizona	Nevada
California	New Jersey
Idaho	Ohio
Indiana	Oregon
Maine	Pennsylvania
Missouri	

As well as materials which reflect employment factors peculiar to the state, some state employment services publish vocational guidance information of a more general nature, such as techniques of getting a job.

Contact the employment body in your state to discover what publications it can provide for your career files.

State merit agencies distribute information about career opportunities in the civil service systems which they administer. The title of the controlling body changes from state to state. It may be the state personnel board, a civil service commission, or a merit system council. Public libraries, academic libraries, and high school libraries should arrange to receive announcements of examinations as well as other descriptive literature available about jobs in the state's civil service system. As with the federal civil service, these materials can serve a two-pronged function. First of all, they inform users of immediate job openings. They also help patrons who are planning ahead for future job possibilities. Because of this second type of usage, it is wise to keep a representative collection of announcements for all state civil service positions, even after examination deadlines have passed.

In collecting state-oriented items, remember that individual agencies such as the public health department or the state police may issue recruiting literature of their own.

Don't overlook the governmental bodies which license or certify members of such occupations as cosmetology, nursing, teaching, and mortuary science. Approach them for printed material on requirements for entering the profession or trade. Some regulating agencies even issue sample tests for applicants.

Local Governmental Units

Large cities sometimes release recruiting leaflets and examination announcements for governmental positions. If you live in a smaller community, it is more difficult to obtain printed material. It is not impossible, however. For example, our local police and fire departments gladly distribute summaries of basic job information to interested adults or students who are considering careers as policemen or firemen. They will provide such material to libraries as well.

It would also be a good idea to check with the personnel departments of your city and county to see if you can get copies of the official job descriptions which have been prepared for positions under the jurisdiction of each governmental unit. If the full set is too massive to duplicate, you can at least obtain copies of the most popular occupations, such as public health nursing.

Organizations

Many societies, institutes, and associations are eager to provide pamphlets and brochures describing career possibilities in their areas of activity. Some labor unions distribute helpful material. Most of the publications are free. There are also career-counseling organizations which have occupational briefs for sale.

A ready-made mailing list covering national associations, societies, institutes, and labor unions can be found in the **Encyclopedia of Associations (84)**, published by Gale Research Co.

Leads to organizations affiliated with various vocations can also be discovered in articles in the **Occupational Outlook Handbook (35)** and in the **Occupational Outlook Quarterly (35)**.

Libraries which own **The Encyclopedia of Careers and Vocational Guidance (85)** will find at the end of the career studies in volume II lists of agencies and organizations to write to for additional information.

For health-related occupations, a free booklet issued by the National Health Council, Inc. cites over 100 organizations which will provide information on particular careers. The title of the booklet is **200 Ways to Put Your Talent to Work in the Health Field (179)**.

The career briefs and monographs for sale by commercial publishers and career-counseling organizations often contain clues to associations connected with a particular occupation.

Here are just a few of the organizations which will furnish descriptive literature about vocational opportunities in their spheres of interest:

> American Chemical Society
> American Society of Civil Engineers
> American Society of Landscape Architects
> American Welding Society
> Association of American Geographers
> Ecological Society of America
> Guild of Professional Translators
> Insurance Information Institute
> National Association of Accountants
> National Association of Broadcasters
> National Association of Purchasing Management
> National Association of Realtors
> National Shorthand Reporters Association
> Piano Technicians Guild

Some nonprofit groups have made a specialty of career information. This is true of Catalyst (52), a national organization that helps women choose, launch, and advance their careers. Catalyst has an extensive publishing program keyed to these goals. Two series of booklets are available which help women explore various career possibilities. Another group of booklets is designed to assist women with educational opportunities in various occupational fields. Catalyst's self-guidance series includes a handbook for planning an effective job-hunting campaign. Other Catalyst materials are described in the organization's publications list.

The B'nai B'rith Career and Counseling Services (31) provides another example of nonprofit organizations which concentrate on vocational data. Two of its publications have already been mentioned in this chapter. They are the **Counselor's Information Service** and **A "Starter" File of Free Occupational Literature**. The organization is also responsible for a series of occupational briefs. The revision of existing briefs has been delayed because of monetary problems. Hopefully, the series can be updated and expanded in the future since it made a special contribution through its assessment of job opportunities for minority groups, as well as for women.

It is important to remember that national organizations are not the only groups active in distributing vocational literature. State associations may also be involved. To illustrate this point, the following groups in Michigan have made career materials available to libraries in the state:

> Mental Health Association in Michigan
> Michigan Funeral Directors Association
> Michigan Hospital Association
> Michigan League for Nursing
> Michigan Pharmacists Association
> Michigan State Medical Society

You will want to check with similar associations in your own state.

Even on the local level, associations may produce publications of value to your career files. Chambers of commerce often prepare lists of local industries, processors, and retail firms which are appropriate for career study as well as being a record of community activity.

Private Businesses and Industries

A number of large businesses and industries publish occupational brochures. They are usually devoted to recruiting for the companies themselves. Occasionally, they will present a detailed study of a career field or will survey occupational opportunities in the industry as a whole. Although they tend to be generalized and overly optimistic, these company publications can be useful, especially if they represent area firms.

Because of the great interest our patrons express in careers as flight attendants, our library has found it profitable to write regularly to the major airlines for up-to-date literature on their requirements and training programs.

Instead of concentrating on career opportunities in its own field, the New York Life Insurance Company has chosen as a public service to issue a series of booklets on a broad variety of occupations. The series is called **Careers for a Changing World**. It is designed to help young people choose productive and satisfying careers. Single copies of the booklets are available free of charge. Write to the New York Life Insurance Company **(191)** for a full set.

The Bank of America produces a publication called the **Small Business Reporter (219)**, which studies specific businesses as well as the techniques of business management. Each issue of the **Small Business Reporter** is, in effect, a substantial pamphlet devoted to a single subject. While some emphasis is placed on California-based operations, most of the material is applicable anywhere in the United States. The **Small Business Reporter** is issued at irregular intervals during the year. In addition to the release of new titles, previous reports are also revised and updated. A publication index distributed free of charge lists all available titles. It is possible to place a subscription for future issues.

Educational Institutions

Colleges and universities frequently publish brochures on the career areas in which they offer training. While the publications are usually concerned with the programs of instruction at the school, they often provide good general information about the vocation itself.

Some colleges and universities have produced studies of current and future employment opportunities in the communities in which they are located.

An outstanding program of occupational orientation is carried on by the Guidance Centre **(115)** of the Faculty of Education at the University of Toronto. It publishes a series of over 200 occupational monographs which give information about careers in Canada. The monographs are frequently revised and republished. The Guidance Centre is also responsible for the **Student, Subject, and Careers Series**. Booklets in this series assist senior high school students in making their future educational and career plans on the basis of special interests or proficiencies in school subjects.

Periodicals

Magazines are fodder for your vocational file since they often run feature articles on interesting careers. The information in such articles is likely to be very current. Magazines also tend to pick up off-beat occupations which are not normally included in more circumscribed sources.

Some magazine articles are useful not only for clipping, but also for the clues they offer to additional information. For example, when **Changing Times** prints articles on careers, they often contain references to agencies or publications that can be of further help.

Reprints of vocational articles which have appeared in magazines are sometimes offered for sale. Send to **Mademoiselle (145)** for a price list of its college and career reprints. Both Chronicle Guidance Publications, Inc. **(56)** and Careers, Inc. **(49)** have reprint programs which will be discussed later in this chapter. As has already been noted, free reprints are available for some articles in the **Occupational Outlook Quarterly**.

School librarians who want to add another dimension to their career files can ask students who have relatives in various occupations to bring in professional journals, trade papers, or union periodicals which these relatives receive. Such publications offer an insider's viewpoint not readily available elsewhere.

Commercial Publishers

The strong and continuing demand for career information has enticed many publishers into preparing series of vocational aids. Some are poorly done and infrequently revised. But a number of career series have established solid reputations over a period of years.

Some of the more widely recognized series will be mentioned here.

Chronicle Guidance Publications, Inc. **(56)** is well-known in library and guidance circles for its **Chronicle Occupational Briefs**, a series of about 470 titles. Most of the briefs are four pages in length. The publisher tries to release about 100 revised briefs and about 15 new titles during each school year. A special price is offered to those who buy a complete set of **Chronicle Occupational Briefs**. However, it is possible to buy the briefs singly. A subscription service is also available to new and revised briefs.

Another vocational series sponsored by Chronicle Guidance Publications consists of **Chronicle Occupational Reprints**. These are reproductions of career articles that have appeared in professional and trade journals. They are available individually, by subscription, or as a complete set.

Careers, Inc. **(49)** features three vocational series composed of approximately 570 publications. **Career Briefs** are eight-page booklets covering general occupational fields or careers requiring extensive description. **Career Summaries** are more compact sketches about specific occupations. They are printed on both sides of card stock. To depict occupations which require only a short period of on-the-job training, there is a third series called **Job Guides**. The publisher claims that all titles are revised within four and one-half years. **Career Briefs**, **Career Summaries**, and **Job Guides** may be ordered as sets, by annual subscriptions, or by individual titles.

Careers, Inc. also prepares reprints of articles on vocations and related subjects. These **Career Reprints** can be obtained on a subscription basis.

Science Research Associates, Inc. **(211)** publishes briefs covering hundreds of occupational areas. Two major series are available. The first consists of 400 **SRA Occupational Briefs** which are four-page surveys written for use by high school students and adults. While SRA would prefer to sell the briefs in sets, they can be purchased individually. Libraries can also subscribe to an updating service which will provide 80 new or revised briefs each year.

The second major SRA series is made up of 340 **WORK Briefs**. Written in a fictional narrative form, they are designed for pupils in grades 6 through 10.

In addition, SRA publishes **Job Family Booklets** dealing with broad fields of work and **Guidance Series Booklets**, some of which cover the general vocational problems of young people.

A veteran name in career publishing is the Institute for Research **(133)**, which has nearly 300 **Careers Research Monographs** for sale. These studies are more elaborate in content and format than the other career series already mentioned. They are sold in groups of five monographs or as individual titles. The publisher offers special discounts for large orders. A continuation order service is also available which will provide for automatic delivery of new groups of monographs as they are released.

While it is important for librarians to be acquainted with the traditional names in the vocational field, it is also important to be on the alert for literature from newer or less well-known publishers.

For example, you may want to send for publicity from Vocational Biographies, Inc. (241). There are 700 **Vocational Biographies** in the basic collection, bolstered by 175 new publications every school year. Each of the four-page **Vocational Biographies** focuses on the career experience of a real person. Such basic topics as job training, work environment, and advancement possibilities are examined in terms of the individual's experiences. The style of writing is informal and conversational.

While **Vocational Biographies** are offered in spiral bound volumes, they can also be ordered unbound for use in vertical files. There is a subscription service to the 175 new **Vocational Biographies** released each school year. Although the publisher prefers to sell the biographies in series or by subscription, individual titles have been made available upon request.

Changing Times Education Service (53) has developed an extensive list of booklets for school use which are concerned with career awareness and career education. The booklets in the **Real People at Work** series range from low second-grade reading level to high sixth-grade reading level. Because of their carefully controlled vocabulary and high motivation level, they may be helpful to older students and adults who have reading or language problems. They are small enough to fit comfortably in vertical files. If you are interested, write for the CTES general catalog and the CTES special needs catalog.

Special Purchase Plans

As has been indicated, publishers of career material frequently offer discounts for large-scale purchases. For example, Chronicle Guidance Publications, Inc. charges $1.00 for a single **Chronicle Occupational Brief** but will provide a full set of about 470 for $120.00. Reduced rates for new or revised titles are also available from some publishers if you place a yearly subscription to their vocational publications.

These are tempting offers. They promise substantial savings in money, as well as in the time spent on tracking down and ordering materials.

On the other hand, these blanket purchases may burden the library with a number of unwanted and unused items. How many calls do you anticipate in a given year for career literature on canoe outfitters, gunsmiths, or art gallery operation? Yet these occupations are all included in well-known sets. When considering a discount purchase arrangement, ask yourself these questions: Can you be ruthless enough to cull out the unneeded titles? Is the discount great enough to represent a bargain price in spite of this weeding?

By ordering a complete set of a publisher's briefs or monographs, you are inevitably going to acquire a substantial number of older titles which are in line for revision. This is a factor to weigh against the savings you are offered.

It is a fact of life that certain commercial firms sell individual titles only with great reluctance because of the cost factor in processing small orders. If inflation continues, there may be increased pressure by both commercial firms and nonprofit publishers to encourage large-scale purchases of career material.

In addition to a simple discount for large orders or for yearly subscriptions, some career publishers offer an assortment of unusual package plans. Depending on the publisher, these plans may feature a mixture of briefs; bibliographies of occupational and counseling literature; reprints; professional newsletters; posters; guides to colleges; guides to training programs; book reviews; and even filing cases.

My reaction to package plans is that most of them are sculptured to the needs of counselors rather than librarians.

If you would like to know more about package plans, consult the catalogs of these publishers:

Careers, Inc.

Chronicle Guidance Publications, Inc.

Science Research Associates, Inc.

EVALUATION OF VOCATIONAL MATERIAL

High on the list of requirements for good career material is currency. In this hyperkinetic world, nothing is so stale as old vocational pamphlets. Salaries, educational requirements, job opportunities, and working conditions are constantly changing. New jobs are springing up which were unknown a few years ago. On the other hand, long-standing jobs have been virtually eliminated or drastically changed.

One of the sterling qualities of career pamphlets is that they are likely to be revised more frequently than books on occupations. It's a simple matter of economics. Pamphlets are cheaper and easier to revise. But don't take too much comfort in that fact. Librarians will still have to work zealously to keep their vocational files timely.

They must become very date-conscious. It is not enough to check the year of issuance of a career brochure. Old statistics can be concealed in a new publication. The significant factor is how recent the data within the pamphlet is. Beware of statistical statements or charts which carry no time identification. A comment that the average union hourly wage for plumbers is $10.40 means little unless you know the year when this wage applied.

Receiving free material that is obsolete is merely annoying. The problem becomes really serious when expenditures of library funds are involved, as is the case with the career series issued by commercial publishers.

The publication dates of briefs or monographs are easily determined when you are ordering them from a guide such as the **Vertical File Index**. Otherwise you will have to ask the publisher for a list of the titles in the series with the copyright dates indicated. In some cases, you will have to be quite insistent. Even this will not protect you from the publisher who fakes a revision or who does a skimpy job of updating. These harsh realities are good arguments for sampling a series before investing heavily in it.

As well as being watchful of new material, the librarian must constantly assess the occupational information already in the files. Career files should be weeded ruthlessly to eliminate outdated publications.

Occasionally there may be overriding reasons for keeping an older publication because of the specialized information it contains—usually a detailed history of the vocation. Under such circumstances, the pamphlet should be clearly labeled with a warning such as this:

> NOTE: This pamphlet was published in 1968. It is still useful for the history of the occupation.

Just as important as currency in a career pamphlet is a concrete, realistic approach. Vague generalities are of little aid to the patron who wants hard facts. Descriptions which gloss over disadvantages and exaggerate benefits are more harmful than helpful. Materials which ignore the lack of jobs in depressed career fields are tragically misleading. These rosy surveys are likely to come from groups with a vested interest in promoting a particular career. Trade schools or business schools are often guilty of this promotional approach in the vocational material they distribute. But institutions of higher education and professional associations have sometimes been at fault, too.

A topnotch pamphlet should be able to weather questions such as these:

1. Does it spell out the physical abilities and personality traits which are important to the job?

2. Does it describe in exact detail the training and experience required?

3. Is it explicit in presenting the kinds of demands the job makes on the individual?

4. Does it give a true picture of salary patterns, not just the higher ranges?

5. Does it depict what beginning jobs are like, rather than concentrating on the glamour positions at the top?

6. Does it present an honest assessment of future employment and advancement possibilities?

7. Does it consider the real prospects for women and minority groups?

8. Does it retain an objective viewpoint, allowing the reader to make his own judgment about the job's desirability?

Style can play an important role in determining how extensively a vocational pamphlet will be used. The narrative approach is most appropriate for elementary school level or for older students with reading problems. A narrative style may also appeal to the teenager who is undecided as to a career choice and wants to explore a variety of vocations in a readable format.

On the other hand, when it comes to writing a report, adolescents want quick, precise facts. So do adults who are facing a career change. So do librarians looking for answers to reference questions. In such instances, a chatty narrative approach can be a hindrance. What is needed in these circumstances is succinct information presented in a simple, straightforward manner.

Libraries should stress materials that concentrate on a particular occupation rather than those which try to survey an entire industry. Studies of broad occupational groups do have special pertinency in the lower grades. Many elementary schools devote part of their curriculum to giving students a generalized overview of the world of work. This approach may be used in the upper grades as an introduction to a more intensive study of careers. Occasionally, a young man will be attracted by a spectacular industry like electronics or aerospace without having a precise job in mind. But aside from these instances, the calls for career information that reach most libraries are for specific occupations. This means that a pamphlet on petroleum engineers is likely to be more popular than one covering all jobs in the petroleum industry.

As indicated earlier, it is essential to examine several selections from a career series before making a wholesale investment in it. It is also vital to calculate what proportion of your total vocational budget you want to commit to a single series. Restricting your vocational collection to one firm's publications is very much like buying the output of only one book publisher. Each series has its strengths and weaknesses. The types of careers covered can also vary from series to series.

If you are interested in more information about standards for occupational literature, you may want to consult the **Guidelines for the Preparation and Evaluation of Career Information Media**, which were established by the National Vocational Guidance Association. They can sometimes be found in books on vocational counseling.

PERIPHERAL INFORMATION

Don't be stereotyped in your thinking about supplementary resources which can be useful in career service.

College and trade school catalogs are a natural adjunct to vocational information.

The annual reports of corporations can furnish insights into company policies and potentials which are helpful to patrons considering jobs with those firms.

A card file listing local residents who are willing to talk to young people about their jobs is an asset to a school library or young adult department.

Materials on labor-related laws are pertinent. For example, pamphlets describing child labor laws, anti-discrimination laws, or provisions relating to the employment of veterans can be very useful.

Booklets on rehabilitation and employment of the handicapped have a contribution to make.

Information on special training and placement programs for the unemployed will be of assistance.

Facts about scholarships, fellowships, student loans, and other methods of financing an education are important to career-minded library patrons.

Material on part-time or summer jobs also has a legitimate place in your files.

Information on service organizations such as VISTA, Project HOPE, and the Peace Corps should be available, since some of your patrons may decide to dedicate a part of their working lives to these programs.

While many of these supplementary resources will be physically separated from your vocational collection, they can still serve as an extension of it.

ORGANIZATION OF VOCATIONAL MATERIAL

A miniature career collection can be incorporated into the general vertical files by lumping the material under a subject heading such as "Vocations." As career resources swell, it is more practical to place them in a separate arrangement.

When an independent career file is established, some means must be found to make sure that folders and pamphlets will be returned to the proper cases.

A distinctive color may be used in lettering pamphlets, folders, and file drawers. Colored labels may also be applied to folders and drawer fronts. Some libraries employ colored stars or dots to distinguish vocational material, but this is a risky system. The stars or dots fall off easily. Furthermore, patrons are likely to pick at them absentmindedly as they read.

Another way of isolating vocational material is to use a stamp with an identifying phrase such as "Career file." To make sure that it will be noticed, apply the stamp just preceding the subject heading on each pamphlet. The stamp should also be used on the folders in the career file.

If the index to the career file is typed on colored cards, it will not be necessary to use any preliminary words such as "Career file" or "Vocations" on the cards.

There are two basic types of filing arrangements for vocational materials. One is alphabetical, the other, numerical.

Numerical plans are usually based on the classification system recorded in the **Dictionary of Occupational Titles (235)**. The **Dictionary** (DOT) is published by the U.S. Employment Service of the United States Department of Labor.

This is a brief and edited sample of the numerical classification code used in the DOT. The sample is carried out to only six digits:

07	OCCUPATIONS IN MEDICINE AND HEALTH
070	Physicians and Surgeons
070.061	Pathologist
070.101	Anesthesiologist
	Cardiologist
070.107	Psychiatrist
071	Osteopaths
071.101	Osteopathic Physician
072	Dentists
072.101	Oral Surgeon
073	Veterinarians
073.161	Veterinary Livestock Inspector
074	Pharmacists
075	Registered Nurses
075.264	Nurse Practitioner
	Nurse-Midwife

(Sample continues on page 128)

Sample (cont'd):

077	Dietitians
077.061	Dietitian, Research
078	Occupations in Medical and Dental Technology

Numerical codes such as this are based on an elaborate classification of job families. Their prime purpose is to keep related occupations in close physical proximity. In fact, the principal argument for using a numerical approach in library files is that it offers a quick overview of jobs that share certain common elements. The excerpt from the **Dictionary of Occupational Titles** shows that anyone who is inspired by the thought of healing people or animals can find a variety of potentially appealing jobs under the broad category of "medicine and health." This correlation of jobs is particularly attractive to vocational guidance counselors.

Numerical arrangements require the use of an alphabetical index to locate specific jobs. If you faithfully follow the classification system in the **Dictionary of Occupational Titles**, you will find a ready-made index at the back of the volume. It is an alphabetical listing of job titles with a notation of the corresponding classification number.

Another type of numerical arrangement has been attempted by school libraries which have assigned Dewey Decimal Classification system numbers to career pamphlets. Usually pamphlets treated in this manner are housed in pamphlet boxes on the open shelves.

After working with both numerical and alphabetical files, I am wholeheartedly in favor of the alphabetical system. The numerical classification used in the **Dictionary of Occupational Titles** offers a tidy way of presenting job relationships, but it does not reflect the manner in which requests for occupational information reach the library. Most patrons want information on a precise job. They are not concerned with the nice interplay between occupations. There are books and pamphlets which are deliberately designed to give broad surveys of major job families. The entire occupational file doesn't need to be organized to offer still another overview.

A strong argument against a numerically arranged file is that it can't be approached directly. In order to trace a particular job, the librarian or patron must first turn to an alphabetical index to discover the proper code designation. Then the code designation must be traced in the files. This procedure is especially troublesome in libraries where patrons serve themselves.

For libraries which rely on the numerical system in the **Dictionary of Occupational Titles**, there is also the problem of dealing with brand-new occupations, since the **Dictionary** is revised only at intervals of several years.

For most libraries, the alphabetical arrangement of career material is the simplest and most productive plan. There are two methods of developing an alphabetical arrangement:

1. The terms used can describe the trade or profession—examples are "Optometry," "Truck driving," and "Surgery."

2. The terms used can describe the worker—examples are "Optometrist," "Truck driver," and "Surgeon."

I recommend using the name of the worker as the subject heading in your files. There are many worker titles which will not gracefully convert into fields of work. It's easy to change the term "Actor" into "Acting" or "Banker" into "Banking," but what would you do with the following titles?

Flight attendant
Waiter or waitress
Curator
Actuary
Ticket agent
Receptionist

The usual treatment would be to bury the material under general subject headings such as "Air transportation" or "Restaurant work." The direct, immediate access offered by worker titles would be lost.

Broad industry surveys pose no problem in files where worker titles are employed. A monograph on career opportunities in the chemical industry as a whole can be headed "Chemical workers."

In setting up an alphabetical filing system, librarians can look for possible subject headings in the alphabetical job index at the back of the **Dictionary of Occupational Titles.** Both base titles and alternate titles are listed in the index. Base titles, which are the most commonly used titles, are capitalized. Alternate titles are given in lower-case letters. In effect, these two types of titles represent subject headings and cross references. Each title in the index is followed by a code number which leads the user to an entry in the classified portion of the book. In the classified entry, the base title is listed first, followed by any alternate titles. A concise description of the occupation is given.

The DOT is significant because it standardizes occupational titles and supplies precise definitions of what various occupations involve. It is particularly useful in dealing with occupations for which there are many names.

An abridged and somewhat modified version of the occupational titles in the DOT can be found in Leonard H. Goodman's **Current Career and Occupational Literature: 1973-1977 (110).**

The **Occupational Outlook Handbook (35)** is another handy guide to subject headings.

For the small collection, limited lists such as those in Goodman or the **Occupational Outlook Handbook** may be simpler and quicker to use.

Some school counselors argue for vocational files that are oriented to the courses taught in the institution. They feel that this helps the student evaluate the career fields that open as the result of following various courses of study.

If the school librarian thinks that such an approach would be helpful in the library, it should be carried out by means of a supplementary index showing the relationship. It would be unwise to arrange the career pamphlets themselves under school subjects.

For the librarian who is desperately short of time or who panics at the thought of organizing a career file, there are commercially prepared shortcuts.

Chronicle Guidance Publications, Inc. **(56)** offers a ready-to-use filing system for career materials. It consists of about 290 manila folders arranged by a numerical classification which is derived from the **Dictionary of Occupational Titles.** A companion set of hanging file folders is also available. Alphabetical access to the folders can be obtained through use of the DOT. Chronicle Guidance Publications also issues an alphabetical guide to its filing plan.

Science Research Associates, Inc. (211) has created a filing system of its own which is centered around six major occupational fields. While it is based on job family relationships, it is not keyed to the **Dictionary of Occupational Titles**. The SRA publicity calls this system an alphabetical filing plan, but it departs drastically from the straight alphabetical arrangement which librarians know. The six major fields which form the framework of the plan are not alphabetized. They are assigned code numbers and are arranged by that number. Under these major headings fall the job families, which, in turn, incorporate individual job titles. It is true that these subdivisions are arranged alphabetically, but only within each area of relationship. The subdivisions are numbered according to this internal alphabetizing.

Printed file folders utilizing the SRA system are for sale. An alphabetical index to the filing plan must be purchased separately.

The **Occupations Filing Plan (30)**, which is sold by Interstate Printers and Publishers, Inc., was last revised in 1968. Some initial overtures have been made which indicate that a new edition may be in prospect for 1979. The possibility of a future revision makes it desirable to introduce you to the present edition, even though it is dated.

The **Occupations Filing Plan**, which was developed by Wilma Bennett, features an alphabetical arrangement by fields of work. The headings were adapted from the **Dictionary of Occupational Titles**, but they were broadened in an attempt to keep related materials together. The DOT code numbers are not used.

Subject headings and cross references are listed in a book from which appropriate terms can be selected for the library's files. It is also possible to order a set of 1,088 prepared labels which are ready to mount on file folders and cross reference guides.

Keep two facts in mind when considering the **Occupations Filing Plan**:

1.   The subject headings are a mixture of terms which describe the worker and terms which describe the trade or profession.

2.   The plan attempts to keep related jobs together under broad headings.

Before investing in any commercially prepared filing plan, try to communicate with librarians or counselors who have had experience with the system. If you have trouble in establishing a contact, write to the publisher for the names of libraries or schools using the plan.

CHAPTER 7

LOCAL HISTORY:
WHY, WHAT, AND HOW

Smaller libraries rarely aspire to specialized subject collections. Their staff members are happy to achieve good general coverage. But there is one area in which any public library—no matter how small—has a responsibility to provide a specialized collection. That area is local history.

Even school libraries are not exempt from this obligation. If instruction is offered in local history or civic affairs, the library automatically acquires a need to gather material that pictures the community.

It's true that there are other agencies on both local and state levels which are concerned with regional historical material. Genealogical societies, historical societies, museums, universities, archival centers, and state historical commissions are among the bodies with a vested interest. But the existence of these groups does not minimize the obligation of the local library to assure the preservation of community history.

WHY THE LIBRARY?

Agencies and organizations at the state level are not always willing to expend time and space on the localized minutiae that are so important to depicting a given locality. They must, of necessity, take a broader approach. While they would snap up the diary of an early pioneer in your area, they are not likely to want to bother with the programs issued by the amateur theatrical group in your community. Yet 25 years from now, when that theatrical group celebrates its silver anniversary, those programs will be an important aid in planning the festivities.

Even the existence of a historical or genealogical society on the local level does not always guarantee the adequate preservation of community materials. The group may restrict itself to narrow fields of interest. It may not want to be concerned with more current items. Rapid turnover in officers and in membership may cause efforts at collecting information to be sporadic and diffuse. Furthermore, the results are not always accessible to the general public.

The public library finds itself nominated by logic and default to play a major role in the field of local history. It is qualified for this participation because it can:

1. Offer continuity to the collection of historical material.

2. Unify diverse efforts to preserve local history items.

3. Represent the entire range of local interests and needs.

4. Furnish personnel trained and experienced in organizing and using information.

5. Provide a central depository open to all citizens.

6. Assure regular hours of service.

Don't ride off to do battle alone on the basis of this list of qualifications. Before initiating a local history collection, your first move should be to contact interested groups and individuals in the community to see what is already being done.

Cooperation rather than competition should be the key word. If the high school library has done a superlative job of collecting material about the origin, staff, students, academic programs, and extracurricular activities of the institution, there is no reason for the public library to duplicate all of these materials so long as they are available to the general public. However, a librarian should never hesitate to duplicate any type of material for which there is a steady demand or which is needed to execute good reference service.

If you represent a small library, the second step to take in preparing yourself for historical specialization is to stop feeling apologetic about what small libraries can contribute. This is one area in which smaller libraries have several advantages over their larger counterparts.

In the first place, residents in small towns think of the librarian as a neighbor. They will often turn over to that neighbor business or family items which they would hesitate to give the librarian in a big impersonal institution. In the second place, the librarian in a smaller community can keep alert to everything going on in the area, keeping aware of governmental, organizational, and private developments which would slip by unnoticed in a larger city. Therefore, the librarian can always be on the spot to acquire materials which will give a comprehensive picture of the community's past and present. In like fashion, local agencies and groups find it easy to remember the library when they have pertinent material to dispense. This happy situation does not prevail in larger cities, where the library may be overlooked in the complexities of urban life.

There is an urgency in collecting historical materials today which is more intense than ever before. When families lived in 12-room houses and stayed in the same location for generations, the materials that feed historical collections accumulated undisturbed in attics or barns. With the advent of small homes, apartment-dwelling, and frequent moves, these accumulations of old materials are being consumed in bonfires or being sold to the junkman. With small home-owned businesses giving way to chains and conglomerates, the records of local firms are also disappearing. Institutions faced with skyrocketing storage costs are destroying their older records.

Every library has a duty to help in preserving vital local information before it vanishes forever. Even if the library does not have ideal equipment or specialized personnel to handle these resources, it does offer a better fate than destruction in a bonfire or deterioration in a damp cellar.

Is a local history collection worth the effort? Ask the people who turn to a typical collection. There is the businessman who is trying to find early pictures of the firm's factory to use in advertisements. There is a doctor reconstructing the controversy which raged around a progressive health officer in the younger days of the city. There are citizens studying issues and candidates in an effort to acquire ammunition for campaign use. There is the genealogist hot on the trail of an early ancestor. There are the visitors hoping to discover the story of the house on the hill that looks just like a castle. There is the newspaper reporter preparing a special feature on Lincoln's visit to the city. There is the graduate student writing a paper about the effect of the Civil War on the local economy. There is the newcomer to the community studying growth patterns and land-use projections in an effort to determine the best place to buy a home. There is the history buff trying to find out how "Whiskey Alley" got its name.

All of the people who figured in these true examples would testify to the importance of a local history collection.

INGREDIENTS OF A LOCAL HISTORY COLLECTION

Any good historical collection should have a sound nucleus of books. If a history has been written of your county or of your city, obtain copies. Histories of your state which pay explicit attention to your community should be represented. City directories are obligatory inclusions. So are collections of phone books for your area. Yearbooks of local high schools and colleges are important. A strong argument can be made for including the books written by local authors even if they don't deal with the community.

Yes, books are essential. But don't sit back smugly once you've arranged for their acquisition. You've only scratched the surface. Most ingredients of local history do not come neatly packaged in tidy volumes. The raw materials of local history must be assembled from a bewildering assortment of items that can range from the yellowed handbill for a local fair to the financial statement of a local bank. These odds and ends are like pieces of a jigsaw puzzle which fit together to present a revealing picture of the community. No book can hope to incorporate the intricate and continually evolving record captured in these miscellaneous materials.

In collecting the miscellany that forms the blood, muscle, and bone of a local history collection, there is one golden rule to follow: Treasure the past but don't forget the present. Tomorrow's history is being made today. The bits and pieces you collect about current activities in your community will be choice historical items 50 years from now. If you doubt this, remember that many things which cause historians to exult were considered trivia at the time of their origin—playbills, political posters, postcards, etc.

This means that even the library in a newly established community can't close its eyes to its historical obligations. There may be no past to preserve except for general area history, but there is a present which will become history in the future.

To illustrate the variety of materials which are qualified for collection as historical records, here is a selective checklist. It is far from comprehensive, but it is indicative:

County, city, village, or township governments
  Charters
  Ordinances
  Directories of officials
  Annual reports
  Special surveys or studies of housing, recreation, etc.
  Zoning and planning reports
  Agendas or minutes of meetings

County, city, village, or township governments (cont'd)
Sample ballots
Organizational charts and booklets describing the functions of
local government

School systems

Annual reports
Minutes of boards of education
Directories of teachers
Superintendents' bulletins
Curriculum guides and studies
Studies of future needs for buildings and capital improvements
Brochures issued when new buildings are opened
School census reports
Student publications
Publicity and programs for student activities such as plays
and concerts
Commencement programs
Evening school announcements
Sample report cards

Businesses and industries

Company histories
Charters
Annual reports
Financial statements
Account books
House organs
Sales catalogs
Advertisements
Speeches describing business activities
Copies of key patents in the firm's development

Political parties, candidates, and interested citizens' groups

Posters depicting candidates
Campaign leaflets
Studies of candidates or campaign issues
Crucial campaign speeches
Records of county meetings of political parties
Ads and program notes for political rallies and picnics
Newsletters from local legislators

Service, social, and hobby groups

Compiled histories of the club or organization
Newsletters
Rosters of members and officers
Constitutions and bylaws
Minutes of meetings
Program notes of theatrical or musical groups; exhibition catalogs of art or photography groups
Literature for fund-raising campaigns

Religious institutions

Anniversary publications
Newsletters
Lists of members
Birth, baptismal, marriage, death and burial records
Minutes of meetings of church officials
Records of clergymen who served the institution
Groundbreaking or dedication brochures
Sermons centered around local events or people
Funeral orations for prominent citizens

Personal papers and memorabilia

(These must either represent prominent citizens or be old enough to justify inclusion because they give the flavor of a past era.)

Diaries
Correspondence
Account books
Scrapbooks
Photographs
Marriage, birth, or death records
Wills
Land grants, deeds, bills of sale
Diplomas

A few sources of historical material deserve a special word of explanation or endorsement.

Older citizens in your community possess memories of times past which will die with them unless you record these recollections. Probably the simplest means of capturing their comments is with a tape recorder. To preserve the tapes and to assure the widest possible use of the information they contain, transcripts should be made for inclusion in your vertical files. Be sure to get legal advice about release forms for tapes and transcripts before you undertake an oral history program.

Graduate students working on research projects involving local history should be approached for duplicates of their completed works. They usually are flattered to receive a request of this sort.

Genealogists tracing ancestors who have figured in the history of your community will be delighted to give a copy of their completed family trees to the library.

Museums, historical associations, or genealogical societies in your area may publish pamphlets or newsletters devoted to subjects of local interest. If significant papers are read at meetings sponsored by these bodies, ask for copies of the presentations.

The area newspaper is one of the kingpins in your collection. It is a treasure house of local news which will mellow into basic history. The use of hometown newspapers will be discussed in greater detail in a later section. In addition to the local newspaper itself, watch for the market surveys which are published by many newspapers to attract advertisers. These brochures usually feature charts, statistics, and photographs of the region served by the paper.

Pictorial materials have a role to play in the enrichment of your local history files. Photographs and postcards add another dimension to your resources since they capture images in a concrete, detailed fashion that cannot be duplicated in words. A postcard showing the corner of Main Street and First Avenue in 1905 is a historic find which will increase in value with each passing year. More will be said about pictorial materials later in this chapter.

Local maps also are important in the historical collection. Seek them out and preserve them, whatever the subject matter. Surveyors' maps, maps showing school boundaries, maps of real estate developments, soil surveys, geological maps, street maps, zoning maps, lake surveys, maps of local college campuses, maps showing locations of landmarks, maps of snowmobile, bicycle, or hiking trails—all of these are grist for your mill. The physical treatment and organization of maps is considered in chapter 8.

As you develop your resources, you will inevitably discover that items of great significance to the historical panorama of your community are in the firm possession of other institutions or individuals. Since you can't own the originals, the alternative is to obtain reproductions if there are no copyright barriers. These reproductions can be made by a commercial photographer, a camera fan on your staff, or by means of a photocopy machine.

EVALUATING MATERIALS FOR INCLUSION

Don't be too restrictive in your interpretation of what constitutes local history. You cannot arbitrarily stop at the city incorporation lines. The first settler in the area may have taken up residence at the other side of the county. Can you ignore him? The resort that flourished at a nearby lake years ago may have been the focal point of summer social life for the town's residents. Will you dismiss it because it was outside your boundaries?

Major emphasis should center on your own snug little community, but its story can't be told without referring to its periphery.

Similarly, it's wrong to be too parochial in your judgment of the type of material which reflects local history. Some historians suggest that the songs, games, and dances prevalent in the early days of a settlement are as historically significant as the establishment of the first blacksmith's shop.

Seemingly frivolous materials can earn a place in your collection by satisfying the curiosity of succeeding generations. For example, in our library we carefully preserve a copy of the popular song, "I've Got a Gal in Kalamazoo," because our city is featured in the lyrics.

The firm standards applied to most library acquisitions in relation to style of writing and quality of printing may have to be waived when it comes to local history materials. Here content takes precedence over form. A pamphlet that covers an obscure episode in the region's past should be coveted despite awkward grammar and poor paper.

Historical gifts may necessitate decisions on the part of the librarian which would tax a Solomon. Some of the material presented by local residents will be useless junk. The librarian must exercise great tact in handling such offers. The right to dispose of inappropriate or unneeded items is one that must be preserved zealously. Remember that while gifts may be "free," their organization and maintenance are not.

If you are a novice at historical collecting, enlist the help of an expert in evaluating questionable items. You can always discard surplus material at a future date, but you can't replace a treasure once it has been tossed out. One of the specialists in our state says that his motto is: "In case of doubt, don't throw it away."

Sometimes groups of historical records will be offered to the library on an indefinite loan basis with the stipulation that they may be reclaimed at any time by the club or institution. This is a risky arrangement. It makes the library answerable for theft or mutilation, but does not give it complete control over the materials. Furthermore, members of the contributing body seem to have no qualms about carrying off sections of the records for study or revision. Many times this is done without notifying the librarian. Sometimes the borrowed items are not returned.

This type of temporary deposit is to be discouraged. However, if the records are an important part of community history and the alternatives are destruction or complete inaccessibility, a library may be forced to compromise its stand.

Libraries may find themselves having to cope with gifts of historical materials which are very massive, very specialized, or very valuable. Should they be kept or not? To deal with this problem you must first establish guidelines for your collection. How far do you want to go in preserving the correspondence of distinguished residents? Do you have the space and staff to handle the business papers of local firms? Do you feel qualified to accept responsibility for a diary which is truly a collector's item?

Once you've established your guidelines, you can turn to other institutions to absorb materials which are beyond your scope. Items which do not fit your focus or facilities will often be welcomed with open arms by state historical societies, state archivists, historical museums, or university libraries.

TECHNIQUES FOR BUILDING THE COLLECTION

A local history collection is like a magnet. Once established, it attracts contributions to itself.

Publicity helps to speed the process. Make speeches at every opportunity about your collection and its goals. Arrange for newspaper, radio, and TV coverage of interesting new acquisitions to the collection. Such exposure inspires further gifts. Send letters to local clubs, businesses, institutions, and government agencies asking to be placed on the mailing list for their publications. Since so much important material originates with governmental bodies, cultivate contacts in key offices who will alert you when new information becomes available. Encourage staff members to participate in societies which have an interest in the history of your community.

Each contact with a patron using the history collection is really an ad for additional materials. The businessman who uses your files to compile a history of a company for an anniversary celebration will be glad to see that you get a copy of the finished brochure. The amateur historian who is tracing the history of plank roads in the area may bring you additional information unearthed in another library.

Flea markets, auction sales, or secondhand stores may be good hunting grounds for historical materials such as postcards or old photographs.

In your search for materials, don't overlook the importance of incidental clues. For example, newspaper articles about local interests are often based on information which can be obtained in its original form. If a feature article about the need for new parks mentions a study of recreational facilities made by the local Rotary Club, follow up this lead by requesting a copy of the study.

At the same time, don't forget the necessity for an orderly pattern of routine acquisition. Maintain a checklist of periodically released items so that you don't miss materials which will be impossible to obtain later on. You can review this checklist at set intervals to discover gaps in your receipts. While such checklists are usually organized on the basis of the issuing body or the title of the publication, it is possible to set up a chronological file to jog the librarian's memory. A "tickler" file arranged by the months of the year will remind the staff that February is the time to watch for the annual public report prepared by the school board.

The burden of keeping up with publications about the area rests very heavily on the shoulders of the librarian. Most of these materials are produced locally for local consumption. They will not turn up in the standard indexes or lists of publications. Most of them are designed for short-term use and the supply is quickly exhausted. You must be constantly on the alert for them and act promptly to obtain them.

Because it is especially hard to keep up with local documents, it may help to work for an ordinance or a state law requiring the deposit of such documents in area libraries. However, laws of this sort usually lack teeth and are not rigorously enforced. As a result, a consistent follow-up is still necessary.

Carefully worded questionnaires are useful devices for soliciting information for the library's local history files. One popular project is to ask prominent citizens to fill out a form devoted to biographical data. A photograph can be requested at the same time. Most people feel complimented to be chosen for this attention. Forms may also be used to solicit the histories of business establishments and clubs.

While techniques of acquisition are important, probably the most significant step in building a history collection is to assign the project to a staff member who is enthusiastic about the undertaking and who is knowledgeable about local history or willing to become so.

TECHNICALITIES IN COLLECTION BUILDING

As your efforts begin to bear fruit, certain formalities become necessary. To avoid future legal complications, have a lawyer develop forms to be used in accepting gifts of any substance. Keep a log of such gifts. This could take the form of an accession book or accession sheets. The record should include identification of the donor; a description of the contents; the quantity and condition of the gift; and any restrictions upon use. Also maintain a donor's file in which significant gifts are recorded under the person's name.

ORGANIZATION

An alphabetical subject approach is the best means of organizing local history files. Dewey Decimal Classification or Library of Congress Classification are completely inappropriate because of the intricate content and local flavor of the resources involved.

In the past, it was possible to neatly divide city and county materials into separate sections of the local history files. This is no longer true in many libraries. Increased mobility, urban sprawl, and the overlapping of problems and activities have made such separation impractical.

It is now necessary in most libraries to think in terms of an extended community. Instead of separate arrangements under city and county, there is now a consolidated file combining both. The file may even extend beyond county lines to incorporate other nearby localities.

If it is considered necessary or desirable, subdivisions can be provided for political units under certain headings.

Despite the trend toward consolidation of city and county resources, it is still important that a separate section of the files be set aside for material about your state or about areas of the state other than your own locality. (The role of state materials in a "local" history collection will be covered more fully later in this chapter.)

Since the emphasis in local history files is on details and specifics, the subjects chosen must be precise and finely honed. If your municipality has adopted a sister city in another part of the world, this concept must be immediately conveyed by the subject heading you select. If your city conducts a "Pioneer Days" celebration each year, there should be a subject heading which mirrors this fact. The more exact your subject headings, the fewer cross references you will need and the less guesswork you will have to do in serving your patrons. Fine subject designations also cut down on unnecessary handling of precious historical resources.

When quantities of newspaper clippings are involved, there are additional decisions to make. Should the clippings under a topic be kept in simple chronological order or should they be broken up into subtopics? Are clippings on the local art center more useful in straight order by date or subdivided into such categories as exhibits, courses, personnel, and construction of a new facility? The first approach gives a progressive picture of the growth of the center. The second arrangement enables you to quickly locate the answer to a single specific question. Your choice of arrangement should be based on the nature of the requests which you receive for information.

Unfortunately, there is no up-to-date list of subject headings specially designed to guide you in setting up your local history files. You may get some help from studying the entries in the **New York Times Index** under the headings of "New York State" and "New York City." While these entries cannot serve as an exact model for your files, they will give you an introduction to the types of activities and agencies which can exist at state and city levels. If you have access to any of the indexes which various libraries have made for their local newspapers, these may suggest patterns which could be modified for your files.

The **Hennepin County Library Authority File (124)**, discussed in chapter 3, might also be consulted for possible clues to handling state, county, and city headings.

The subject headings you use in your local history files should be recorded in a card index. The complexity of these headings makes a written record indispensable. Generous cross references will help to unravel the complicated interrelationships.

Your vertical files may be a way station for some material. For example, the minutes of the city council may be housed there until a year has elapsed. The accumulated minutes can then be bound, cataloged, and placed on the open shelves. Rather than attempting to give prime file or shelf space to a long run of annual reports from the parks department, you might keep only the current edition in your vertical file. Previous reports can be shifted to a separate storage room from which they can be retrieved when needed. Having the latest edition in the vertical files will alert you and your users to the existence and nature of the publication without usurping undue space in your service area.

Special gift collections pose peculiar problems of organization. If your library is housing the papers or records of a family, company, organization, or institution, you will have to make allowances for the unique character of these holdings. Archivists and historians warn that these collections should be kept intact, if possible.

Such collections can be represented in the card catalog. The number of entries will depend upon the nature and importance of each collection, as well as the philosophy of the library itself. The records of the Ladies' Literary Society might be noted in the catalog by a single card indicating the name of the group, the character and extent of the holdings, and the period of time covered. Since a single card of this type requires the user to know the exact name of the group, many librarians would add alternate approaches such as "Lake City—Women's clubs."

It is possible to assign a Dewey or Library of Congress number to special collections, but it isn't necessary. They are usually housed in a separate closed area. A simple location note or symbol on the catalog card is sufficient. A cutter number may be added to provide further identification.

Catalog cards of the type described above give access to a group of papers or records, but they do not help to pinpoint valuable bits of information within a particular collection.

Since it is important to preserve the unity of these special collections, access to individual items of interest will have to be provided by additional finding aids.

Notes referring to selected items in a collection may be inserted at appropriate places in the vertical files. Pertinent portions may be photoduplicated for inclusion in the files. An index may be created for each collection. Or entries describing certain items in a collection may be added to an existing index.

These additional finding aids can greatly enrich historical coverage.

For example, the records of the local Men's Club may detail the campaign which its members conducted for a municipal swimming pool. While this material is important as part of the overall history of the Men's Club, it is also important as part of the story behind the construction of the swimming pool. Means of retrieving such information should be provided.

The complexity of local history materials points up the need for organizing holdings thoroughly and carefully. Too many libraries have relied on the memory of a single staff member as a key to these resources. Librarians do move away or retire or die. For the sake of continuity, your local history collection must be able to stand on its own two feet despite changes in staff.

HOUSING AND PRESERVATION

In a public library, the local history collection should be housed in a separate room or concentrated in a clearly defined area of the general room. This will serve to dramatize the collection and point up its special nature.

There is no way to completely stop the physical aging of a library's historical treasures. Even the most elaborate methods can only retard the process. Furthermore, many advanced techniques such as the deacidification of valuable papers are not economically feasible for many libraries. However, there are practical steps which most libraries can take to promote the well-being of their historical holdings.

If your building can boast of adequate temperature and humidity controls, the historical materials you own will be assured of a better chance at longevity. Using the proper air filters will also help. Another important conservation measure is to protect historical resources from the destructive impact of light. Be particularly careful to shield them from sunlight. Be sure that fluorescent lighting is filtered to reduce ultraviolet emanations.

In dealing with items of vertical file format, steel files may be used to protect historical materials from dust, light, and physical manhandling. Files equipped with locking mechanisms provide extra security.

Physical protection can also be provided by acid-free storage boxes constructed with metal clips rather than adhesives. The boxes manufactured by the Hollinger Corporation (129) are well-known.

Boxes are available which can be used for horizontal or vertical storage.

If materials are to be stored vertically in boxes, care must be taken to make sure that papers do not sag in the containers. If boxes are not filled reasonably full, papers may have to be "blocked up" to provide support.

Archivists point out that there is less physical strain on important papers when they are stored flat instead of being housed in vertical filing cabinets or in vertical storage boxes. However, horizontal boxes consume more space. If horizontal boxes are stacked, they are also extremely difficult to manipulate.

Compromise seems to be the best solution. Vertical filing cabinets can be used for historical materials which are in active use. It is easy to retrieve materials from vertical files, and it's equally easy to add new resources to growing headings. Materials which are in less demand can be housed in vertical storage boxes in a behind-the-scenes area. The few delicate or precious pieces that justify flat containers may be placed in flat storage boxes.

Be generous with your use of folders in the vertical files. Do not overload them. Attempting to economize will invite damage to the contents. To provide additional protection for unusual items, envelopes may be fastened inside file folders. In order to slow deterioration, all paper folders and envelopes should be made of acid-free stock.

Plastic may also be used to protect historical materials in files. A simple way is to employ holders of polyester or cellulose acetate for valuable or awkward items.

A recent innovation carries the use of plastic containers one step further. Archivists and history librarians are excited about a new process called encapsulation. This consists of encasing a paper between two sheets of chemically inert polyester film. Double-coated tape is used on all four sides to hold the two layers of film together, making a container that protects the document from air, dirt, and handling. Even brittle paper can stand rough treatment once encapsulated.

The document itself remains in its original physical condition. It can be removed from the "capsule" whenever desired. However, it must be stressed that unless papers are deacidified and buffered before encapsulation, deterioration from acid will continue inside the container.

Because encapsulation does not involve the use of heat and does not alter the physical format of the document itself, many archivists are opting for its use in place of lamination whenever possible.

Descriptive literature about encapsulation can be obtained from the Hollinger Corporation (129). The Library of Congress has a working paper on the technique which is available free of charge (201). It also has announced that it will devote one of its future **Preservation Leaflets (204)** to the subject.

Acid and other impurities can migrate from one piece of paper to another. This is another reason for isolating deteriorating materials and high-acid items such as newspaper clippings in separate folders, envelopes, or capsules. Interleaving sheets of acid-free paper between historical materials is another way of combating this destructive migration.

All acquisitions should be unfolded and flattened before storage.

Metal paper clips, metal staples, and rubber bands are to be avoided in storing historical items, because they will eventually cause discoloration and deterioration. Plastic clips are available, although they are not very effective.

Marks of ownership and location should be applied with great discretion and care to avoid defacing important historical resources. Some archivists and curators even urge that marking of valuable material be restricted to the envelope or folder housing the item because of their fear of disfigurement or damage. However, the problem of theft has become so overwhelming that ownership marks may be unavoidable. Certainly every effort should be made to avoid marring the face of pictorial material which might be needed for duplication in books, magazines, or newspapers. Caution should also be exercised so that the mark does not obliterate any part of the text.

Working jointly, the Government Printing Office and the Office of the Assistant Director for Preservation at the Library of Congress have developed an archivally safe ink. This ink will be made available without charge. The formula for the ink is being kept secret to prevent thieves from devising means of eradicating identification marks made with it. This ink, as well as other means of marking, are described in the Library of Congress publication, **Preservation Leaflet Number 4: Marking Manuscripts (204).**

To protect very fragile items from wear, it may be desirable to make photoreproductions which can be used for ordinary consultation. Of course, any photoreproduction must be in accordance with copyright regulations. If photocopies are made, it is preferable that they be on permanent/durable or acid-free paper.

Another way of handling fragile or theft-prone material is to place a referral note in the vertical file indicating that an item has been transferred to a special storage area and may be obtained by contacting the librarian. The simplest kind of referral note is a photocopy of the cover or title page with a sentence of explanation written on it.

More information on the physical management of historical maps, pictorial materials, and clippings can be found in the individual chapters on these subjects.

As you work with your historical collection, you will be faced with many questions about conservation and restoration. The best course to follow is to do nothing until you're sure that you know what you're doing. Background reading can be helpful. Mention has already been made of some titles in the **Preservation Leaflets** series **(204).** This free series will give you a quick introduction to some of the problems and processes connected with the conservation of library and archival materials. The series is produced by the Office of the Assistant Director for Preservation at the Library of Congress. Five titles have been published, and ten more are projected.

In addition, don't hesitate to consult the experts. Turn to your state library or to conservators at major libraries or museums in your section of the country. Check to see if there are any regional facilities in your vicinity, such as the New England Document Conservation Center.

You can seek advice from the Office of the Assistant Director for Preservation at the Library of Congress **(22).** Or you can direct your questions to the ALA's Committee on the Preservation of Library Materials **(58).** In addition, there are commercial firms which specialize in preservation and restoration techniques. Check with other librarians for their recommendations of specific firms.

Because your local history collection is a promise to the future as well as a tool for the present, mass circulation cannot be justified in public libraries.

If you cannot resist the pressures for circulation, try to accumulate duplicates of frequently requested materials. If permitted by copyright, photocopies of popular items can also be made for circulation. Providing a duplicating machine for public use will help to compensate for circulation restrictions.

School libraries may be more liberal in their circulation policies, since their local history materials do not represent a commitment to the community as a whole. In addition, the school librarian can assume that the public library will act as a backup to his/her collection. If, however, the school library is the major depository for information on the history of the school, careful consideration should be given to protecting this collection from the hazards of random circulation.

SPECIAL RESOURCES

Newspapers

The history of your community cannot be adequately told without the help of the local newspaper. It is like a group diary, recording events and thought in your area.

One method of presenting the contents of your local paper is to clip significant articles and file them by subject in the local history files. This system provides quick, easy access for the user. Clippings from a number of dates are brought together for instant retrieval. The reader can quickly scan the articles for precious pieces of information not even hinted about in the headlines. The system does have certain disadvantages:

1. Clippings take up a great deal of room.

2. Clippings are vulnerable to damage, theft, and deterioration.

3. The physical process of clipping is time-consuming, and if clippings are mounted, even more time is consumed.

4. The sheer bulk of articles makes it almost impossible to clip all stories of possible interest.

The cost of this operation can be lowered by utilizing volunteers such as retired people to do the mechanical processing of clippings. Mounting expenses may be curtailed by letting clippings age a while before pasting them. Many times summary articles will appear which will permit the discarding of preliminary clippings.

As indicated earlier in this book, there has been experimentation in photocopying clippings and disposing of the originals.

A clipping program is most easily managed in smaller communities where local news is fairly limited. In larger cities, articles of local interest are so numerous that the cutting and mounting of clippings becomes an operation of massive proportions.

The processing of clippings is discussed in detail in chapter 5.

To avoid the problems associated with clippings, some public libraries have resorted to indexing the local newspaper instead. Since newsprint deteriorates so rapidly, these libraries usually microfilm their newspaper holdings for use with the index. In cities where newspapers have more than one edition a day, the edition indexed must be the one which is being preserved on microfilm.

The traditional newspaper index consists of cards topped with subject headings. The date and page of each article on the subject is entered below the heading. There are two techniques for adding entries to the index. One method calls for pulling subject cards one by one as the indexer proceeds from article to article. Under the second system, the indexer first types all the new entries on a sheet of paper before turning to the index file. If there is sufficient staff time to support this nicety, it helps to record a few key words from the headline to give a clue to the contents of each article. Noting the exact column in which an article appears is a refinement which also will depend upon the time available.

Clerical help can be employed in some phases of the indexing operation. For example, the librarian can mark subject headings on the articles in the newspaper which are to be covered. The typing of entries on the index cards themselves can then be turned over to a clerk or student assistant.

Some libraries are indexing local newspapers using computers. The resulting indexes are printed on pages which can be bound into book form.

The indexing method, if combined with microfilming of the newspaper, is a great space saver, but this approach has its drawbacks, too:

1. Many people dislike using microfilm, as they find it difficult to read.

2. Indexing reveals only the general content of articles, whereas to trace a particular fact, it is often necessary to put reel after reel of microfilm on the reader.

3. Microfilm use is restricted by the number of microfilm readers which the library owns, and users may have to wait until machines are free.

Despite these disadvantages, indexing may be the only choice possible as the municipality and the local newspaper grow larger and larger.

It's a common predicament for libraries to find themselves with newspaper runs covering many decades when absolutely no clipping or indexing was attempted. Most libraries have all they can do to cope with the current year's paper without tackling this backlog. And yet those early newspapers are studded with vital information about the region.

To tap this resource, try to enlist the efforts of interested citizens in your community. History buffs or retirees with academic backgrounds may be delighted to tackle these intriguing old papers under the supervision of the library staff. The indexing they do may not be perfect, but it will be infinitely better than having no subject approach to these papers at all.

To quiet any skepticism, let me point out that our museum which is a part of the local library system has sponsored a project to index the early years of the **Kalamazoo Gazette**. The initial indexing has been done by inmates at one of our state prisons.

If you are not ready to tackle a major indexing of back issues of your local paper, you can build up a partial index by asking patrons and staff members to jot down the location of any helpful newspaper articles which they are lucky enough to stumble upon.

Pictorial Materials

To preserve a visual image of the community, the librarian must make a conscious effort to build up the pictorial portion of the local history collection. A collection cannot rely on gifts alone, as important as they may be. The librarian must make the rounds of dime stores, drug stores, and newsstands to locate picture postcards depicting the community. Also, canvass local restaurants, hotels, and motels, since they often furnish postcards to customers which feature pictures of their establishments.

Make arrangements with the editor to obtain copies of historically significant photographs which have appeared in the local newspaper.

If individuals in the community own choice pictures they don't want to part with, try to get permission to have prints made for the library's collection.

Any major events taking place in the community should alert the librarian to picture leads. When a local industry has an anniversary celebration or the Chamber of Commerce organizes a street fair, the library can contact the sponsor for copies of photographs taken in connection with these activities.

Because this is an age of constant and devastating change, every library should initiate an organized campaign to preserve the present-day community on film. The demolition of an ancient structure, the leveling of an impressive hillside, the relocation of a monument, or the remodeling of a government building should send the librarian or his agent scurrying to photograph the edifice or terrain before the face of the city is changed forever.

In fact, one of the finest projects the library can organize is a systematic photographic inventory of the city. A local camera club or a budding young amateur photographer can be enlisted to carry on this undertaking. Public buildings, parks, monuments, historic houses, factories, stores, and schools are among the landmarks which should be included in this photographic survey.

One word of caution! Photographs taken for library use must be fully identified and carefully dated. The name of the photographer should be noted also.

Photographs which reach the library as unsolicited gifts can be mixed blessings. Among them may be treasures that will add luster to the collection. But there will also be shots of family pets and rose bushes in bloom. The librarian will have to screen gift pictures carefully to make sure that they really justify inclusion in the library's files. Are the people or locations pictured historically significant? Or does the picture warrant inclusion because it depicts the clothing, equipment, or activities of a particular era in the community?

Oftentimes the big stumbling block in making full use of gift photographs is that the scenes and people shown are not identified. Older residents of the community can be of inestimable help in solving these mysteries.

In order to squeeze the greatest benefit from your collection of pictorial materials, make sure that they are indexed thoroughly. You may be keeping pictures of dwellings either for their historic importance or their indication of architectural trends. The indexing might be expanded to include references to these pictures from the name of the original owner, the style of architecture, or the location.

If you are interested in reading about the techniques used at one major library for indexing its local history pictures, you can consult **Picture Indexing for Local History Materials**, by Karen Diane Gilbert **(109)**. This booklet describes a system developed at the Newark Public Library.

You will find more information about pictorial materials, particularly photographs, in chapter 9.

Special Indexes and Directories

Special card files or indexes can add greatly to the scope of your local coverage.

Some libraries maintain obituary indexes to death notices which have appeared in the newspaper.

An index to street name origins is extremely useful.

A card file recording early cemetary inscriptions is an intriguing possibility. The location of each gravestone should be indicated on the cards. This is a project which might be carried out by the local historical society or even by an American history class in the community high school.

An index to early county records of marriages, births, and deaths would be a boon to researchers.

A card directory of local clubs and organizations serves a double purpose. It can be helpful in furnishing current information about officers and meetings. Superseded cards can be preserved to form a historical record of these groups.

In an effort to provide a centralized approach to all of their holdings in the area of local history, some libraries have developed a single index for pamphlets, photographs, maps, periodical articles, clippings, and parts of books. The various types of reference aids may be distinguished by file cards of different colors. If a library chooses, instead, to list everything about a given subject on a single card, symbols or descriptive abbreviations must be added to the entries to identify the nature of each resource.

Resource indexes do not need to be limited to the holdings of your own institution. A record of community information available through other agencies and individuals is an excellent backup tool. Where are the birth records housed? What early church documents are kept at the First Presbyterian Church? Which resident is an expert on the history of railroads in the area? What materials with local implications are in the state library collection? These are all bits of knowledge which may prove invaluable.

State History

The emphasis which you place on local affairs should be supplemented by special attention to materials about your state. There are good reasons for this focus.

Being a part of a local community obligates a library to record that community's present and its past. Similarly, being situated in a particular state obligates a library to interpret that state to local residents.

Furthermore, the events which have shaped your state have also molded your city. The history of the one is the history of the other.

In acquiring material about your state, concentrate on what is currently being published. Leave the pursuit of rare old items to the historical library.

While discussions of the state's past are obviously a part of "state history," don't ignore the publications which consider present-day economy, culture, government, population, etc. These accounts are initially helpful in answering reference questions about current developments. They are also the history of tomorrow.

Because of the mass of material available, the average library will have to be selective in its choice of publications about the state. It should concentrate on the more basic items. Since major libraries in the state will be collecting and preserving state information, there is no compulsion for the local library to acquire anything that does not fall into its normal pattern of reference service. Interlibrary loans and photocopying arrangements will satisfy the occasional requests that involve highly specialized materials.

Official state publications are basic ingredients for your files. The **Monthly Checklist of State Publications (163)** is one way to keep abreast of current state releases although it is not all-inclusive. Our state library in Michigan issues a periodic list of state documents which it has received. It also serves as a clearinghouse for supplying documents to local libraries. You will want to check with your state library to see if it provides similar services.

Judging from our experience, it is possible to be placed on the mailing lists of some state agencies, although many are not responsive to such long-term commitments.

The publications lists issued by some state bodies are wonderful shortcuts to ordering materials.

Clues to new state publications can be obtained from newspapers, since they often report the printing of documents that are of interest to the general public.

A good method of surveying the agencies which might have publications of interest to your patrons is to obtain an organizational chart of the state government. The secretary of state may be able to provide such a chart.

If your state has an official handbook or manual, it will also give you an overview of agencies and their responsibilities. These guides may be called by different names in different states. They are familiarly known as "blue books."

Official state telephone directories offer another good way to survey the various departments, bureaus, and offices of the state government.

State Administrative Officials Classified by Functions (223) will also introduce you to key governmental bodies in your state.

State historical commissions and state historical societies are particularly good prospects for bolstering your files, since they usually have extensive lists of publications relating to state history. Many are inexpensive but authoritative booklets which will be first-rate additions to your collection. Museums and universities are also likely to sponsor historical publications.

A helpful guide to historical organizations can be found in the **Directory of Historical Societies and Agencies in the United States and Canada (5)**, a publication of the American Association for State and Local History.

Don't overlook the federal government in your search for state information. For example, the United States Environmental Data Service publishes **Climatological Data** for each state. There are monthly issues and an annual summary. Single copies or subscriptions can be purchased through the Environmental Data Service, which is a part of the National Oceanic and Atmospheric Administration. Representative of the coverage offered on special topics from time to time by the federal government is a recent series on the legal status of homemakers in each state. These studies sponsored by the National Commission on the Observance of International Women's Year are for sale by the Superintendent of Documents.

You will also want to investigate the commercial publishers or distributors who specialize in state history. In our state, Hillsdale Educational Publishers, Inc. **(128)** concentrates on Michigan interests. Comparable firms exist in other parts of the nation. They often exhibit their wares at educational meetings or state library conventions.

Newspapers represent an important source of state information. Subscribing to a newspaper from the state capitol or the largest city in the state will enable you to supplement the state clippings from your local paper.

If you're lucky, you may find that some group or agency within your state has published a bibliography which includes free and inexpensive materials about your state. In Michigan we are very fortunate. Our state library publishes a quarterly called **Michigan in Books**, which, despite its title, also offers good coverage of new pamphlets about Michigan. Our state library has also produced general bibliographies about Michigan from time to time. Your state library may provide similar lists.

SPECIAL LIBRARIES

While this chapter has concentrated on the role of public libraries, special libraries may also find themselves involved with local history materials. Their assignment may be no more than clipping and preserving newspaper articles about the institution, organization, or business which they serve.

On the other hand, many special libraries are given the responsibility for maintaining the historical records of the parent body.

This responsibility is a major one, since archival materials may include items which are voluminous and varied. Examples are correspondence files, research reports, employee newsletters, speeches, and statistical records.

Special librarians faced with the task of operating archival collections should develop retention and disposition schedules in cooperation with the administration. Such schedules should indicate which items are of only temporary interest and which are of long-term value.

Accession records should be made for any materials transferred to the archives.

The traditional method of handling archival material is based on two concepts. The first is the principle of provenance, which means that materials are grouped by source. Under this principle, acquisitions from each department or division are kept intact in a record group. Access by subject can be achieved only through the creation of special finding aids.

Grouping by source is supposed to provide an orderly picture of the nature and development of each unit within an institution or business. Furthermore, it is claimed that users accustomed to the organizational structure of the body will have a particular division or office in mind when they approach the archives.

The second basic precept followed by archivists is to retain the original order of the records as much as possible. The theory behind preservation of original order is that it demonstrates the interrelationships between individual items, thus making them more meaningful.

Perhaps the most persuasive argument advanced for the traditional archival approach is that archival holdings are usually so overwhelming in volume that there is no other practical way to handle them.

On the other hand, Knox College in Galesburg, Illinois, has had a successful experience with organizing the college archives by subject in vertical files **(118)**. The archivist admits that the initial filing may be slower under this plan. However, this time loss is offset by eliminating the need to create complicated finding aids. Specific information can be quickly retrieved by consulting the headings in the files.

It must be admitted that Knox College represents the exception rather than the rule. Although they may display some local modifications, most collections of archival materials are still dominated by the principle of provenance and dedication to original order.

Under the traditional approach, archives are usually placed on shelves in acid-free boxes.

Because needs differ so greatly, shelving schemes vary from one archival center to another. Most systems roughly parallel the organizational structure of the institution, business, or association. These systems represent a simple form of classification although archivists prefer to call them "arrangements." The notation symbols may be numbers or letters or a combination of both. A separate symbol is assigned to each key unit in the institution or organization. Subdivisions can be used to provide a further breakdown under key units. These subdivisions might represent subordinate agencies or special series of records. Classification symbols are noted on the boxes or folders in which materials are stored. They are also added to any finding aids which are developed.

The type and number of finding aids which can be developed depend upon the time and money available. Among the devices used are inventories, card catalogs, and indexes. Some special libraries with access to the necessary equipment have even developed key-word computer indexes.

FOR FURTHER READING

Enid T. Thompson has written a down-to-earth handbook for the novice which touches on all aspects of the collection and management of local history materials. It is titled **Local History Collections: A Manual for Librarians (228)**. While old hands in the field may not agree with every one of the author's suggestions or conclusions, this book does offer a quick and practical introduction to the art.

CHAPTER 8

MAPS

Among the resources of any self-respecting library should be a representation of maps. Too often we tend to think of maps in terms of travelers only. Maps are also valuable to businessmen, government officials, historians, speakers, students, hobbyists, homeowners, and people with ties in other lands.

USES OF MAPS

Here are some examples of map use taken from actual library experience, which illustrate the variety of services these resources can provide:

1. To pinpoint the location of communities for businessmen who are trying to arrange for shipments to distant points.

2. To supply the altitude in a given location for the proud recipient of a new barometer.

3. To help the convention-goer who wants to find a hotel within walking distance of the auditorium.

4. To assist the timid driver in finding the easiest way to get to Greenfield Village or the Chicago Art Institute.

5. To locate places of current interest ("Just where did that earthquake strike that I heard about on the 12 o'clock news?").

6. To aid people who have friends or loved ones in other countries ("Can you locate this settlement in Africa where my daughter will be stationed with the Peace Corps?" "Where is the town in which my pen pal lives?").

7. To help the historian who wants to determine the precise spot where the first city hall stood or to trace the bed of an early railroad that once served the city.

8. To reinforce the hobby interests of patrons, such as the rock collector who studies geological maps or the sailor who looks for nautical charts or the scuba diver who uses the shipwreck maps of the Great Lakes or the hiker who searches for new trails to conquer.

9. To help government officials plan the future of the area—old maps showing the composition of buildings razed many years ago helped our city officials determine what kind of support they would need for a projected parking ramp.

10. To add interest to the speech of a clubwoman who wants a large map of Brazil for her talk to a women's study group.

(List continues on page 152)

11. To provide a decorative background for the businessman who wants to build a window display around imported gift items.

12. To serve as a model for the climatic map of Africa which Johnny needs for his notebook in order to get an "A" in social studies.

13. To dramatize the printed word for the reader who has just finished a book about General Custer and wants to know exactly where the famous last stand took place.

14. To assist the English teacher who wants to spice up a bulletin board with pictorial maps showing the location of literary landmarks.

15. To guide the amateur genealogist trying to trace the settlements from which that person's ancestors came.

16. To furnish background information for citizens organizing protests against the location of a new airport or a new highway.

Do you really need individual maps if you have some good atlases in your library? The answer is a resounding yes! Single maps are like zoom lens cameras which zero in on details and small areas that the generalized maps in atlases overlook. They can concentrate on special subjects, such as housing characteristics, which are not covered in the broad overview taken by most atlases. Furthermore, single maps can be readily circulated and displayed.

Entire books have been written about map libraries and map librarianship. The most recent and comprehensive text is Mary Larsgaard's **Map Librarianship: An Introduction**, published in 1978 by Libraries Unlimited, Inc. Such texts are keyed to the needs of institutions with massive map holdings. The comments in this chapter are directed to the library with more modest plans.

Whether massive or modest, a map collection exists to serve a particular group of people. The first step in collecting maps—whether you're in a school library, a public library, or a business library—is to determine the particular map needs of your particular group of people. It boils down to this: "Who wants maps or could use maps? What maps will satisfy them?"

MAP SELECTION

Selecting maps need not be a harrowing project. Don't worry too much about the fine distinctions between types of maps such as physical, political, economic, pictorial, historical, social, statistical, etc. Just concentrate on acquiring the maps for which you have a demonstrated or projected need. Don't become frantic about the complex technicalities of different map projections. Just turn to reputable sources.

Map scholar, Lloyd A. Brown, has a word of comfort for the novice:

A map is supposed to convey a picture. If it does this clearly, without confusing the reader, the chances are it is a good map. And if a map is drawn to scale, with clean lines carefully laid down, with parallels of latitude and meridians of longitude indicated, the chances are it will be a fairly accurate map, though not necessarily so. Whether we realize it or not, all of us are capable of editing a map or chart which is badly done. Good maps are almost never badly printed! **(32)**

There are some easy guidelines which even the beginner can follow in selecting maps. Be alert to these key characteristics in the maps you consider adding to your collection:

1. *The reputation of the publisher.*

2. *The date of the map.* In these days of rapid change, the more recent the map, the better. Of course, currency loses its importance in the case of reproductions of early maps. Your patrons, for example, might be interested in the concepts of the world shown in reproduced maps of the sixteenth century. And as far as maps of your own community are concerned, older maps are precious acquisitions.

3. *The geographic area covered.* Does the map properly emphasize the area in which you are interested?

4. *The subject covered.* Does your collection need a thematic map showing traffic flow or the distribution of older Americans across the nation?

5. *Detail included on the map.* The fine points to observe will vary with your purpose in acquiring the map. If, for example, it's a state map, does it show railroads? Does it define counties? Does it indicate park and forest areas?

6. *Scale.* What is the relationship between a given measurement on the map and the actual distance on the ground? This may be expressed in miles per inch or kilometers per centimeter. Or it may be expressed in a ratio such as 1:24,000. The larger the scale, the more concentrated the coverage (a scale of 1:24,000 is more sharply focused than a scale of 1:250,000).

7. *Use of color.* Are the variations distinctive enough to isolate physical features, political units, or thematic characteristics?

8. *Use of other symbols.* If symbols other than color are used, are they easily located and easily interpreted?

9. *Textual information.* Are place names or other word designations on the map clearly printed and readily legible? Are adequate explanations and instructions provided? Are textual portions of the map in English or in a foreign language?

10. *Indexing.* Does the map carry its own place name index? If not, is there a separate index available? The importance of having a good index can't be overemphasized. Not only does a detailed index help you locate points on the map, but it also serves as a mini-gazetteer when you're trying to track down an elusive town that evades identification.

11. *Special features.* Some maps carry extra bonuses such as mileage charts or enlarged inserts of important areas.

12. *Format.* How large is the map? Is it cloth-backed? Does it have a protective plastic coating? Is it flat or folded? Or in rolled form? Is the format suitable for your storage facilities?

13. *Price.*

MAP SOURCES

How do you go about building up your map collection? Even the newly minted librarian knows that a subscription to that old stalwart, the **National Geographic Magazine**, will bring maps neatly tucked in the pages of the periodical. Five map supplements are usually included each year.

The removable maps are carefully compiled and are valuable additions to your collection. Happily, all **National Geographic** maps are clearly dated. Unhappily, a name index is rarely provided on the maps themselves.

It should be easy to fill in gaps or duplicate popular items. Many people in any given community subscribe to the **National Geographic Magazine**. Since this is not a periodical which people dispose of lightly, there should be basements or attics loaded with back issues and their accompanying maps. Patrons are often glad to share this bounty with the library.

The National Geographic Society publishes a list of all the maps which it has for sale currently. With rare exceptions, these maps are duplicates or modifications of the maps sent to subscribers to the magazine. Some of the maps distributed with the magazine can be purchased in enlarged form. Many **National Geographic** maps can be ordered in a protective plastic format.

Separate indexes have been prepared for certain maps. They are available for an extra fee.

Commercial Publishers and Distributors

Where do you turn once you've decided to venture beyond the security of **National Geographic** maps? There are many commercial map publishers eager to sell their wares, and some of their wares cost a pretty penny. This is particularly true of the wall maps designed for classroom use. Many are handmounted on cloth. They frequently are attached to wooden rods or to spring rollers. Some are placed in folders after being dissected, backed with map cloth, and fitted with eyelets for hanging. Publishers offer protective plastic surfaces or overlays, which make maps markable and washable. Certain maps are especially tear-resistant. Maps may boast of special features such as thematic overlays for added information or raised relief which provides feeling as well as seeing. The text may be bilingual or entirely in a foreign tongue to facilitate language and cultural studies. It's quite common for maps designed for school use to fall in the $30.00 to $70.00 price range.

What is your position in relation to these maps? If you are employed in the media center or instructional materials center of a school, there are good arguments for purchasing as many of these maps as the budget will allow. However, you may want to weigh the merits of map transparencies as against those of wall maps.

Map selection in a school should, of course, be geared to curricular needs. Since so many of the wall-type maps being produced today are aimed at school use, it will be an easy matter to find maps which fit neatly into the teaching patterns in your school. Their sturdy format will absorb the buffeting of being shifted from classroom to classroom. Protective coverings will enable instructors to write or mark on the maps for more creative teaching.

If your school library budget cannot bear the heavy weight of such an investment, there often are special funds in administrative or departmental accounts to take over the burden.

If you are interested in maps for classroom use, write for catalogs to such firms as:

American Map Company, Inc. **(12)**

George F. Cram Company, Inc. **(66)**

Denoyer-Geppert **(75)**

Hearne Brothers **(123)**

Nystrom **(192)**

Rand McNally & Company **(206)**

Weber Costello **(247)**

On the other hand, public libraries should be extremely cautious about investing in expensive, school-oriented maps. The demands a public library faces are much broader than those of a school library, which can restrict its map buying to curricular requirements. Can you really justify spending your map budget on a few high-priced maps rather than on a variety of maps to meet a variety of needs?

Investing in expensive maps places a heavy responsibility on the librarian who is working with a modest public library budget. To warrant the initial outlay, the librarian must make sure that selections will keep their informational value over a period of years. This automatically curtails the choices that can be made. A costly political map depicting a part of the world where boundaries are unstable is a poor investment. Maps which feature changing factors such as airline routes or rail networks are not worth heavy raids on the library budget.

Maps in which a library has sunk sizable sums can turn into white elephants. Librarians often hesitate to discard them even when they become dated. It seems wasteful to throw away anything that expensive. Unfortunately, the same exaggerated prices which impede weeding also prevent frequent replacement with new editions.

Added to these problems is the fact that some maps designed for school use may be troublesome to public libraries because of their format. Roller maps, for example, are difficult to store and circulate.

Luckily, there are still some useful series available from commercial publishers at modest prices. Relatively inexpensive maps depicting the world, regions of the world, and selected countries can be obtained from:

American Map Company, Inc. **(12)**

Hammond Incorporated **(117)**

Rand McNally & Company **(206)**

For topics in the news, **Headline Focus Wall Maps (120)** are useful acquisitions at a reasonable cost. While designed for teaching purposes, they can be helpful to public libraries as well. They are published biweekly during the school year.

Some commercial publishers specialize in city maps and street guides that sell for moderate amounts. Among these are:

Arrow Publishing Company, Inc. **(19)**

Dolph Map Co., Inc. **(77)**

Geographia Map Co., Inc. **(104)**

Hagstrom Company, Inc. **(116)**

Rand McNally & Company **(206)**

Public libraries have a special obligation, of course, to collect city maps and street guides for the area in which they are located. These resources have a twofold contribution to make. They can be useful now to direct people where they want to go. They will be equally useful in the future as historical records of the community.

Find out what firm specializes in publishing maps for your area. It may be a small local business. Or it may be a company with statewide or regional emphasis. Check the yellow pages in phone books for listings. See what maps are for sale at local newsstands, bookstores, and office supply stores. Contact the public utility firms to see what maps they find useful.

Typical of such specialized publishers is Metro Graphic Arts, Incorporated **(155)**, which concentrates on metropolitan area maps and street guides for the Midwest. These maps are available in the form of inexpensive folding maps or as wall maps on heavy paper with hanging rods. The wall maps generally range in price from $38.00 to $43.00.

Here my reluctance about costly maps for public libraries vanishes abruptly. Good wall maps of your local community are an excellent investment. And price be hanged! In fact, you would even be justified in investigating the city-county maps published by Hearne Brothers **(123)**. These 50x68-inch cloth maps are laminated and mounted on spring rollers. They are fully indexed. They currently sell for $152.50.

Foreign publishers deserve the attention of any library building up a map collection. Expert cartography and low production costs combine to make some of their maps real finds. Many of these maps offer minute coverage of areas which are unavailable elsewhere.

My one real argument with certain foreign publishers also applies to many map sources in the United States—namely, a reluctance to date maps. In ordering maps from some countries, there is also the possibility of encountering place names which have not been anglicized—as, for example, "Wien" for "Vienna."

Road maps and city maps of other countries are particularly desirable items for a public library. There are a number of series available from foreign publishers who have outlets in this country, among them:

Bartholomew
Maps distributed by American Map Company, Inc. **(12)**

Falk
>Maps distributed by Larousse & Co., Inc. **(140)**

Hallwag
>Maps distributed by American Map Company, Inc. **(12)**

Kummerly & Frey
>Maps distributed by Rand McNally & Company **(206)**

Michelin
>Maps distributed by Michelin Guides and Maps **(159)**

Patria
>Maps distributed by American Map Company, Inc. **(12)**

Foreign publishers even have special resources to offer the school librarian. Excellent wall maps appropriate for classroom use are available through agents in our country such as Nystrom **(192)**, Denoyer-Geppert **(75)**, American Map Company, Inc. **(12)**, and Rand McNally & Company **(206)**.

In dealing with commercial map publishers, whether in our country or abroad, the initial procedure is to write for lists or catalogs of their publications so that you can study them. Be sure to include an explicit request that publication dates be indicated for the maps. Perhaps all you will get is a general statement about the firm's policy of revision, but that will at least give you a guideline for judging currency.

Sample a publisher before investing heavily in its maps. Order one map. Examine it for content and for quality of printing. Make sure that it lives up to the claims made in the catalog or advertisement. If the map is not dated, conduct spot checks to see if recent changes or developments have been incorporated. These tests are essential before you make a wholesale investment in a map series.

United States Government

Our federal government is a major producer of maps. These maps are authoritative, well-printed, and inexpensive. What map-hungry librarian could ask for more?

To harvest this bountiful crop of United States government maps, your first move should be to consult **Subject Bibliography 102, Maps (United States and Foreign) (226)**, which is issued annually by the Superintendent of Documents.

It is important to understand the purpose and limitations of this bibliography. It reports maps which are for sale by the U.S. Government Printing Office. The entries include such practical items as weather maps of the United States and such exotic listings as reproductions of original Civil War maps.

But beware! **Subject Bibliography 102** records just a portion of the output of federal maps. Map experts estimate that more than one-half of the United States government maps are *not* available through the Government Printing Office.

Some are sold only through the individual mapping agencies themselves or through their authorized agents. This is true of such important map producing units as:

Defense Mapping Agency

Geological Survey

National Ocean Survey

U.S. Army Corps of Engineers

Other federal agencies have arranged for free distribution of their maps through their own facilities. This is true of the Soil Conservation Service.

As you must suspect by now, there is no quick and easy way to keep abreast of United States government maps.

The **Monthly Catalog of United States Government Publications (162)** is a great disappointment as a source for locating maps. **Selected U.S. Government Publications (216)** includes occasional map entries.

There are three survey publications available which give an overview of federal map production. One is the **National Ocean Survey List of Frequently Used Federal Government World, United States and Historical Maps.** This free list from the National Ocean Survey **(182)** includes addresses.

Another summary is provided by the U.S. Geological Survey. It is titled **Types of Maps Published by Government Agencies.** A single copy can be obtained free **(171).** As well as listing categories of maps, it indicates the publishing agencies and distributing agencies. Addresses are given.

A third aid originates with the Geography and Map Division of the Library of Congress **(105).** This free compilation by Donald A. Wise is called **United States Official Mapping Agencies.**

A major effort to coordinate information about United States government maps is now being conducted by the National Cartographic Information Center **(171).** This agency was established by the U.S. Geological Survey in 1974. Its goal is to serve as a national information service for cartographic data of the United States. It hopes eventually to become a one-stop information *and* ordering center. If you have questions about federal mapping programs, this is a good place to turn for information or referral.

It would be a wise move on your part to familiarize yourself with the federal map series which are most closely allied to normal library needs. Fortunately, the larger map-producing agencies publish lists or indexes. To keep up with agencies that issue only an occasional map, look for leads in the tools described in chapter 1.

The most famous of the United States government maps form the **National Topographic Map Series,** available from the U.S. Geological Survey. These magnificent maps are sometimes called the "mother maps" or "master maps" of the country. The detail shown on large-scale maps in this series is awesome. Not only do they indicate the shape and elevation of the land surface, but they pinpoint such specific features as gravel pits, oil fields, cemetaries, and schools. The goal of the Geological Survey is to depict all of the United States, Puerto Rico, Guam, American Samoa, and the Virgin Islands in these maps.

There is a free index map and order form for each state and each of the outlying territories **(171).** The index indicates which quadrangles have been mapped and the date of the mapping. The indexes and order forms identify other Geological Survey maps available for the geographical unit. These may be topographical maps on other scales, specialized maps of certain areas and features, or photomaps in quadrangle format.

As well as requesting the index and order form for your state, you should think about getting a complete set of these tools. Library users often want to order personal copies of maps for other parts of the United States. If your library has the necessary indexes, your users will be able to do this promptly and easily.

You will certainly want to obtain the quadrangle map for your area. The price of the standard quadrangle map is only $1.25. Consider expanding your coverage to the neighboring quadrangles. In this mobile civilization, our local patrons are often concerned with the possibility of vacation homes, business investments, or camping trips in more distant regions.

While you're building your map resources, remember that the Geological Survey also issues free indexes to its smaller-scale maps in the 1:250,000 and 1:1,000,000 series (171).

If you're interested in topographic maps of national parks, monuments, and historic sites, the Geological Survey has a special order form for its maps of these features (171).

The Geological Survey also has for sale selected maps prepared for the **National Atlas** and published as separate sheets. Mapping is underway for a new edition of the **Atlas** projected for 1985. To obtain a list of the maps available in individual format, ask for the order form for **National Atlas Separate Sales Editions (171)**.

Many highly technical maps are published by the Geological Survey. Among them are maps relating to the geology and mineral and water resources of each state. A new project involves the compilation of land use and land cover maps for the entire United States.

To keep up with the many materials issued by this agency, ask to have your library placed on the free mailing list for monthly issues of **New Publications of the Geological Survey (189)**.

The National Ocean Survey **(182)** is another federal agency which has an extensive publishing program. One of its responsibilities is the production of charts for the coastal waters of the United States and for the Great Lakes and adjacent waterways. If your library is located in a coastal region or near one of the lakes or rivers covered by the National Ocean Survey, you may want to consider buying the charts for your area.

Of special interest is the series planned for recreational boaters. These guides are called **Small-Craft Charts**.

Even if you do not choose to invest in these nautical charts, your library should have descriptive material on hand for boaters who want to purchase their own. Ordering details for the navigational guides of the National Ocean Survey are given in the **Nautical Chart Catalogs**, which you can obtain free of charge. Since obsolete information is dangerous for navigation, a quarterly bulletin titled **Dates of Latest Editions, Nautical Charts & Misc. Maps** is published in addition to the catalogs. It also is free.

The National Ocean Survey also has for sale an extensive collection of aeronautical charts covering the world. They are designed for flyers but are popular with non-pilots as well. Of greatest interest are the sectional and local charts which cover the various parts of the United States. Once again, your library should be able to supply ordering data even if you decide not to buy samples of the charts themselves. A free catalog of aeronautical charts and related publications is available. To update the catalog, NOS regularly issues a list called **Dates of Latest**

Editions, VFR Aeronautical Charts. The list is free. The National Ocean Survey also publishes a list of authorized sales agents for its aeronautical charts.

The U.S. Army Corps of Engineers **(64)** is also actively engaged in producing charts and maps of the waterways under its jurisdiction. These publications are concerned with navigation and flood control. Determine which district office serves your area and ask for a list of publications covering that region.

While the Defense Mapping Agency **(73)** is one of the crucial mapping arms of the United States government, it offers relatively slim pickings for the small- or medium-sized library. It does designate certain items for public purchase which may be of interest. They can be found in the **Price List of Maps and Charts for Public Sale**. The list is free.

The Central Intelligence Agency has released a series of multicolored relief maps of foreign countries. They indicate transportation networks, ports, airfields, and urban areas. Insert maps provide additional information about such characteristics as population, land utilization, and economic activity. A nice feature of this series is that it provides sizable maps of some small countries, such as Honduras. The maps are very inexpensive, presently ranging from $0.70 to $1.25 in price. They are sold by the Superintendent of Documents. To determine the maps in print at any one time, check the latest edition of **Subject Bibliography 102, Maps (United States and Foreign) (226)**.

The national forests administered by the U.S. Forest Service prepare maps of great appeal to hikers and other outdoor enthusiasts. You may be able to obtain some small maps free, such as the mini-maps prepared by the Eastern Region to help in making preliminary plans. Large maps of the forests, however, cost $0.50 each. They can be purchased from forest supervisors, ranger district offices, or the regional offices of the Forest Service. A free list of Forest Service field offices is available **(95)**.

The Agricultural Stabilization and Conservation Service is a source of aerial photographic maps. Each ASCS county office and Agricultural Service Center has a photo index of the county or counties it serves. The index is a composite picture at a reduced scale of all the aerial photos covering the county. By consulting this photo index, you can determine the order number of any photograph you want. These offices also have order forms for your convenience.

It is possible to buy copies of the photo indexes themselves if you don't want to invest in the individual maps.

Among the users of aerial photomaps are farmers, conservationists, government planners, and citizen action groups. The aerial photomaps are also of historic value. When a new set of photos was produced for our county, a staff member at the local ASCS commented about the startling changes which have taken place since the last group of photographs was made. Aerial photo negatives from earlier studies through 1941 have been transferred to the National Archives **(51)**. Copies of these now historic photographs can be ordered from that agency.

The ASCS **(3)** has a free pamphlet describing its aerial photo program.

Since 1899 the Soil Conservation Service of the U.S. Department of Agriculture has been publishing soil surveys, which include county or area soil maps. However, the maps are bound right into the reports and are not available separately.

Many of the older soil surveys are now out of print, but new studies are being completed at a steady pace. If you are lucky enough to obtain a soil survey of any vintage for your region, treasure it. A **List of Published Soil Surveys** can be obtained free from the Soil Conservation Service **(221)**. Soil surveys which are in print are distributed free of charge by local and state offices of the Soil Conservation Service.

You'll also want to find out whether a generalized soil map has been completed for your state. If so, you can get a free copy from your state SCS office.

A new undertaking of the Soil Conservation Service is an inventory of prime and unique farmland. This project is producing large maps detailing the extent and location of important rural lands in counties and parishes. The maps which have been published for each state are available free from the state SCS office.

The Bureau of the Census produces maps based on the information it collects as it profiles the nation. Of particular interest are the display maps which make up the GE-50 and GE-70 series. They show the distribution in the United States of demographic and economic characteristics. Among the inclusions are maps showing persons of Spanish origin by county, per capita retail sales by county, and trends in the type of home heating fuel used. These maps are sold by the Superintendent of Documents. Order forms listing the maps may be obtained from the Bureau of the Census **(40)**.

Libraries in the western states may want to investigate the maps of surface and mineral ownership which have been prepared by the Bureau of Land Management of the Department of the Interior **(36)**.

While the Library of Congress is not a publisher of maps, it is a collector of maps. Its Geography and Map Division has custody of more than 3½ million maps and charts. This fact is significant to your map holdings because it is possible to order photoreproductions of those maps in the Library of Congress which are not protected by copyright.

Although there is no comprehensive catalog of the cartographic holdings of the Library, many maps are described in special lists prepared by the institution. These guides are included in the free publications list issued by the Geography and Map Division of the Library of Congress **(105)**.

Some of the compilations in print or in preparation at this time are:

1. **The American Revolution: A Selective, Annotated Bibliography of 18th Century Maps in the Collections of the Library of Congress.** Free from the Geography and Map Division **(105)**.

2. **Railroad Maps of the United States: A Selective Annotated Bibliography of Original 19th-century Maps in the Geography and Map Division of the Library of Congress.** For sale by the Superintendent of Documents. $2.60.

3. **Land Ownership Maps: A Checklist of Nineteenth Century United States County Maps in the Library of Congress.** For sale by the Superintendent of Documents. $2.75.

4. **Ward Maps of United States Cities: A Selective Checklist of Pre-1900 Maps in the Library of Congress.** For sale by the Superintendent of Documents. $0.95.

5. **A Descriptive List of Treasure Maps and Charts in the Library of Congress.** For sale by the Superintendent of Documents. $0.70.

6.   Civil War Maps: An Annotated List of Maps and Atlases in Map Collections of the Library of Congress. Revision in preparation. Will be for sale by the Superintendent of Documents.

The National Archives and Records Service is another repository of vast and unusual cartographic treasures. In its Cartographic Archives Division, you may find priceless maps which correlate with the history of your own area. The agency offers photoduplication service. Since most of its holdings are part of the public domain, there are usually no restrictions in the way of acquiring reproductions for your collection.

A booklet on the resources and services of the Cartographic Archives Division is available free (51). It names the guides, inventories, and lists which describe the holdings of the Division.

Typical of these publications are the following titles. Single copies can be obtained without charge as long as supplies last:

1.   Cartographic Records of the Bureau of Indian Affairs (Special List 13)

2.   Pre-Federal Maps in the National Archives: An Annotated List (Special List 26)

3.   List of Selected Maps of States and Territories (Special List 29)

The roll call of federal units which produce maps could go on indefinitely. For example, we might refer to the maps of reclamation projects, reclamation dams, and power facilities provided by the Bureau of Reclamation (39). We might mention the maps of Indian land areas which the Bureau of Indian Affairs has for sale through the Superintendent of Documents. All federal maps cannot be recorded here, but the examples show how naturally the activities of a federal agency can culminate in the production of maps.

The moral of this lesson is clear. If you can't find the map you want, contact the federal office most intimately involved with the subject or turn to the National Cartographic Information Center (171). Chances are good that some sort of map or chart has been compiled that is related to your needs.

State Governments

Governmental map publishing isn't limited to the federal level. State agencies also are aggressively involved in map making.

The best-known example of this is the official highway map issued by most states. These maps are important because of their detailed, authoritative coverage of roads and communities within the state. The place name indexes are useful in locating very small communities. Many maps offer additional features such as:

Mileage charts

Hunting and fishing information

Insert maps of cities

Summaries of traffic regulations

Points of interest for travelers

Lists of campgrounds and parks

State symbols such as the official bird, tree, flower, seal, and flag

The title of the issuing agency varies from state to state. Usually, it is the governmental unit in charge of highways or transportation.

Most states update their maps frequently and are very gracious about distributing them. As new editions of these maps are released, many of them are recorded in the **Monthly Checklist of State Publications (163)**. However, there is often a time lag. Furthermore, inclusion in the **Checklist** is not automatic. It is wise to inventory your state road maps once a year to determine how up to date your holdings are.

Some librarians are convinced that they receive a faster response to their requests for state highway maps if they write to the agency responsible for tourist promotion or economic development, even though the map may be produced by the state highway or transportation unit.

Closely related to the state highway maps are turnpike or toll road maps. In some instances, they may be issued by the state agency in charge of all highways. More often, they are put out by the turnpike commission or authority itself. For aid in obtaining copies, turn to the tourist office of the state in question. Turnpike, toll road, or thruway maps can earn a place in a public library collection by helping the careful traveler who wants to plan ahead.

State highway agencies may be a source for maps of counties and cities within the state. The **Monthly Checklist of State Publications** will furnish leads to some of these maps. However, since your major interest will center on your own state, the best procedure is to write to your state highway authority for a price list of any county and city maps that may be available.

Roads are far from being the only focal point of mapping activities on the state level. The possibilities are endless. You will want to study the various departments and commissions within your state to see which jurisdictions have a natural affinity for map making.

Terminology varies from state to state, but certain key words should alert you to possible leads. Agencies charged with responsibility for the following areas are prime prospects for your map gathering:

Mining and mineral industries	Tourism
Geology	Commerce or economic development
Agriculture and soil study	
Natural resources or conservation	Planning
Water resources	Railroads
Lakes and streams	Public utilities
Waterways	Education
Forestry	Taxation
Lands	State history
Parks	Aeronautics
Wildlife	Environment
Fisheries	Energy

Fortunately, there are tools to aid you in tracing state bodies which are potential map sources. If you should want to collect maps from states other than your own, a good list of contacts is available free from the Geography and Map Division of the Library of Congress **(105)**. It is called **Sources of Official State Maps**. For an extensive survey of the units of government responsible for specific activities in each of the 50 states, turn to **State Administrative Officials Classified by Functions (223)**. To get a concentrated look at agencies in your own state, use the official handbook or directory for your state.

Local Governmental Units

Local governmental units—county, city, township, village, school—are also involved in map making. Road commissions, planning bodies, engineering departments, park boards, county surveyors, and assessors are all good prospects for map hunting. A small number of cities issue street maps for use by local residents and for publicity purposes outside of the community. School districts often prepare maps depicting boundaries and buildings. In large cities, transit authorities may distribute detailed maps showing bus and subway routes.

Street maps and transit system route maps are valuable to travelers and, therefore, concern any library which has patrons planning to visit the cities covered. Aside from such uses, the maps issued by local governmental units rarely are of interest to any libraries except those in the immediate vicinity. But to these area libraries, they are of utmost importance both for current reference value and future historical use. Establish firm liaison with the various governmental agencies in your bailiwick. Often the maps they publish are not widely publicized, particularly if they were designed primarily for internal use. It may take some ingenuity and persistence to obtain such maps, but the rewards are worth the effort. Under certain circumstances, you may even be justified in paying for photographic copies of maps for which no duplicates exist.

Foreign Governments

In their efforts to promote goodwill and help prospective visitors, some foreign governments distribute travel maps of their countries. This can be a boon to libraries as well as to tourists.

Possible sources for these maps are the embassies, consulates, information services, and travel bureaus of these nations.

Lists of agencies representing foreign countries are found in the:

1. **Congressional Directory (59).**

2. **National Directory of Addresses and Telephone Numbers**, edited by Stanley Greenfield **(114).**

3. **Information Services and Embassies in the United States of Members of the United Nations (232)**, issued by the Office of Public Information of the United Nations.

4. Yellow pages of the phone books for major metropolitan areas, particularly those of Manhattan and the District of Columbia.

Remember that foreign governments are interested in much more than tourist maps. The Canadian government, for example, has a vigorous publishing program which parallels many of the mapping activities of United States officials. You may not want to acquire specialized foreign maps for your library, but you will want to be able to guide businessmen, investors, students, and prospective emigrants in their efforts to acquire them. This means that if you live in a northern border state, you may want to obtain the free indexes to the topographical maps of Canada **(44)**.

Businesses and Associations

Businesses and associations offer rich possibilities for acquiring maps.

For a broad collection of city maps, write to the chambers of commerce in the metropolitan areas you want represented. Occasionally, you'll receive a reply indicating that maps are for sale only. But chances are good that these organizations will furnish you with free maps. As added lagniappe, they'll probably toss in lots of descriptive brochures, too. A public library will want to approach the chambers of commerce in all cities within its own state. Beyond that point, it should contact chambers of commerce in cities across the nation which its patrons are likely to visit or where they are likely to have business dealings. **The World Wide Chamber of Commerce Directory (255)** offers a shortcut to the addresses you need.

Rising costs have diminished the steady stream of free maps formerly distributed by major petroleum and refining companies. However, city, state, and regional maps are still available at many service stations. The majority charge a small fee for maps. Other stations provide maps free if a customer has purchased gas or arranged for car repair or servicing.

The clubs affiliated with the American Automobile Association have a wide range of maps for free distribution to their members. These maps would make valuable additions to a library's collection. There are maps of states, counties, cities, and recreation areas in the United States, as well as some maps of foreign countries. If you have staff members, trustees, or patrons who are AAA members, they may be glad to give their maps to the library once their trips are over. Certain AAA offices have been willing to supply free maps directly to their local public libraries.

Rent-a-car services have maps for use by their customers. Libraries should encourage returned travelers to contribute these maps for possible inclusion in library files.

Reflecting their professional interest and know-how, the American Association of Petroleum Geologists **(7)** has prepared a series of eleven geological highway maps covering various sections of the United States. Their purpose is to present the general geology of different regions of the country in an interesting and colorful manner, simple enough to be understood by the general public but detailed enough to be useful to science students and geologists. The price of each map is $3.00, plus a handling charge.

As well as tapping sources which are extensively involved in map distribution, librarians should be alert to the occasional map offered by a business or association as a natural outgrowth of its activities. One example is the **Map of Malaysia**, offered by the Malaysian Rubber Bureau **(146)**.

If these occasional maps are issued by nationally known organizations or firms, leads may be discovered in periodicals or in bibliographies of supplementary materials.

When it comes to local businesses and associations, you will have to rely on a mixture of luck, grapevine information, and constant inquiry. It's helpful to know that city maps are frequently distributed as publicity items by banks, savings and loan associations, and realtors.

ON THE TRAIL OF MAPS

Some ways of finding various types of maps have been indicated in this chapter.

However, it must be pointed out that there is no comprehensive clearinghouse of information about all kinds of maps.

Long-range plans call for the National Cartographic Information Center **(171)** to coordinate mapping data about the United States that originates with state and local agencies and private sources as well as with federal units. But even when achieved, this coordination will not furnish universal control over mapping information.

Map libraries have unique tools and techniques which they employ for locating maps. They may consult acquisition lists from other map libraries. They may turn to geographical and cartographical serials. Most of their tools are too specialized for use by libraries with smaller collections of maps.

Nevertheless, if you have a map library in your area which owns **International Maps and Atlases in Print (254)**, it might be worth your while to look through this huge volume. You would, if nothing else, get a sense of the immense mapping effort going on throughout the world.

If you live in the western part of the United States, it would also be useful to locate a map library that has the **Information Bulletin** of the Western Association of Map Libraries **(132)**. You will find some valuable clues in its column, "New 'Mapping of Western North America."

Where else can you turn?

As stressed earlier in this chapter, it is important to collect catalogs and lists from dealers, publishers, agencies, and organizations involved with maps. The "Short Lists" published by the Geography and Map Division of the Library of Congress **(105)** are good places to find names and addresses. As well as the state and federal lists mentioned in previous sections, the Division issues a compilation of **Selected United States Private and Commercial Map Publishers.** There is also a **Selected List of United States Dealers in Out of Print Maps and Atlases.** Both lists are free.

As you use the source guides described in chapter 1, watch for occasional entries for maps. The **Vertical File Index**, for example, now lists the Michelin maps.

Travel provides exposure to opportunities for map acquisition.

Librarians vacationing or attending conventions in certain major cities such as Chicago or New York will find specialized map stores which are a delight and a revelation.

When you visit a big city, don't forget that large bookstores are likely to have a broad variety of maps on display.

Map hunting isn't a simple task, but it's a rewarding one.

HOUSING OF MAPS

Obtaining maps can be a problem. Coping with them in the library poses still other problems. Because of their specialized nature, their diversity of size and physical make-up, and their lack of hard protective covers such as books have, the treatment of maps calls for some deep thought on the part of the librarian.

The first decision you will have to make is how to house your maps. Housing can be as simple or elaborate as your needs and budget indicate. Factors which will influence your choice include:

1. The format of maps in your collection.

2. The size of the collection.

3. The purpose and use of the collection.

4. The nature of your library quarters.

Most map authorities agree that the best housing for maps consists of storing them flat. Folded maps may eventually weaken and tear along the creases. Rolled maps are likely to deteriorate if left rolled for long periods of time.

The equipment most commonly suggested for map storage is a horizontal metal filing case with large shallow drawers. While there is not complete agreement among map librarians or equipment manufacturers, the happy medium seems to be a drawer two inches deep with inside dimensions approximating 43x32-inches. This size can accommodate maps up to 40x30-inches in size.

The cases usually come in units of five drawers each. They can be stacked. A two-unit combination will provide a convenient counter-height surface upon which to examine maps.

Horizontal cases are available from firms which supply libraries, offices, architects, and engineers. They may be labeled as map cases, blueprint cabinets, or flat files.

In selecting a map case, be sure that the drawers are carefully aligned and that they operate in a smooth and easy fashion.

Some map cases offer extra features such as:

1. Drawer stops to prevent accidental spillage.

2. "Lock-out" devices to hold drawers in open position while the contents are being examined.

3. Hinged metal weights at the front to hold maps in place.

4. Fabric covers for dust protection and for securing maps more firmly.

5. Metal hoods at the backs of drawers to keep maps from curling up.

6. Drawer dividers to aid in housing small maps.

For the library with a limited budget there are alternatives to metal cases. You may want to investigate the fiberboard flat files available from such suppliers as the Highsmith Co., Inc. **(126)** or the Fidelity Products Co. **(89)**. These fiberboard flat files may be purchased in five-drawer stackable units.

In the absence of filing cases, folders made of sturdy materials such as heavy red rope paper may be used to store maps. If the folders are constructed with overlapping flaps or in envelope form, they will offer added protection from dust and damage.

It is quite possible that flat storage of maps, no matter how highly acclaimed, may not answer all or any of your needs.

Suppose that you have maps on sticks or spring rollers which can't be stored flat. The large map firms and many school supply houses sell special cases or racks for spring roller maps. Suppliers serving architects and engineers offer roll files which are large enough to hold maps. But librarians have often skirted these commercial offerings to come up with solutions of their own to this dilemma.

Some are quite conventional such as storing rolled maps on open shelves; in long shallow drawers; on top of cases; in roomy cupboards; or laid on pairs of wooden pegs. On the other hand, some methods display a great deal of ingenuity.

Libraries have experimented with placing rolled maps in vertical containers much like giant umbrella stands. There have been attempts to adapt the traditional newspaper rack for storage of rolled maps. Other solutions have been to build diagonal shelves in a cabinet or employ a sloping rack spaced with dowels to support the maps.

A popular technique for storing rolled maps is to fasten a screw eye to the end of the inner map stick and suspend the map from a hook attached to a low ceiling, to the underside of a high shelf, or to a specially constructed crossbar. Some libraries attach a screw hook to the end of the map stick and hang the maps from a rod or heavy wire. This method is less desirable since an exposed hook on a portable map can be a hazard.

If you're tempted to try some of these ideas, please keep certain admonitions in mind. Standing a map on end may eventually result in warping the map stick. Storing roller maps horizontally on pegs or by any other method which exerts pressure on the map itself may cause wrinkles where the support depresses the map. Hanging a map by a single screw eye tends to cause the map to droop spirally unless it is tightly bound. Maps stored this way should be tied at both ends. Another solution is to insert screw eyes in both ends of the map stick and suspend the map from both screw eyes.

Unfortunately, there is no one simple answer to all the problems of storing rolled maps.

As we have just seen, horizontal map cases do not meet all of the needs of the library which prefers to keep some of its maps on sticks or spring rollers. Even for the housing of sheet maps, you may decide that horizontal filing is not the answer for your library, despite the recommendations of the map experts.

Some libraries cut maps into sections, mount them on a flexible backing, and insert the folded maps in protective covers so that they can stand on the open shelves with corresponding books. Others have turned to cases with narrow vertical compartments in which they file maps mounted on heavy cardstock. Some libraries use pamphlet boxes for special sets of maps.

I even know of a school librarian who punched holes in the reinforced edges of his sheet maps and hung them by shower hooks from clothes hangers. The oversized hangers which cleaners use for draperies are preferable for this sort of use. Spring clothes pins offer another means of attaching the maps to the hangers.

The vertical file provides still another alternative to horizontal map storage. It's true that unless oversize files are used many maps will need to be folded several times. This raises the possibility of hastened deterioration. But there are mitigating factors which may make the use of letter- or legal-sized vertical files very attractive:

1. Most of the maps which the typical library possesses are not rare or precious maps, but are free or relatively inexpensive maps which can be replaced easily. In fact, they should be replaced frequently to keep up with changes in this frantic world.

2. If maps are circulated, they usually must be folded anyway so that the patron can carry them.

3. When maps stand folded and upright in a vertical file drawer, the cover or title section of the map offers a quick preview of the nature and contents of the map.

4. Smaller maps are less likely to be overlooked among their big brothers if they are housed in ordinary vertical files.

5. It is easier to remove and refile maps when they are stored in vertical files rather than in horizontal arrangements.

6. Standard vertical files are cheaper than good map cases.

There are some highly specialized types of equipment on the market which can be used to provide vertical storage for maps. The best-known is the vertical plan file which has long been in use by architects, engineers, and surveyors. It is a large, steel container filled with sturdy pockets which, in turn, would hold folders full of maps. Other types of vertical containers suspend maps by holding devices which attach to the maps themselves. These unique pieces of equipment are of interest to the map scholar but of more dubious value to the average librarian.

ARRANGEMENT AND CATALOGING

Your map collection will earn its keep only if you can find the map you want when you want it.

The arrangement you choose for your maps is an important factor in determining how close you will come to achieving this goal.

Libraries with very small map collections sometimes add their maps to the vertical file folders used for pamphlets on the same subject. In other words, pamphlets, clippings, and maps on Bermuda would be in one folder. The only exceptions made are for maps which are physically unmanageable for such inclusion. This merger of materials is particularly appealing to school librarians, who are anxious to bring all their resources on a given topic together for quick consultation by teachers and students.

Public libraries with modest collections often file their maps under the "Ms" in the alphabetical sequence in their vertical files. With this approach all maps stand together under the heading, "Maps," and are then subdivided.

As map resources grow, it becomes more practical to isolate them. Trying to cope with large numbers of maps in the general pamphlet files can be awkward and frustrating.

Even separate map files do not solve all of the many problems facing map librarians. They've been arguing furiously for years over the best method of organizing maps.

Map libraries of substantial size classify their maps. Many types of classification exist. If you read the literature, you'll find such schemes mentioned as that of Boggs and Lewis, the Library of Congress G schedule, the Dewey Decimal Classification, the Universal Decimal Classification, and the American Geographical Society system. Each of these approaches has drawbacks as well as strengths. As a result, map libraries have resorted to modifications which are sometimes radical to adapt systems to their own needs.

Attempts at classification of maps have not been limited to institutions of higher learning and big public libraries. Some smaller public libraries and a number of school libraries have classified their map holdings also. These efforts usually involve the Dewey Decimal Classification system, although Library of Congress Classification is occasionally used. The hope is to correlate map holdings with book holdings.

A few school librarians have even resorted to assigning arbitrary number symbols of their own devising to continents and countries.

A common element in all of these classification schemes, whether unassuming or complex, is the feeling that maps should be arranged regionally. This means that they should be organized first by continent, then by country, and finally by units within the country. One of the arguments advanced for this concept is that it brings together as closely as possible those maps which people use most frequently in relation to one another.

It is true that teaching units are often organized by major geographical areas. It is also true that a traveler planning a lengthy trip may occasionally want to survey broad geographical reaches.

But years of experience in both school and public libraries have left me convinced that the bulk of requests involving maps center on a single country, or city, or river rather than on a series of interrelated geographical regions. I would like to argue for a simple alphabetical arrangement of maps, using the names commonly associated with the various geographic entities.

A straight alphabetical arrangement offers a direct and immediate approach. It eliminates the need for mechanical symbols to designate class divisions. These artificial symbols only interpose an extra barrier which needs to be interpreted before finding what you want. Furthermore, mechanical schemes are subject to breakdowns when changes such as the creation of new countries occur. Nor will they always expand comfortably with your collection.

For most libraries, an alphabetical arrangement is the most practical means of handling maps.

A few libraries have in essence said, "A plague o' both your houses." They have not attempted to arrange maps either alphabetically or by a classified approach. Instead they have assigned sequential numbers to the maps much like the accession numbers used with books. The maps are arranged by these numbers. Such libraries rely entirely upon catalog entries to relay the contents of their collection. While there are merits to this plan, it does have drawbacks for the busy school or public librarian who must produce maps for immediate use while a crowd of customers clamors for attention at each elbow. The system does serve to emphasize the importance which cataloging can assume in manipulating maps.

A map catalog can function as a finding device, indicating whether or not you have maps on a particular area and where they are housed. It can serve as an inventory record, helping you discover when maps are missing. It can assist as an ordering tool by revealing gaps in your collection or by pinpointing maps that need updating. It can offer physical protection to maps by eliminating the wear and tear that results from random pawing through the collection.

Should you try to establish a catalog for *your* maps? The decision depends on the size and nature of your collection and the time you have available. If your map holdings are very small, there is little need for a catalog. As collections become larger and more complex and more valuable, a catalog can be an important aid in controlling them. Sometimes a happy compromise can be reached, limiting cataloging to the map resources which can justify this treatment and can benefit from it. There is one exception to this flexibility. All libraries, large or small, should attempt to keep a full and accurate record of the maps which are a permanent part of their local history collections.

Map cataloging differs sharply from book cataloging in certain respects. In book cataloging, the author is the pivotal point for the cataloging process. In map cataloging, the "author" is usually the publisher. Few patrons ask for maps by publisher. Titles are also of less importance since they are little more than a statement of the region or theme depicted by the map.

The basic cataloging information about a map is the area covered. It takes precedence even over the kind of information depicted on the map. In other words, a map about railroads in Scotland is significant, first of all, because it is about Scotland and only secondarily because it is about railroads. If you are attempting to set up a very simple sort of catalog for your maps, you may settle for a single subject card bearing the heading, "Scotland—Railroads." If your catalog is more ambitious, you may make a second card referring from railroads to Scotland.

For the average library, there is no need to go beyond the making of subject cards for maps. Leave the more complex cataloging to large, specialized libraries. For your purposes, the geographical area is the main entry. In fact, it should be the only entry except for occasional cross references. The only deviation might be a series entry for important sets of maps.

A prime bit of map knowledge which must appear on catalog cards is the date. This is of great significance in determining pertinence of information recorded on the map. A street map dated 1920 obviously will be of no value in directing a patron to a new subdivision, but it might be of great assistance to the historian trying to chart city growth. Unfortunately, dates are frequently omitted from maps. In such instances, you will have to guess at the date of issuance from clues such as population figures on the map. Your catalog cards should use brackets and question marks to indicate conjectural dates. If no hints at all are discernable from the map, you should at least record the date of receipt. The urgency of establishing a time relationship for maps is an added reason for stamping each map with the date of receipt as soon as it arrives.

Your catalog cards should indicate the source of each map. In some cases, the distributor is as important as the publisher, or even more so. This is true of the free street maps distributed by local businesses.

Map size is an added item of interest which often appears on catalog cards. Many libraries also record the scale of the map. Scholarly libraries even note the type of projection, although this technical information is of little significance to smaller libraries. If a map is published in sections, you will want to record the number of sheets.

If you have maps in several locations, it will be necessary to mark your catalog cards with place symbols. There is no set formula for these symbols. You can make up your own. "PB" might stand for maps in pamphlet boxes and "H" for maps suspended from hooks.

Maps which come in large sets—such as the U.S. Geological Survey maps—pose a special cataloging problem. A cataloging shortcut is available for many of these extensive sets. Frequently there are index maps or diagrams published for the maps in the sets. In such instances you can type a single catalog card for the set as a whole and mark the index map to show your particular holdings. If a library owns just a handful of the maps in a given set, it would, of course, be better to catalog them individually.

Some libraries, particularly school libraries, incorporate their map cards directly into the main card catalog. In this sort of amalgamation, it is necessary to mark each card with a word or symbol showing that it refers to map holdings. The clue might consist of an abbreviation, "M" or "Ma," or the word, "Map," typed or stamped on the upper left-hand corner of the card.

It would be presumptuous of me to try to establish a master map card for you. The choice of inclusions is a highly individual matter based on circumstances peculiar to your own library. All I can do is to show you what a catalog card *might* look like. You may want to delete items of no significance to your library. You may want to add other descriptive information of value in your own unique situation.

Location
symbol if
needed

Heading

Title. Publisher or source. Edition and date.

Scale. Size. Number of sheets.

Descriptive notes.

A catalog card can be adapted to facilitate ordering. For example, the price or free status of a map could be indicated. The card might carry a note about frequency of publication, such as "Revised biennially." If a map source is difficult to trace, the full address might be included on the catalog card to expedite replacement or updating. A penciled note could be added to the card when a new edition has been requested.

Certain large map libraries have developed preprinted form cards for their map catalogs to save time and utilize less highly-trained personnel. The samples that I have seen are too elaborate and too technical for use by smaller collections.

Suitable housing, a sensible pattern of arrangement, and a good map catalog aren't enough to assure that maps will be easy to find. The maps themselves must be carefully and clearly marked. In addition to the subject heading, the notation should include any necessary location symbol. The date of issuance should be a prominent part of the label.

The type of housing you use will determine the location of the heading. For example, maps in horizontal cases are usually marked on the reverse side of the map at the edge nearest the front of the drawer. The letters should face the front so that they can be read easily. They should start at the left-hand corner. Maps housed in vertical files should be labeled in the upper left-hand corner in the same manner that pamphlet material is marked.

PRESERVATION OF MAPS

Maps, being the fragile creatures they are, have called forth a great body of literature on their care and preservation.

Except for select items in a local history collection, the average library is concerned with the ordinary, utilitarian type of map. This means that we can ignore the real intricacies of map preservation and concentrate on a few basic principles and techniques.

The rejuvenation of maps may have to begin the moment they reach the library. Most maps come folded in containers or rolled in tubes. This means that they may be curled or may display excessive folds. Experts agree that the curls and unnecessary folds should be eliminated, but they are not in agreement as to the method. Some processes call for equipment available only to specialized libraries. A simpler solution suggested by one experienced map librarian is to place the map face down on an ironing board and press it with a steam iron set on "steam" and "wool." Another authority disagrees with this suggestion because of the exposure of the map to the heat of the iron. Her recommendation is to let the map rest on a clean, flat surface under weights for two or three weeks. A third expert recommends reversing rolled maps and putting the unfolded maps under heavy weights for a few hours. She deals with stubborn creases by dampening the map with a wet sponge along the folds or even over the entire surface before placing it under weights. You'll just have to take your choice among these possibilities. My one caution would be to test the ink on your map before applying moisture.

What about the folding of maps? In their book, **Conservation of Library Materials**, George and Dorothy Cunha express this opinion: "A single fold does little harm to a map. Double or triple folds are particularly damaging where the creased edges meet and should be avoided." **(68)**

Clara Egli LeGear, one of the great names in map circles, had this comment to make:

Unmounted maps which are too large for the files may be folded, preferably with the grain of the paper. They should be folded a minimum number of times to fit the files. A fold made with the grain of the paper is sharper and smoother than one made against it, and is less likely to break. The grain is comparable to the warp in woven fabrics and runs in the direction of lesser resistance to folding. To accommodate extra large maps, right-angle or cross-folding may be necessary, but some libraries prefer to dissect such maps. A little trim from wide margins may obviate folding map sheets which are only slightly larger than file drawers. Trimming should, however, be done with discretion. Maps to be mounted on cloth should be sectioned and hinged if folding is required. Cross-folded paper maps break eventually at the weakened points, and unsectioned mounted maps crack in the folds. **(142)**

The sectioning and hinging which Clara LeGear mentions is a technique which calls for mounting a map in pieces with about a ¼-inch space between the sections to allow for folding.

Even when storage cases are used which minimize the need for folding, some libraries go one step further in attempting to protect their maps. They enclose them in heavy paper folders within the map drawers. These folders prevent any damage to the maps that might be caused by sliding them in and out of the drawers. They also help to keep the maps from slipping around within the drawers. Since the contents are indicated on the outside of each folder, map librarians claim that this facilitates the finding of maps and cuts down on unnecessary handling of these resources.

It is recommended that the folders for horizontal files should be at least two inches shorter and narrower than the inside drawer dimensions of the cases to allow for maneuvering.

For the preservation of important items such as rare maps of your locality, acid-free folders should be considered. The Hollinger Corporation **(129)** produces such folders.

Is storing maps in rolled form really bad for them? Some map experts think it is very bad. In fact, they suggest removing the maps from their rollers and cutting them so that they will fit in storage drawers. However, one authority argues against this treatment because cutting up maps may impair their legibility and reduce the chances of using them for accurate measurements of distance.

Most public and school libraries will continue to use rolled maps if they find this format convenient. It is only when a map of permanent significance is involved that the damage caused by rolling will become of prime importance to them. Usually, this concerns a historical map of the community.

For maps that are deteriorating or subject to heavy use, some type of reinforcement is indicated. This often takes the form of strengthening the edges, folds, and areas of strain with adhesive cloth tape. A more permanent solution lies in mounting the maps. Since this process involves a considerable investment in materials and time, it would be foolish to consider mounting maps which can be easily replaced or which have only passing value.

The time-honored method of backing maps has been to hand mount them on muslin or linen, although one authority feels that good quality backing paper will outlast fabric. The traditional method of mounting maps is a time-consuming and messy process. It requires great skill and a large working area. If you are curious about the process, there is a detailed description in Clara LeGear's **Maps: Their Care, Repair, and Preservation in Libraries (142)**.

Luckily, there is an alternative to this laborious method of wet mounting. Seal, Incorporated, manufactures a dry backing cloth called **Chartex®**, which serves as a very satisfactory reinforcement for maps. It makes a sturdy but pliable mount which does not dry out or become brittle with age. Since **Chartex** is applied dry to a dry map, there is no expansion or shrinkage to cause curling or buckling. Best of all, it is such an easy process. An ordinary electric hand iron may be used to apply **Chartex**; however, a dry mounting press is preferable if you have access to one. **Chartex** is available from firms which handle photographic, school, and library supplies. Write to Seal, Incorporated **(212)** for a descriptive handbook and a free sample.

Many other materials have been tried through the years for backing maps. Cardboard is one. However, map experts point out that there are perils in using cardboard. In time, poor cardboard becomes brittle and cracks with handling, breaking whatever is mounted upon it. If you do decide to use a stiff paper backing to mount your maps, be sure to choose stock of good quality.

Libraries wanting stiff mountings for their maps have also experimented with plywood and wallboard. These materials offer sturdy support, but they may create storage problems.

Even window shades have served as a base for maps. Can you think of a cheaper way to get a roll-up map? Brackets to hold window-shade maps can be mounted on a small piece of wood. With hanging devices such as hooks or screw eyes inserted in the top of the board, the entire display unit is ready to travel wherever it is needed. It has been suggested that two rubber suction cups might be substituted for the hooks, but my experiences with rubber suction cups have not been happy ones. Window-shade maps are particularly suited to school library use.

Mounting may help to solve the problem of the small map. Not only are small maps likely to be completely lost among the larger sheets in a map drawer, but they are also vulnerable to crumbling and creasing. Filing them separately by size only creates another place to look. By mounting these small maps on large backings, they will be able to hold their own among the big maps. It may be a temptation to just dispose of small maps as nuisances, but sometimes these diminuative publications are the only resources available for offbeat places or specialized information.

Frequently, there is a need to protect the surface of a map. Varnish and shellac have been discredited except for maps which are expendable, because with time they turn brown and brittle.

Clear plastic sprays are available which offer a degree of protection from dirt and moisture. There are certain precautions to take in using such sprays. Experiment with the best distance from which to spray in order to prevent too much penetration. Don't try to put on too thick a coat in one application. Two or three thin coats are better than one thick one. Before spraying an important map, make a test run to determine the compatibility of the spray with the paper and ink.

Plastic film which has been coated with a pressure-sensitive adhesive can also be used to make a protective covering for maps. A backing sheet conceals the adhesive until the film is ready to apply. Since correct placement is a tricky process, it is fortunate that there is now a film with a delayed action adhesive. Because the adhesive doesn't set immediately, it gives you time to make adjustments.

The use of this self-adhesive film is sometimes called "cold lamination."

It shouldn't be confused with the technique of lamination, which utilizes heat and pressure to bond a map to a protective plastic film. This process offers the ultimate method of protecting map surfaces. Laminate may be applied to one side only, but better protection is offered by sandwiching the map between two layers of film. A cloth reinforcement may also be added.

Since a laminated map is protected from air, moisture, and dirt as well as being strengthened against tears, its life expectancy soars.

Happily, lamination offers a perfect solution for the map which can't be mounted because of important material printed on the back. Laminated maps also boast of surfaces which can be marked and later wiped clean. This is important in teaching.

Lamination can be done on a laminating or dry mounting press. Smaller items of a flexible nature can be laminated on thermal copy machines.

While results will not be so professional, lamination can even be applied with an ordinary laundry iron. For a detailed description of laundry iron lamination suitable with any flat illustrative material including maps, consult Dr. Herbert E. Scuorzo's article, "Plastic Picture Protection," in the **Grade Teacher** (September 1963).

If you are interested in lamination, contact photographic, school, or library supply houses for equipment and materials. In ordering laminating film, remember that if you're willing to pay a premium price, it now comes in matte finish as well as the regular glossy finish.

Lamination is not an inexpensive undertaking, but it is a boon to libraries which can afford it.

Preservationists still worry about the acid which is left in the paper after lamination. They claim that this acid will continue to cause deterioration over a long period of time. But except for precious local history maps, this long-term fear need not concern the average librarian. There are deacidification processes which can be used before lamination, but they're too expensive for smaller libraries to employ.

Maps of great historical interest do present special preservation problems. There is now much discussion about the wisdom of laminating such unique treasures at all. The primary concern stems from the exposure of these items to the extreme heat necessary for lamination. There is also fear about doing something to a historically important item which can't be undone.

The solution for fragile maps may be encapsulation, the process described in chapter 7. If copyright is not a problem, a corollary to this solution would be to make photoreproductions of the maps so that the originals can be protected from unnecessary handling.

Repair of delicate maps of historical importance is another matter of great concern. It is an undertaking not suited to amateurs. It is suggested that you contact your state library for assistance. There are firms which specialize in such repairs. A few areas of the country also have regional conservation centers for library materials where restoration can be undertaken.

CHAPTER 9

PICTORIAL MATERIALS

Many librarians who enthusiastically cultivate other supplementary resources avoid any commitment to pictures. They are frightened by the physical and organizational requirements of such collections.

What a treasure they're missing!

To begin with, pictures have a definite contribution to make to the information services of a library.

Don't be browbeaten by accounts of the complex methods and equipment employed by very large libraries. No matter how Spartan your treatment of pictorial materials has to be, they can still add a new richness to your resources. In the beginning stages, they can even be housed with pamphlets on the same subject if no better arrangement is possible.

VALUE OF PICTORIAL MATERIALS

If you are dubious about the contribution which pictures can make to the reference function, look at these examples of picture use in a public library:

1. Period costumes for a local theatre group staging *Oklahoma!*

2. The exact colors in the traditional depiction of Uncle Sam for a commercial artist planning a full-color advertisement.

3. A fireplace for a new recreation room which would look "colonial" but not old-fashioned.

4. Danish Christmas decorations for a December club meeting featuring the community ambassador to Denmark.

5. The "litterbug" symbol for use in a cleanup campaign.

6. Window curtains of the 1850s for the restoration of a historic homestead.

7. Pictures of a chimney sweep for the business card of a young man going into this occupation.

8. Interior and exterior colors of a 1939 pickup truck for a hobbyist restoring such a vehicle.

Not only do pictorial resources earn their keep by helping to answer reference questions, but they also serve as valuable raw material for building effective exhibits and displays. In addition, they can be used to dramatize speeches and oral reports.

The current popularity of posters, especially among young people, illustrates another contribution which pictorial materials can make. Through the philosophy, humor, or beauty which they depict, posters can bring a new dimension to the lives of library users. They can also act as a magnet for people who might not otherwise be attracted to the library.

PICTURE SELECTION

The first step on the road to assembling a good picture collection is to gather materials energetically but with discretion. Pictorial resources need to be subjected to some of the same critical evaluation that is applied to books. Not all colorful magazine illustrations are suitable for inclusion in your files. Nor does every attractive bit of publicity that comes through the mail deserve a permanent place in the picture collection. Processing, housing, and maintenance involve the expenditure of time, money, and space. The touchstone of judgment should be the extent to which a particular picture will meet the needs of your clientele.

The decision becomes particularly crucial when mounting is involved. Some librarians sharpen their powers of selectivity by letting clipped pictures "ripen" a while before they make a final evaluation about their suitability for mounting.

The larger your collection becomes, the more discriminating you will have to be. Almost any picture of a reindeer is precious when you've been struggling along with none. But when you have acquired ten or fifteen, you'll want to concentrate on keeping only the best.

Aesthetic considerations really take a back seat in the selection of materials for most subject areas in the picture collection. The clarity of the image, the authenticity of the portrayal, and the demands of your public have priority.

Artistic standards do come to the fore when choosing reproductions of paintings and other art objects. Here the artistic quality of each reproduction becomes important.

Color enhances most pictures and usually increases their value to the user. For your collection, choose color representations if you can find them.

Special libraries must exercise particular care to correlate their picture collecting with their sharply focused areas of emphasis.

For example, a business or institutional library might concentrate on:

1. Pictures that present a consecutive history of the organization.

2. Pictorial material that could be used in publications of that body.

3. Pictorial material that can be used for training purposes.

4. Pictorial material that can be used in research.

PICTURE SOURCES

The process of acquiring pictures is one that will vary with the librarian's ingenuity and budget.

With a Pair of Scissors in Hand

You can cut your way to an effective picture collection!

Magazines offer the most obvious way of expanding picture files. There are many published today which feature illustrations potentially useful to a picture collection. Among the most evident are:

American Artist	Life
American Heritage	Look
American History Illustrated	National Geographic Magazine
Art in America	National Wildlife
Audubon	Natural History
Gourmet	Smithsonian
House & Garden	Sports Illustrated
Ideals	Travel/Holiday

While the previous list was composed of periodicals published for "grown-ups," there are children's magazines which are also noteworthy for their pictorial value. Representative of these periodicals are **Ranger Rick's Nature Magazine** and **National Geographic World**.

As you search for picture possibilities, be alert to area publications as well as national magazines. **Arizona Highways**, the **Louisiana Conservationist**, and the **Michigan Natural Resources Magazine** are examples of handsomely illustrated periodicals that focus on one portion of the country.

The bulletins which major museums issue for their members usually contain significant pictures. The Metropolitan Museum of Art **(158)** in New York City and the Field Museum of Natural History **(90)** in Chicago are typical of the institutions which produce memorable bulletins.

While rising costs have diminished the production of colorfully illustrated house magazines by business enterprises, there are still some available. For example, you may find some good picture prospects in the "house organs" of airlines, automobile manufacturers, and petroleum companies. **The Lamp (139)**, published by the Exxon Corporation, is a particularly fine sample of a house publication which contains clippable pictures. Tools giving access to house magazines are discussed in chapter 5.

Aside from the free periodicals offered by some businesses and associations, most pictorial magazines cost money. Some affluent libraries maintain extra subscriptions to periodicals such as **National Geographic Magazine** for picture clipping purposes. But you can do very nicely without such expenditures. First of all, establish a pattern of screening any magazines your library is discarding to salvage any usable illustrations. Secondly, start a campaign among your patrons to contribute back issues of magazines to the library. Don't be scornful of duplicates. It is good insurance to keep two copies of heavily pictorial magazines since you will often find desirable pictures on both sides of a page.

In schools where paper drives are common, school librarians can arrange to have promising runs of magazines set aside temporarily until they can be assessed by the library staff.

Newspapers offer some potential for clipping, especially when it comes to the colored illustrations in the Sunday supplements. Newspaper illustrations of local personalities, landmarks, and events are of special importance. The big drawback to newspaper pictures is the poor quality of the paper.

To increase the odds for locating choice newspaper and magazine illustrations, alert your staff to hard-to-find subjects so that they can be watchful during their leisure-time reading.

Librarians traditionally raise their hands in horror at the thought of anyone cutting up books. But this heretical behavior opens another avenue for acquiring pictures for your files. When books containing good illustrations become candidates for discarding, they should be screened for clipping. It's only fair to point out that a book scheduled for discarding may be in such bad condition that the pictures will be worthless.

Some large libraries with ample budgets buy copies of pictorially noteworthy books solely for clipping. This is beyond the realm of possibility in most libraries, except for inexpensive paperback volumes or books on remainder lists.

The richly illustrated travel booklets from chambers of commerce or state tourist offices are worth screening for pictures. So are the brochures issued by the national tourist agencies of various foreign countries.

Calendars are first-rate resources for clipping. Despite increased costs, some private enterprises are still distributing beautifully illustrated calendars to their customers as a publicity effort.

The lavish calendars displayed in bookstores and magazine agencies at Christmas time make delightful additions to picture collections. While you may not be able to buy them for your files, you can urge your public and your staff to contribute them to the library once the year is over. If you do have some funds at your disposal, you may find leftover gift calendars for sale at a fraction of their original cost in the spring.

Your scissors can also come in handy for salvaging the pictures of authors which appear on book jackets. While duplicate jackets are no longer freely distributed by publishers, plastic-covered jackets usually survive circulation well enough to justify clipping when the books are discarded.

Seed and nursery catalogs might augment your picture files. Annual reports from corporations are usually filled with glossy prints. The promotional ads you receive from publishers sometimes contain excellent pictorial presentations.

The prospects for creating a picture collection by clipping are broad and exciting if you don't allow yourself to become stereotyped in your thinking. Almost any illustrated or decorated piece of paper is a possibility. Greeting cards can be clipped for art reproductions or symbolic representations. Even well-designed wrapping paper is worth saving for interpretations of holiday themes. You'll understand what a blessing these simple items can be if you've ever had to produce several versions of a Thanksgiving cornucopia for a harried artist.

Despite its importance, clipping is not the only method of building a picture collection. Many sources offer "ready-made" pictorial material.

The Business World

To expand the horizons of your picture collection, you will want to investigate the pictures, posters, and charts offered by businesses and industries in an effort to sell their products and build goodwill.

Typical of such productions is the set of historic airplane pictures offered without charge by United Air Lines (231). The Ford Motor Company (94) distributes a free chart which shows the history of measurement. With the compliments of the Washington National Insurance Company (243), you can obtain reproductions of paintings depicting episodes in the life of George Washington. The Hershey Foods Corporation (125) will provide a free wall chart about the history and manufacture of cocoa and chocolate.

Don't overlook the promotional posters and prints prepared by the publishers of children's books. Announcements sometimes appear in library and publishing periodicals. Library conferences, particularly the annual ALA conference, offer excellent opportunities for acquiring these pictorial materials.

Special Interest Groups

Associations, societies, councils, and institutes which represent special fields of interest are potential sources for pictorial material.

A choice example is the American Quarter Horse Association (15) which offers free a set of beautiful horse paintings as well as charts of quarter horse bloodlines and horse anatomy.

The National Safety Council (184) has a tremendous collection of safety posters which are available for a small charge. The National Dairy Council (174) and its state affiliates sell posters and study prints that deal with nutrition and health. The National Audubon Society (170) will furnish a catalog listing the many charts and other pictorial aids it has for sale in the area of nature study. From the American Humane Association (11), you can obtain modestly priced posters and prints which deal with pets and kindness to animals. The American Classical League (9) sells posters which emphasize the Greek and Roman languages and cultures. Multicolored charts about population issues and trends can be purchased from the Population Reference Bureau, Inc. (202).

To single out just a few more possibilities, the American Paper Institute, Inc. (14), the National Cotton Council of America (173), the American Forest Institute (10), and the Wheat Flour Institute (252) all have large wall charts which would make excellent additions to a library's files. Single copies are free, except for a $0.10 charge for the Wheat Flour Institute publication.

Closer to home, investigate the posters which your area chapter of the American Cancer Society has for distribution, and inquire about the charts at your area unit of the American Heart Association.

For pictorial material about your own state, be sure to check with the state historical society to see what it has available. As an example, the Minnesota Historical Society has for sale a spectacular array of color prints and black-and-white drawings portraying the history of that state.

Art Museums and Art Centers

Since art is a visual experience, it is only natural that pictorial reproductions of artistic works should be a major emphasis in most picture collections.

Some of the most distinguished museums in North America sell pictorial copies of major works of art. It's true that the large-scale reproductions meant for framing are relatively costly. But these institutions also publish small color prints and postcards which are well within the means of any library.

Among the museums which have lists of reproductions for sale are:

Art Institute of Chicago **(20)**

Detroit Institute of Arts **(76)**

Freer Gallery of Art **(98)**

Metropolitan Museum of Art **(157)**

National Gallery of Art **(176)**

National Gallery of Canada **(177)**

Libraries should acquire the catalogs of reproductions which are issued by such museums. Not only are they useful as ordering tools, but they also serve as authoritative guides to important artists and works of art for the librarian building a new picture collection.

Clues to help you determine which museums in the United States and Canada have pictorial materials for sale can be found in **Museum Media (245)**, by Paul Wasserman and Esther Herman.

The art centers in smaller cities can also be fine sources for obtaining reproductions. These centers often have gift shops which offer good quality reproductions in the form of note cards and small prints.

United States Government

To anyone who thinks of the federal government as a statistic-oriented establishment, it may come as a surprise to learn how deeply it is involved in the production of pictures, posters, and pictorial charts. In fact, it is one of the best sources you can tap, because the pictorial material is well-planned, well-printed, and inexpensive. We've already touched on the offerings of the National Gallery of Art and the Freer Gallery of Art, but that's only a beginning.

To take advantage of this bonanza, the first move is to obtain a free copy of **Subject Bibliography 057, Posters, Charts, Picture Sets, and Decals (226)**. Don't rely exclusively on this publication since there is a time lapse between editions. Furthermore, it does not list all items produced by governmental agencies. Watch **Selected U.S. Government Publications (216)** for additional announcements. Write for descriptive literature when you have reason to believe that a federal agency is actively engaged in picture production.

So broad is the participation of federal agencies in picture publishing that it is difficult to single out any one unit as being the most outstanding. Here is a random sampling.

The Soil Conservation Service of the U.S. Department of Agriculture has assembled a series of 52 striking photographs representing each state plus Puerto Rico and the Virgin Islands. The set is called "America the Beautiful." Reproductions of the pictures are for sale by the Superintendent of Documents.

Tree growth, tree products, and forest land utilization are the focus of posters developed by the Department of Agriculture's Forest Service (95). Single copies are available free from that agency.

Man's space efforts are recorded in pictures originating with the National Aeronautics and Space Administration. Posters, charts, and sets of pictures are for sale by the Superintendent of Documents. **Subject Bibliography 020, America in Space (226)** will help you with ordering information.

Our armed forces are also active in producing pictorial material. For example, the U.S. Army has released three sets of paintings titled **The American Soldier**. These paintings trace the evolution of the Army and its uniform. They are supplemented by a group of pictures portraying scenes from the American Revolution. The U.S. Navy has developed sets of color prints depicting its history. The development and activities of the U.S. Air Force are shown in an extensive series of color lithographs, as well as in black-and-white photographs. The Marine Corps is also represented by a collection of lithographs. All of these pictorial materials sponsored by the armed forces are for sale by the Superintendent of Documents.

The National Marine Fisheries Service of the Department of Commerce has issued a series of multicolored wall charts featuring marine animals of the Western Hemisphere as well as fishes of the Great Lakes. Also devoted to animal life are the full-color pictures in the **Wildlife Portrait Series** produced by the United States Fish and Wildlife Service of the Department of the Interior. The materials from both agencies are sold through the Superintendent of Documents.

An intriguing chart is issued each year by the Federal Highway Administration of the U.S. Department of Transportation. It shows license plates in color for every state, the District of Columbia, the Canal Zone, Guam, Puerto Rico, the Virgin Islands, American Samoa, and the provinces of Canada. The chart is for sale by the Superintendent of Documents.

The Bureau of Engraving and Printing (33) will send you a price list of engraved and lithographed printings which it has available. Included are presidential portraits, portraits of chief justices, vignettes of government buildings, government seals, and miscellaneous documents. These items can be ordered directly from the Bureau.

Posters of historic sites and subjects as well as natural and recreation areas are prepared by the National Park Service of the U.S. Department of the Interior. They are for sale by the Superintendent of Documents.

The National Archives and Records Service is a good place to turn for historic materials. For example, it offers faithful facsimiles of such celebrated documents as the Emancipation Proclamation. It has reproductions of war-time posters. It can even furnish photographs of Abraham Lincoln and Robert E. Lee taken by the renowned Mathew Brady. Send for a free copy of its reproductions list, **Documents from America's Past (168)**. For more specialized guides to the pictorial holdings of the NARS, write to the Still Picture Branch, Audiovisual Archives Division (224) for copies of its **Select Picture Lists**.

This sprinkling of federal publications only hints at the wealth of pictorial resources available from the United States government.

Commercial Publishers and Distributors

Any library seeking to broaden its picture resources should become acquainted with the wide range of materials for sale by commercial sources. Approach them with a judicious mixture of enthusiasm and caution. Some offerings are modest in price, but others are very expensive. Some can be put to a wide variety of uses while others are designed primarily for classroom instruction.

Certain publishers specialize in inexpensive reproductions of art works. For 75 years, a firm called University Prints (238) has been providing low-cost visual materials on the art history of the world. It offers over 7,000 small prints for only a few cents apiece, most in black and white but some in color. They cover a broad variety of art forms from dance masks and totem poles to painting, sculpture, and architecture. Artext Prints, Inc. (21) features color prints of various sizes depicting well-known works of art. Imported color postcards are offered, too.

Because pictures of famous personalities are a particularly troublesome area, the Gale Research Company (100) inaugurated the International Portrait Gallery. At the end of 1978, there was a base collection plus seven supplements. The complete collection totals 3,350 pictures. At this moment, the base collection is selling for $150.00, while each supplement costs $90.00.

Regional interests are of special concern to school and public libraries, as well as some special libraries. If you're lucky, you may find one or more commercial publishers in your state who specialize in historical or contemporary pictures of your part of the nation. For example, in Michigan, we have a firm called Hillsdale Educational Publishers, Inc. (128), which sells prints and postcards with a Michigan flavor.

Of particular interest to school libraries are the innumerable sets of study prints developed to fit instructional needs. Some of these prints may be candidates for purchase by public libraries, but sets should be carefully screened to determine what contribution they can make to a general purpose library. Most sets of study prints are far from being cheap. However, study prints offer quick, selective, and organized access to pictures on a given subject. They are usually printed on better stock than stray magazine illustrations. They also eliminate the labor costs involved in searching for pictures to clip from random sources.

Some publishing companies which have gained recognition for their study prints are:

David C. Cook Publishing Co. (63)

Encyclopaedia Britannica Educational Corporation (83)

Nystrom (192)

Society for Visual Education, Inc. (220)

School media centers may find themselves involved in the purchase of wall charts specifically designed for instructional use in such areas as anatomy, mathematics, and botany. These wall charts are first cousins to the wall maps described in chapter 8. In fact, wall charts are often sold by map companies. For example, wall charts are available from the American Map Company, Inc.; Nystrom; George F. Cram Company, Inc.; and Denoyer-Geppert. Like wall maps, they can be expensive. They also present some of the same storage problems. Yet, like wall maps, they can enrich the teaching program.

The current popularity of posters both for school and private use has sparked a lively response from commercial publishers and distributors. Some of the firms currently active in producing posters are:

Argus Communications **(18)**

Giant Photos, Inc. **(107)**

Perfection Form Company **(199)**

In your search for posters, don't overlook the occasional items that develop as spin-offs from other publishing activities. For example, **Automobile Quarterly (25)** has developed a series of posters about automobiles from the photographs and paintings which have appeared in the magazine and its **Library Series** books. Franklin Watts, Inc. **(246)**, has used two of its talented illustrators, Brian Wildsmith and Eric Carle, to produce some charming posters for children.

As you build your poster collection, be sure to visit your local bookstores and discount stores. Because of the demand, many of them are carrying large selections of posters.

Picture Postcards

Librarians can profit by repeating that old bromide, "Drop me a postcard," to all of their vacationing friends. For travel postcards can become a valuable adjunct to the library picture collection. They record natural wonders, historic landmarks, and city scenes that are often impossible to find pictured anywhere else. Many times such postcards are for sale only at the site. That is why it is so important to cultivate the assistance of staff, friends, and library users in feeding the postcard collection.

Postcards which depict the local community are worth their weight in gold.

Postcard reproductions of works of art have already been mentioned in this chapter. They can be used to reinforce weak spots in your collection of larger reproductions.

Tracking down Pictorial Material

Unfortunately, there is only one recently revised compilation of pictorial resources on the market at this time.

Dale E. Shaffer's **Posters for Teachers and Librarians (217)** offers a quick survey of display material. Despite the title, the list includes pictures, study prints, charts, and maps as well as posters. The entries are arranged under 212 subject headings. According to the compiler, 332 sources are represented. While the cover and foreword describe this compilation as a sourcebook of "free and inexpensive" items, some of the inclusions are substantial in price.

Scattered references to pictorial resources can also be found in the location aids discussed in chapter 1.

Be particularly alert to ads and announcements in periodicals published for librarians, teachers, and the book trade.

HOUSING

Cardboard containers, wooden crates, pamphlet boxes, and other oddities have been commandeered to house pictorial materials. It's better to have a picture collection stored in a stray carton than to have no picture collection at all.

Libraries which have a choice usually turn to steel filing cases. Some attempt to make do with letter-sized files, although larger drawers are overwhelmingly preferred. While legal-sized files offer a greater horizontal capacity, they are still limited as to "head room." Much more flexibility is provided by an oversize or jumbo file, which can accommodate considerably larger mounts.

Naturally, such extra-large cases are going to be more costly than more commonplace equipment. However, they promise efficient, easily accessible storage for larger pictures which might otherwise have to be stacked on shelves.

Because of the weight which a drawer full of mounted pictures represents, it is wise to inquire about optional vertical file equipment such as sway blocks or dividers, which help to support heavy or bulky materials. A clever and inexpensive trick to help in preventing sliding and buckling in picture files is to place strips cut from rubber matting on the bottom of the drawers.

Hanging file folders are recommended by some librarians as a good way to distribute the bulk and weight of mounted pictures within a vertical file. Frames and folders are available which fit filing cabinets from letter to jumbo size. If the picture collection is a large one with substantial numbers of pictures on a given subject, it would be prudent to inquire about hanging folders of the box bottom style.

While many libraries attempt to house postcards in their regular files, others turn to special card files which are designed for the Lilliputian dimensions of the postcard. These files are small enough to store on top of other cases or on tables.

Giant-sized resources such as posters and large charts call for special handling. They can be folded and inserted in regular files, but folding creates unsightly creases that diminish their display value. Folded paper is also subject to more rapid deterioration. If posters and charts are mounted on stiff backings, folded storage isn't even a possibility.

Unmounted and laminated items of large size may be rolled for storage. However, rolling makes it difficult to flatten materials for exhibition. It also calls for special storage facilities. There are roll files sold by office supply firms which can be used with rolled posters and charts. These roll files are available in steel or fiberboard. Librarians with more ingenuity than money have invented their own form of rolled storage. For example, they have used plastic wine racks or empty tennis ball containers set honeycomb fashion into wooden frames.

For the physical welfare of charts and posters, horizontal storage is much better than rolling or folding if it can be arranged. Map cases, flat files, portfolios, or even deep storage shelves can be used.

Librarians with a flair for woodworking have designed swing-out units which house large items vertically. These structures usually involve a door which pulls forward. It is fastened securely to the base of the case but is free at the top except for a chain. Sturdy leaves or dividers may be provided inside the case to support and separate the contents.

There are libraries which use a wide variety of storage equipment to house their pictures. These are usually extensive collections of many years standing. Letter-sized files, legal-sized files, oversize files, card files, and horizontal units are all represented. Resources are assigned to the file which best suits their physical makeup.

On the other hand, vertical files of a single uniform size are used for the bulk of pictorial holdings in many libraries. Unmounted pictures, small mounted pictures, and larger mounted pictures stand together in the drawers. Only jumbo visuals such as posters are isolated for special storage, with some libraries also providing separate housing for postcards. The arrangement of materials under a given subject often follows this sequence:

1. Small mounted pictures.

2. Larger mounted pictures.

3. An envelope or other device containing unmounted pictures.

This system is employed not only in smaller libraries but also in some major collections. It works best, of course, with larger file drawers.

For the average library, this combined housing of pictures provides the most practical type of storage. If the librarian is skeptical about interfiling mounted and unmounted pictures, they can, of course, be arranged in two separate alphabets.

Some school libraries carry this trend toward the merger of resources to its ultimate point. As far as is physically possible, all materials—whether they are pictures, pamphlets, clippings, maps, transparencies, or flannel board sets—are gathered together in vertical files by subject. The theory is that a teacher or student hunting for resources will need to turn to only one spot to find this hoard of study aids.

More by necessity than choice, small public libraries may also house pamphlets, clippings, and pictures side by side in the same file drawers. This can create problems because of the diverse physical nature and organizational requirements of these items. Separate folders for pictures and pamphlets may help the physical situation. But joint housing makes it impossible to allow for desirable variations in subject headings between picture resources and pamphlet resources.

While filing cases are important to the organization and protection of the picture collection, there are also internal devices which help to facilitate the accomplishment of these goals.

Unmounted pictures are customarily housed in envelopes, pockets, or folders.

Folders open at the top and on both sides are awkward to use because the irregularly shaped pictures are likely to spill out at both ends, giving a ragged appearance to the files and exposing the clippings to damage.

A popular substitute is a homemade container open at only the top and the right-hand side. These storage units can be made from strong paper stock folded in half lengthwise and taped shut at the left side.

Commercial sources will supply vertical file pockets which are closed on both sides. For subjects on which there are a great many unmounted pictures, file pockets of the expanding variety are most suitable.

Containers resembling large correspondence envelopes are also sold by library and office supply houses for use with unmounted pictures.

In making your choice from among these possibilities, remember that containers open at the top can be time-savers because they permit easy refiling of materials.

Libraries which house all of their pictures in common files often place the envelope or pocket containing unmounted pictures behind the larger-sized mounts on the subject. In such a progression, there is good reason to match the size of the container to the large mounts which it follows. This coordination will aid visibility and add to a sense of order in the files.

Plastic containers are still another device used in the storage of pictures. Some of the commercially published study prints used by school libraries come already equipped with plastic envelopes or pockets. School librarians themselves have constructed containers of cellulose acetate or other plastics to protect pictures and keep small groups of related visuals together. The edges are sealed with **Mystik**® cloth tape or with plastic electrician's tape. These pockets and envelopes have been found useful for storing pictures in vertical files or on open shelves. They can be used to circulate the pictures, thus continuing their protection.

File guides in the picture files serve as handy road signs. Use them generously. Guides of heavier materials such as pressboard not only aid in locating pictures and separating categories, but they also offer physical support to the pictures.

As well as using file guides in their picture files to designate subject headings or letters of the alphabet, some libraries record cross references on them in addition. File guides can also contain scope notes which explain the exact range or nature of a subject heading.

PHYSICAL PREPARATION

If variety is the spice of life, librarians have certainly added considerable flavor with their physical manipulation of picture collections. I am not disturbed by this wide diversity. The test of any approach is not whether it conforms to what other libraries are doing, but whether it works well for *your* library. My goal will be to introduce you to various possibilities and let you choose the methods which hold the most promise for your circumstances.

To Mount or Not to Mount

Librarians run the gamut from those who proclaim that any picture worth saving is worth mounting to those who have collections composed almost entirely of unmounted pictures.

The arguments for mounting are these:

1. Mounting protects the picture.
2. It adds to the attractiveness and effectiveness of the picture.
3. It makes the picture easier to use.

The opponents of wholesale mounting make these points:

1. Mounting is expensive and time-consuming.
2. Mounted pictures take up more space.
3. Users prefer to choose their own backing colors for bulletin board displays.

Most libraries compromise, incorporating both mounted and unmounted pictures in their files. The ratio depends upon two factors: the budget and the librarian's interpretation of what is of permanent value.

Some librarians use the unmounted collection as a proving ground from which pictures graduate to the mounted state. If certain pictures circulate well or if they fill gaps that have developed in the mounted collection, these illustrations are then singled out for backing.

My personal reactions to the mounting controversy are mixed. While I campaign for the mounting of all newspaper clippings, I realize that there are moderating factors at work in the handling of pictures. The items which libraries choose for their picture collections are usually printed on better paper than newsprint. In most libraries, unmounted pictures are not mixed with heavy, odd-sized pamphlets, as newspaper articles are. Picture mounts are likely to be heavier than news mounts and therefore more of a storage problem. In short, the mounting of pictures is desirable but not mandatory. Let the popularity and uniqueness of the picture be your guide.

Choosing Mounts

Type of Mount

The high-water mark of individuality among librarians is demonstrated in their selection of mounts for pictorial resources. Just note this list of materials which practicing librarians have recommended for mounting various types of pictorial holdings:

Cover paper	Poster board
Bristol board	Kraft paper
Chipboard	Illustration board
Mat board	Show-card board
Tag board or manila tag	Railroad board
Construction paper	Lined pulpboard
Poster paper	Binders board

Even with this splintering of opinion, there are still a few basic guidelines which can be followed. First of all, select mounts that will be substantial enough to protect the pictures but not so bulky as to clog valuable storage space.

In the second place, it is wise to standardize your selection. If you operate an elementary school library which has only a small picture collection, you may be able to experiment with all sorts of novel materials in reinforcing the pictorial holdings. But in a public library or a school district resource center with a picture collection numbering into the hundreds, there is a real need for a uniform type of mounting which will permit mass processing.

Choosing the perfect mounting paper is a complex chore. Your first task will be to decide upon the variety of paper you want. Then you will have to determine the ideal weight or thickness for your purposes. Here you can become bogged down in a maze of paper trade terms such as points, ply, basis weights, and weights per M.

If there is a paper processor or wholesale paper merchant in your town or in a nearby city, the best procedure is to seek advice. Explain your needs. Ask what materials might meet them. You may find that you can make better arrangements with a local firm than with national suppliers.

My own preference for mounting standard-sized pictures is a good grade of cover paper. Paper of 65-pound weight offers support without too much bulk. If you are building a collection of pictures with long-term usefulness, you may want to consider buying acid-free mounts. Such mounts will help to slow the deterioration of the pictures.

It is possible to order mounts with holes punched in the corners. These holes are meant to permit the use of thumbtacks without damaging the mounts. They would also make it possible to hang the pictures from strings. This practice may have merit in a small school where the librarian has close contact with users and can reinforce proper practices for picture display. However, our experience with public library borrowers is that they remove pictures from bulletin boards by taking hold of a corner and pulling. If the mount is held to the board by thumbtacks inserted through holes in the mount itself, the pulling process is likely to cause tearing of the paper.

Large items such as posters and charts pose a special problem. If they justify the cost, oversized materials can be mounted on a sturdy backing such as manila tag. If you decide to use makeshift mounts such as stray pieces of cardboard, remember that you can expect no guarantees of longevity. Poor grades of cardboard, despite their thickness and seeming show of strength, soon break and crumble.

Posters and charts with stiff backings are difficult to transport. This may not be a problem in a school media center where such items are intended for classroom use within the building. However, in a public library where posters and charts are made available for outside circulation, this factor assumes more importance.

Flexible cloth backings may be applied to posters and charts. The use of traditional cloth backings such as linen or muslin requires great skill, time, and space. Chartex® would be a much easier cloth mounting to employ for extra-large items. The use of these special backings is discussed more fully in the chapter on maps.

Although lamination is primarily considered a means of protecting the surface of a graphic, it can serve as a substitute for mounting if it is applied to both sides of the item. Used in this fashion, it strengthens and supports in much the same way as a mount. Reinforcement by lamination is particularly appropriate for oversized materials such as posters and charts.

Mount Size

When it comes to mount size, librarians once again go riding madly off in all directions like Stephen Leacock's famous character. There is no consensus as to the ideal size or sizes to use in mounting pictures.

Librarians seem to be guided in their choice of backing dimensions by such diverse factors as these:

1.   The physical measurements of storage facilities which are available.

2.   The size categories into which most of their mountable pictures fall.

3.   The aesthetics of various mount sizes and shapes.

4.   The need for economical division of mounting paper purchased in large uncut sheets.

Some libraries use a single mount size for all pictures except posters and charts. Others employ a variety of different backing sizes.

The advantages of using a single mount size are that it eliminates the need for individual decisions and also simplifies filing. On the other hand, the one-mount method is criticized as being wasteful of backing paper and blind to aesthetic principles.

Since there is no agreement among librarians about mount sizes, what is the best policy to follow?

Utilize the space your storage facilities offer to the fullest extent. Get out your ruler and determine what is the largest mount your files will accept. Don't take anything for granted. I've discovered, for example, that there is a variation in the inside drawer dimensions of even such standardized items as letter- and legal-sized metal files. This deviation is evident among different makes and sometimes even among different models from the same manufacturer. The variation is slight but it is significant enough so that a mount which will slip into one file will not fit into the next one.

Make sample mounts in the largest size your files will house and experiment in using them with expendable pictures. If this maximum-sized mount is not pleasing to your artistic eye, trim it to more attractive dimensions. Don't forget that a mount should look good with both vertically and horizontally placed pictures.

If your basic mount is sizable, you may find that it does not flatter small pictures. In this case, it is desirable to provide an alternate mount of smaller dimensions. In trying to find the easiest method of accomplishing this, many libraries just cut their larger mounts in half. Others provide an in-between size which they feel is more attractive and more practical.

Over a span of decades, our library has been faithful to two mounts: 10x11½-inches and 11x14-inches. But this formula is not necessarily the answer to your needs. Your physical facilities and your artistic judgment should dictate your choice of mount size.

As has been indicated, some libraries order mounting paper in large uncut sheets for reasons of economy or because it allows them flexibility in mount sizes.

If you have quantities of uncut sheets, try to obtain access to a power paper cutter. It will do a faster and much more professional job. These paper cutters are found in many printing establishments.

Mount Color

In mounting a picture, you are in essence creating a "frame" for it. From the artistic viewpoint, the color of this "frame" should be individually selected to best complement the picture. Unfortunately, the strictures of time and money do not always permit this coordination.

Even if you are forced to standardize your choice of mount color, it is still possible to present your pictures in an attractive manner.

Remember that the backing color you choose should emphasize the picture rather than dominating it. Your purpose is to "sell" the picture, not the mount. Mounts in the neutral tones will provide this subtle background and at the same time blend nicely with a wide range of illustrative material. Tan, gray, brown, buff, and cream are frequent library choices. Black and white are also popular.

In making color selections, librarians should keep in mind that very light mounts will soil more rapidly than darker ones.

Most public libraries hold to a single color for all their mounting. This makes for a simpler and quicker operation.

Some school libraries have been more adventurous, using a variety of colors in their mounts. Their selection is usually directed toward finding a backing that will harmonize with tones in the picture. However, with holiday subjects they are likely to give precedence to the spirit of the occasion. As a result, Christmas pictures are often pasted on red or green mounts while orange figures prominently as a backing for Halloween illustrations.

No outsider can determine which color or colors will be most suitable for your collection. Once the practical considerations have been met, this becomes entirely a matter of taste.

Trimming

No matter how steady your hand is, a pair of shears is not the ideal tool for trimming pictures in preparation for mounting. A manual paper cutter will do a much neater and faster job. Be sure that the model you choose is big enough to handle large pictures efficiently.

If a paper cutter is unavailable, a razor blade in a special holder or a sharp cutting knife such as the **Lewis Safety Knife®(213)** may be substituted. A steel-edged ruler, a steel straightedge, a T-square, or a steel carpenter's square can be used to guide the blade.

As you trim, don't neglect to salvage any text which serves to identify or explain the picture. In the case of a magazine picture, this includes the name and date of the periodical.

It has been suggested that leaving a narrow white margin around pictures makes them stand out more clearly from their mounts. Another recommendation has been to leave a substantial margin on heavily used pictures to facilitate their removal when mounts need replacement. But these procedures are not the usual rule. Most libraries trim pictures closely before mounting.

Pictures which are destined to remain unmounted will, of course, profit considerably from a wide margin since this surplus will serve to protect the picture itself from wear and tear.

School libraries which mount pictures for use in opaque projectors face special trimming requirements. The usual aperture on such projectors is 10x10-inches. This means that the picture must be trimmed to fit these limits if it is to be seen in a single exposure.

Picture Placement

It's usually best to place only one picture on a mount. Occasionally, two or three small pictures on the same subject may be grouped. This has added justification when all the pictures are from the same source.

The key rule for placement is that the bottom margin must be slightly wider than the upper to give a proper sense of balance. As far as side margins are concerned, libraries usually try to center the picture between them rather than attempting to create an off-center effect.

Holding to horizontal mounting so far as is possible will make it a bit easier to leaf through pictures in the files or in a pack on a table. But this temporary convenience is not important enough to justify placing a picture in an awkward, unattractive position on a mount. If a picture looks better in a vertical arrangement, it should be pasted with the long side of the mount turned vertically. Of course, there are pictures which *must* be pasted vertically because of their height.

You can rely on your innate sense of proportion or a trusty ruler when you determine the precise location of a picture on its mount. But some librarians have developed ingenious devices to expedite this process. One of the most intriguing is a homemade scale suggested by Carl J. Giganti **(108)**. He states that this instrument can be made by "taking a white card the same size as the card being used and marking it off, along the four edges very accurately, with the zero in the middle. With this device, one can use it either vertically or horizontally and note at a glance whether the picture is properly centered." A version of this homemade scale is shown on page 195.

After finding the desired spot for your picture on the mount, make light tick marks or corner lines on the backing paper to guide you once you've applied adhesive to the picture.

In attempting to deal with as many pictures as possible within the confines of the regular files, libraries often turn to an accordian type of mounting for large pictures or panels. The illustrative material is pasted in sections on two or more mounts. The mounts are joined together by hinges of adhesive cloth tape or pressure sensitive book tape. The tape should be applied when the mounts are closed so that there will be adequate leeway in the hinge to allow flexing.

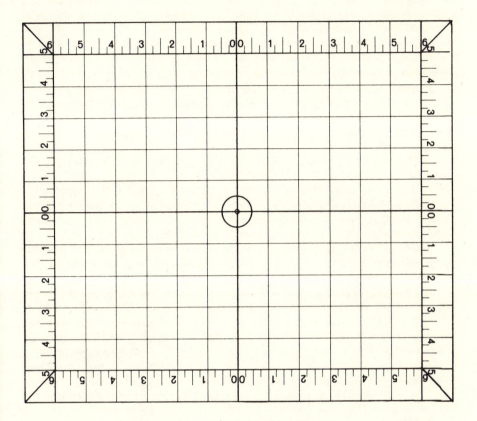

Attaching Pictures to Mounts

To a large extent, the discussion of techniques for mounting clippings in chapter 5 is pertinent for pictures as well.

The same problems persist in the use of rubber cement, tape, and spray adhesives. Similarly, the liquid adhesive I have found most satisfactory for mounting newspaper articles is also my favorite for pasting pictures. It is a "white glue" called "Yes"®, which is manufactured by Gane Brothers & Lane, Inc. **(101)**. As was indicated in the chapter on clippings, "Yes" is more expensive than many library glues and pastes, but it does a commendable job. However, it must be pointed out that **"Yes"** is not recommended for mounting photographs.

If you can afford the necessary equipment and materials, dry mounting is the ideal method of attaching pictures. Properly done, it creates a perfect bond which is neat, smooth, and secure. It also makes possible the successful mounting of pictures which are on thin paper. This process is described in more detail in chapter 5.

In attempting to find a bargain treatment for pictures, libraries have been known to resort to stapling their pictures to mounts. This method should be avoided no matter how tight the budget. As well as being unattractive, it is hazardous. Staples frequently tear loose, mutilating the picture in the process.

Tipping pictures with paste or glue at the four corners is another economy move which is unacceptable. This attachment is not strong enough to absorb the wear which most library pictures receive. Like stapling, it leaves the edges of the picture loose so that they are vulnerable to snagging. One argument advanced for tacking is that the picture will be easy to remove when the mount is worn. My feeling is that pictures fastened in this manner are likely to succumb faster than the mounts.

The only proper way to mount a picture is to see that it is attached firmly and fully on all four sides.

The strongest seal is one in which the adhesive is applied to the entire back of the picture. But this practice is far from being universal among libraries. While they make sure that the picture edges are secured, many libraries elect not to coat the whole picture with paste or glue. Instead, the adhesive is applied only to a strip along each edge. A token dab may be given to the center. Usually this procedure is adopted to save on adhesives or staff time, but the decision may stem from a fear of wrinkling or curling.

Oversized materials or those with extra thickness present a special problem. They are likely to demand overall pasting to compensate for their spread or weight.

Pictures prepared for showing in an opaque projector need individual consideration. The intense heat generated by this machine will loosen many adhesives. If you are furnishing mounted pictures for prolonged exposure in an opaque projector, it would be wise to test your adhesive for resistance to heat. Otherwise, you will have to resign yourself to cheerfully repasting the pictures each time they come loose. Substituting a permanent dry mounting tissue such as **Seal MT5®** in place of glues and pastes will help to eliminate this hazard.

Pictures printed on thin, absorbent paper sometimes present a problem because they may begin to curl even while a liquid adhesive is being applied. One solution is to cover the back of the picture with a clear plastic spray before attempting to use paste or glue. The spray will slow the absorption of the adhesive, giving you time to position the picture. As indicated earlier, dry mounting tissue rather than liquid adhesives is the best choice for such pictures.

To insure a tight, even attachment when using a liquid adhesive, a paste cloth or paper towel may be used to smooth the picture after it is placed on the mount. Some librarians prefer, instead, to apply pressure with a brayer. The most knowledgeable technician I know recommends a tongue depressor or a bone folder. She claims that it's easier to control the amount and direction of pressure with these instruments than with a brayer. Tongue depressors should be sanded before use if they exhibit rough spots.

Pictures should be placed under weights until they are thoroughly dry. If they are stacked, waxed paper should be used to separate the sheets.

Edging

Because of the expense and effort involved in mounting or laminating large posters and charts, many libraries resort to partial reinforcement by placing cloth tape or some other variety of tape along the edges on the reverse side.

Protection of Picture Surfaces

The best form of picture protection is "hot" lamination. This is a relatively expensive process, but its fans argue that the extended life span of pictorial materials helps to amortize the original investment. They also point out that lamination helps to preserve pictures that are difficult or even impossible to replace.

Lamination may be applied to both unmounted and mounted materials. Since the laminating process involves high temperatures, any adhesive used to mount pictures must be able to withstand the necessary heat. Permanent dry mounting tissue is probably the only bonding agent you can be sure about.

School libraries have taken the lead in laminating pictorial resources. They usually reserve this treatment for their most precious or most popular pictures. Since manpower for such projects is limited, one junior high school has successfully employed the help of a service corps of students who are given academic credit for dry mounting and laminating materials for the school library and the teaching staff.

Public libraries have been a bit slower to become involved with the lamination of pictorial materials. However, there is some movement in this direction.

The principal impetus in public libraries is the growing popularity of posters, especially among young adults. The cost of posters and the heavy physical wear and tear to which they are subjected have led many public libraries to laminate these resources. Libraries which do not own the necessary equipment have arranged to have the laminating process done by commercial firms or by school agencies in their communities.

Librarians are particularly satisfied with polyester film for laminating posters. A medium-weight film is desirable, one that is strong but flexible. Try to obtain laminate wide enough so that no seams are necessary. This will improve the wearing quality of the finished product. Laminate is available in both gloss and matte finish. The matte finish is preferable because it eliminates any distorting glare; however, it is more expensive than the gloss finish. For superior protection, the poster should be placed between two sheets of laminate to form a "sandwich" effect.

After lamination, some libraries punch two holes at the top edges of the poster. The holes are made with an eyelet punch and reinforced by metal eyelets. Eyelet punches are for sale in sewing stores. These eyelets make it possible to use tacks to display a poster without harming its surface. Hanging a laminated poster by string from these eyelets is less satisfactory. The poster tends to buckle.

Since tape will not mar polyester laminate, your patrons will probably be glad to settle for this method of hanging if you don't want to fuss with eyelets.

There are commercial hanging devices available for posters, which consist of plastic rods into which the top and bottom edges of the poster are slipped.

However, while there has been some library experimentation with these devices, they are too expensive for mass use by most libraries.

Although "hot" lamination in public libraries is usually limited to popular posters, a few institutions have experimented with selective lamination of their mounted pictures. One large public library which I have visited applies lamination but limits it only to the surface of the picture itself. The picture is then dry mounted to an unprotected mount. This technique certainly reduces the amount of film consumed. However, mounts take a lot of abuse. It's quite likely that they will not last as long as the laminated pictures they carry.

"Cold" lamination, involving the use of plastic film coated with a pressure-sensitive adhesive, is another method which is used to protect pictorial resources.

For more information on lamination, see chapter 8.

A more modest type of protection from moisture and dirt is achieved by coating picture surfaces with clear plastic spray.

School libraries sometimes make use of transparent covers into which they slip pictures before they're taken to the classroom. Vinyl picture covers such as those sold by Demco (74) permit pictures to be passed from hand to hand with no fear of damage.

Identification and Labeling

Any textual information that will help to clarify the significance of a picture should be placed on the mount along with the picture itself. Without this descriptive material, a picture loses much of its value. You may have a perfectly spectacular picture of Indians in full tribal dress, but unless the picture is accompanied by a caption identifying the tribe and the occasion, your picture is little more than a pretty decoration.

While most libraries are content to rely on the information which is printed with the picture, some do added research on their own. In mounting reproductions of paintings, for example, such libraries will search out the life dates of the artist and the school of art to which that person belongs.

Usually the printed explanation accompanying a picture can be transferred directly to the mount. On occasion you may find it necessary to retype the information if the format of the original is poor or if you want to edit the comment.

Some libraries prefer to place longer descriptions on the back of the mount. However, titles or brief captions should always be pasted on the front.

Source and date of publication are vital facts which should be recorded somewhere on the mount, perhaps on the picture caption or even on the subject label. Do you question the need for this citation? Knowing the source can be essential to an author who wants permission to reproduce a particular picture in a book. The date is equally important to the set designer trying to find typical room interiors of the 1940s.

Some major picture collections have established source files to expedite processing and to assure access to bibliographic information necessary to obtain clearance for picture reproduction. A code number is assigned to each book from which illustrations are clipped. The code number is recorded on each picture taken from a particular book. A card file is maintained that gives full bibliographic information about each book clipped. The cards are arranged by the code numbers.

When it comes to the location of subject headings on picture mounts, librarians line up like two opposing football teams. One side insists that subject labels should be placed on the *front* of the mount. This will permit mounts to be filed so that the pictures face the user. As a result, it is easier to consult the pictures while they are still in the drawers.

Other librarians are convinced that subject headings should always be recorded on the *back* of the mount. They argue that subject headings deface the front of the mount.

I'm inclined to agree with the supporters of back labeling. The subject heading is not an integral part of the illustration or the explanatory text that accompanies it. It is merely a device to help locate the picture. Placing a subject label on the front of the mount does detract from the attractiveness of the finished product without adding anything to the message conveyed by the picture.

There is no escaping the fact that back labeling requires mounts to be filed with the pictures facing the rear of the drawer. This causes a measure of inconvenience because pictures must be removed from the files to be studied. However, this removal also has its advantages. The drawers are quickly freed for others·to consult. Packs of pictures run less chance of being bent and torn when they are examined away from crowded drawers.

Subject headings should be applied to the upper left-hand corner of the mount *as it will stand in the drawer.* The use of the left-hand corner is appropriate because we are conditioned to turning our eyes to the left for books and catalog cards.

Usually all full-sized mounts are placed horizontally in storage files. This means that vertically pasted pictures will be turned sideways. To prevent further dislocation, be sure that all vertically mounted pictures face in the same direction before applying subject headings. Otherwise, patrons will have to do a good deal of head bobbing as they examine a group of pictures.

The subject heading may be written directly on the mount in ink or it may be typed on gummed or pressure-sensitive labels.

Many libraries prefer to print or type subject headings for mounted pictures entirely in capital letters. Their hypothesis is that taller letters are easier to see. To further augment the legibility of their labels, some libraries use large-print typewriters.

When gummed labels or pressure-sensitive labels are used, it is wise to leave a small margin between the label and the edge of the mount. Labels placed at the very edge are likely to separate from the backing. Libraries which record subject headings on the front of mounts may avoid this peeling by using labels which fold in the center to fit over the top of the mount.

All pictorial material should be stamped on the back with the ownership symbol of the library.

In the case of graphics which are to be laminated, the identification mark must be applied before laminate is affixed to the area.

Unmounted pictures pose peculiar labeling problems because of their physical characteristics. Their labeling is a haphazard affair in most libraries. The usual procedure is to record pertinent information either in margin areas on the front of the pictures or in free spaces on the back. A mixture of these locations can really slow up the filing process. One major library applied gummed labels to all of its unmounted picture clippings in an effort to provide a uniform location for subject headings. Most libraries, however, would hesitate to make this investment in a resource which they obviously think of as temporary and expendable.

The labeling of unmounted pictures is customarily done with pencil. When headings are faint or blurred, the handling of these awkward materials is made even more difficult.

Because of their format, postcards are immune to any controversy over front or back labeling. They must always be sourced, dated, and headed on the back of the card.

ORGANIZATION

Most libraries arrange their picture collections alphabetically by subject.

Division of pictures by broad subject categories is a common practice. This is ironic, because there is nothing so specific as a single picture capturing a single idea or moment in time.

What could be more definite than an illustration of a motorcycle? Yet many libraries will hide it under a broad class heading such as "Transportation" or "Motor vehicles."

There are serious drawbacks to this generalized approach to the picture collection. It presents no problem when a student rushes in to say, "My teacher told me to get 25 pictures on architecture." But when specific items are needed, this type of organization puts obstacles in the way of finding them. If intricate subdivisions are not provided, it means leafing through stacks of pictures to find the desired illustration. If detailed subdivisions are employed, they are often so involved and awkward that they become stumbling blocks themselves.

Why should it be necessary to look under "Physiology" for a picture of an ear or under "Games and amusements" for illustrations of the Olympic Games? Is it really sensible to put fireplaces under "Architectural detail—Fireplace?" Is the best place for pictures of military tanks really under "Armament?" These subject assignments are all recommended in a standard list of subject headings for picture collections.

It is generally acknowledged that when out-of-school adults consult pictorial materials, they are usually looking for very specific topics. With changes in teaching patterns, this has become increasingly true of school-affiliated patrons, too. In libraries which encourage the public to serve itself, there is even more incentive for establishing a direct approach to the subject content of pictures.

I must hurry to point out that there are areas in a picture collection which almost demand broad class groupings. Paintings offer one example. Sculpture is another. Depictions of famous and infamous people also fall into this pattern. The inclusions in these areas are so complex and varied that they would be difficult to handle separately. In effect, they are almost distinct collections within a collection. Some large libraries even provide separate housing for their picture holdings in such distinct categories as paintings and people.

The happiest solution to the problem of subject assignment for the picture collection lies in compromise. Stick to direct, specific subject headings whenever possible. Group pictures under broad generic headings when it is illogical to disperse them.

School libraries may decide that arrangement by curricular units is more appropriate for their needs, but even the strongest advocate will run into trouble with this plan. Many pictures are pertinent to two or more units. Should the cotton gin go under "Inventions" or "Textiles"? Should a picture of a pony express rider be placed under "Frontier and pioneer life," "Postal service," "Transportation," or "Communication"? What sounds gloriously simple in theory becomes complicated in practice. The saddest feature of this plan is that pictures which could add sparkle to a certain unit may be entirely overlooked because they're buried in the resources for another unit.

A published list of subject headings employed in the highly respected picture collection at the Newark Public Library has appeared in many revisions through the years. A sixth edition edited by William J. Dane was released in 1968. **The Picture Collection: Subject Headings (72)** is a helpful guide in establishing subject heading terminology and in discovering useful cross references. But it is based on a "scheme whereby small and fragmented topics are grouped under major headings." Be prepared to edit this list to fit your own philosophy and your own needs. The publisher has not yet decided whether an updated edition of this resource will be undertaken.

A compilation of subject headings is also offered in **The Picture File: A Manual and a Curriculum-Related Subject Heading List (127)**, by Donna Hill. This list of subject headings is tailored to the needs of school libraries and teacher-training institutions. Small public libraries may also find it worth consulting. It attempts to strike a judicious balance between specific headings and broad headings with numerous subdivisions. The author has incorporated both types, making her choice on the basis of what she felt was best for a curriculum-oriented situation.

Clues to subject headings may also be gleaned from the **Readers' Guide** and from other more specialized indexes such as the **Art Index. Sears List of Subject Headings (214)** is useful in determining related topics.

Standard reference books may be of assistance in verifying correct entries for such items as artists' names, mythological citations, and botanical terminology.

There should be a separate card index to the subject headings employed in the picture collection. When all picture holdings are not filed in one consecutive series of drawers, the index cards should reflect this fact. The location of various picture resources on a given subject should be indicated. This might be done by a number code, assigning a separate numerical designation to each special storage unit. Or it might be done by a simple cross reference: Castles SEE ALSO Postcard collection.

Referral cards may be inserted in the card catalog, directing the patron to the pictorial resources available on a certain subject. A typical card might read like the one on page 202.

Many school libraries employ more elaborate means to promote use of their picture holdings. They often classify and catalog pictorial resources as though they were books. This is most likely to occur with sets of study prints and with

TREES

Consult the picture files for illustrated material.

substantial items such as posters and large wall charts. The entries in the catalog may be distinguished by the use of colored cards or by color-banded cards. Usually a symbol, such as "P" or "Pi," precedes the classification number.

Some special libraries may attempt selective cataloging of individual pictorial resources. Special libraries may also resort to coordinate indexing, assigning serial numbers to pictures as they are added to the collection and using a card index to provide access by subject. Appropriate pictures are tracked down through the serial numbers placed on the subject cards. A picture may be entered on more than one subject card. For example, there might be entries for the same picture under a geographical location, a time period, an activity, and a person's name.

Dale E. Shaffer has proposed a different sort of numerical arrangement in his booklet, **The Library Picture File (217)**. His plan calls for placing mounted pictures in stacks of open bins with a separate bin for each topic. The bins are numbered consecutively. Subjects may be alphabetically assigned to the bins at first, but this pattern cannot be maintained for subjects added later. Pictures are assigned numbers to match the subject bins in which they are to be housed. In addition, each picture within a particular bin is given an additional number to distinguish it from its neighbors. A notebook provides a list of the subject areas covered and the number assigned to each. There is also an entry for each picture, giving its description and location number.

While Shaffer originally sold the storage units used in this system, he no longer does so. Instead, he suggests that school maintenance departments can easily build the devices using the dimensions given in the book. The units are 18-inches wide, 24-inches deep, and 85-inches high. Each unit has 19 open bins.

Shaffer stresses the accessibility of the picture collection under his plan. It is only fair to point out that this system could result in a considerable investment of money and space, since only 19 subject areas can be covered in a single unit. Furthermore, a library may neither have nor need enough pictures on a given topic to fill a bin.

The growing involvement of public libraries with popular posters has not as yet created any uniform approach to the organization of these resources. Thus far, the only common concern is for circulation control. Some libraries place a code equivalent to an accession number on the back of each poster and maintain a shelf list geared to these numbers. The shelf list records title, source, price, and date of acquisition. If posters have been commercially laminated, the cost of this process can be noted also. Instead of preparing new shelf list cards, you may be able to use the original order cards for this purpose, thus saving time and money.

If you do decide to use a number code for posters, remember that such information must be applied to a poster before it is laminated.

To provide a record of its poster holdings, the children's department at the public library in Red Wing, Minnesota, has created a picture index. A colored photograph is taken of each poster. The photographs are placed in a photo album next to the poster shelving. The photographs are numbered to correspond to numbers on the posters themselves. Children can leaf through the album to make their selection.

CIRCULATION

Most libraries concern themselves with the total number of pictures borrowed on any one subject rather than with each individual item. For circulation purposes, pictures are treated as sets rather than isolated entities. Thus a group of three pictures on skiing might be recorded only as "3—Skiing."

While this does not provide indisputable identification of the pictures which are in circulation, it may be the only practical procedure to follow. Because pictures are often borrowed in large packs, an attempt to tally each item separately would be a staggering task. So librarians make a simple notation and say a little prayer. Remember that the finer your subject divisions are, the closer you can come to pinpointing the exact nature of items in circulation.

Smaller libraries are likely to use the same type of circulation slip or card for all of their supplementary resources. These devices are discussed in chapter 2. Larger libraries may design a special form for hand charging that clearly indicates that pictorial resources are being circulated.

Some libraries have turned to a fixed card system in the circulation of pictures. Each envelope reserved for picture circulation is assigned its own number. The number is repeated on a charging card, which is kept with the envelope until it goes into circulation with a group of pictures. At the time of circulation, the librarian records on the card the number of pictures taken, the subject of the pictures, the date due, and the patron's identification. Cards may be housed with general circulation records under the date the material is due or they may be placed in a separate tray until the envelopes are returned. The card pictured on the top of page 204 is typical of those used with this system.

PICTURES		#3
9-15-79	John Smith ·	6
	103 Main St.	Birds

When school libraries assign Dewey Decimal numbers to sets of study prints or to large posters and charts, they usually equip these resources with cards and pockets so that they can be circulated like books.

In libraries which use photocharging for all of their circulating materials, the simple form shown below can be used to expedite picture circulation.

The form should be of a size to fit a standard book pocket.

Once filled out, the form can be placed under the camera when the photographic record of the loan is made. The transaction slip and the form can then be placed in a pocket on the envelope containing the pictures. If envelopes are meant for short-term use only and have no pockets, the transaction slip and picture form can be stapled to the envelope itself.

```
┌─────────────────────────────────────────┐
│                 PICTURES                 │
│                                          │
│   Subjects                  No. Borrowed │
│   ────────                  ──────────── │
│                                          │
│                                          │
│                                          │
│                                          │
│                                          │
│                                          │
│                                          │
│                                          │
│                                          │
│                                          │
│                                          │
│                                          │
│                                          │
│                                          │
└─────────────────────────────────────────┘
```

The circulation of popular or decorative posters presents some special considerations. They can be charged out on the circulation forms used for other pictures. The title can be substituted for the subject. If the poster is accessioned, the accession number should be recorded.

Another solution for accessioned posters is to institute a fixed card system with a separate card for each poster. Cards of a particular color can be chosen to differentiate these materials from other media. Each card would bear the accession number and at least part of the title of the poster it represents. These cards would be kept together in order numerically. When a poster was chosen for circulation, the appropriate card would be pulled. The borrower's identification and the date due would be recorded on the card. The date due would also be stamped on a date due slip fastened to the back of the poster. The poster card would then be transferred to a section of the tray representing those materials in circulation. When the poster is returned, the patron's identification is crossed off on the card and the card is returned to the "in" file.

For photographic charging, a pocket bearing the accession number and short title can be taped to the back of each poster. If it is felt necessary to supply further identification, the word, "Poster," can be typed on the pocket. When a poster is selected for circulation, the pocket is placed under the camera for photographic recording. The transaction slip can then be placed in the pocket.

Various types of carrying devices have been used in the circulation of pictures. Old mailing tubes may be saved for transporting charts and posters. However, the use of mailing tubes can result in considerable damage if posters and charts are carelessly inserted or removed. Most libraries that have laminated posters just roll them up, secure them with a rubber band, and let it go at that. If you're not satisfied with that arrangement, you might investigate the long plastic bags used by some poster stores or narrow paper bags of the sort once used for curtain rods.

Large paper envelopes are appropriate for circulating mounted or unmounted pictures. These can be either used mailing envelopes or specially purchased envelopes. Expanding red rope envelopes with string ties are particularly sturdy and protective.

School libraries sometimes resort to plastic pockets or holders.

Libraries may even utilize picture envelopes of cloth. Our library is fortunate enough to still have denim carriers which were sewn some years ago in the workshop of a state mental hospital. They have an overflap which fastens securely with twill ties. The inside is reinforced with a rectangle of corrugated cardboard which fits loosely against the back of the envelope. A date due slip is pasted to the cardboard. These denim envelopes have given excellent service.

In making or buying envelopes, remember that they should be one or two inches longer and wider than the pictures they will contain.

Be sure that the identification mark of the library appears on carrying devices such as envelopes.

Because of the misuse to which pictures are subjected when they are exhibited, some libraries attach a list of suggestions for safe display techniques to the carriers in which the pictures circulate.

When pictures are charged out, the date on which they are due should be indicated on the carrying device. The number of pictures taken should be recorded there also.

In addition to circulating pictorial material, some school librarians have pictures which they are willing to give away. In their efforts to serve students in every way possible, these librarians save pictures which are not needed in the library's collection. Students are free to use these excess materials to illustrate notebooks or reports. The pictures are also in demand as ingredients for collages prepared in art classes.

PHOTOGRAPHS

Photographs about the local community form a very special kind of picture collection. Extra care is necessary to insure the survival of historically important photographs, since they are vulnerable to light, harmful chemicals, excessive heat and humidity, careless handling, and dirt or dust.

Envelopes will help to protect them. Under optimum conditions, each unmounted print stored in a vertical file should be placed in a separate container. If paper envelopes are employed, they should be made of acid-free paper. Be sure that the adhesive used in making the envelopes does not adversely affect the photographs. The Hollinger Corporation (129) is one source of paper envelopes which meet these requirements. If prints are on thin paper, they may have to be supported by stiff sheets slipped into the envelopes. The support sheets should also be of acid-free materials. Any descriptive notes on the envelopes should be made in pencil or typed with a carbon ribbon.

In place of paper envelopes, some experts prefer protective holders made of plastic materials, such as cellulose triacetate or polyester. One advantage is that they allow examination of the print without its removal from the protective covering. However, it is difficult to apply labeling to these containers. Plastic holders may also be less desirable under conditions of high humidity. They can also build up static electricity, which attracts dust.

A seamless paper envelope developed by the Department of Special Collections at UCLA has been termed suitable for use with both prints and negatives. These envelopes can be ordered according to your specifications from supply houses such as the Hollinger Corporation. Or you can elect instead to order the acid-free paper and cut and fold your own envelopes. Detailed information about the construction of these envelopes is contained in the following sources:

1.   "Technical Notes." **American Archivist**, July 1975, pages 403-405.

2.   Weinstein, Robert A., and Larry Booth. **Collection, Use, and Care of Historical Photographs (249)**, pages 138-140.

While it is essential to know the exact content and history of each photograph, it is risky to attempt writing all of this information directly on the back of an unmounted picture. Writing may raise ridges on the face of a print. Inks of a volatile nature can damage photographs. Authorities recommend that any necessary labeling be restricted to the outer edge of the reverse side. To prevent damage, lay a single print at a time face down on a clean sheet of glass and write with a soft pencil.

Some libraries type the descriptive material on a separate strip of acid-free paper using a carbon ribbon. The strip is then dry mounted to the back of the print.

Another solution is to file the photographs numerically. Under this arrangement, only a number needs to be penciled on the back margin and repeated on the envelope if one is used. Complete information about the photographs can be recorded on cards numbered to correspond with the photograph numbers. A subject index will provide access to the pictures. Since a single photograph may contain several historically important features, multiple subject cards may be used for one print, if necessary.

Dealing with historical prints by mounting them on supportive mats is a method that arouses great support and great opposition. Proponents point out that the mounts protect the prints by providing a sturdy backing. Margins supplied by the mounts minimize possible damage to prints by contact with the human hand. Mounts help to counteract the tendency of prints to curl. They provide ample space for captions. Supporters of picture mounting suggest using acid-free museum mounting board. They recommend dry mounting tissue to attach the prints to the mounts.

Opponents argue that historic prints should not be tampered with by mounting. They argue that to mount a print of this sort is to destroy its historic integrity. Furthermore, they point out that many prints have historically important notations on the reverse side. Opponents are not completely satisfied that dry mounting is safe for all historic prints. They also note that if a mount has to be replaced, the print will have to be removed by means that may threaten the photograph.

There is a good solution to this controversy, although it does involve the expenditure of money. Duplicate prints can be made of the original pictures. These duplicate prints can be mounted to make a collection of working pictures for the public to use. The unmounted originals can be preserved in their unaltered form in a separate storage area. Precious prints may be stored horizontally, as many conservators suggest. Under this system, the original photographs will be available for serious scholars but will not be subject to the deterioration that frequent handling would cause.

Having mounted duplicate prints means that you can offer your public liberal access to a collection arranged by subject for quick retrieval.

Whether you intend to mount pictures or not, you should give serious consideration to the development of duplicate prints for your important historical pictures. Pictures do deteriorate. They do get damaged. They do get stolen. Interestingly enough, new prints may turn out to be clearer than the original if the reproduction is handled by a skilled technician.

For reasons of security, you should also have a negative made of any significant print which reaches your collection without one.

Because of their extreme sensitivity, negatives pose even more of a problem for libraries than prints do. They should be stored separately from prints. Each negative should be placed in an individual protective holder. Paper jackets are most commonly used. Envelopes of acid-free paper with nonacid side seams can be obtained from such firms as the Hollinger Corporation (129). You may also want to consider the seamless paper envelopes described earlier. To minimize handling, negatives can be filed numerically. A card index will enable you to retrieve negatives by referring you to the appropriate numbers. The numbers assigned to negatives should be noted on the corresponding prints.

Color film presents special difficulties for libraries hoping to preserve historic pictures. Colors may fade or change, particularly in older films. Experts urge that black-and-white copy negatives be made to serve as backups.

Among their historical acquisitions, librarians may even find themselves faced with the need to cope with nitrate base film or glass plate negatives. Nitrate base film is extremely inflammable. It can also harm other film as it deteriorates. Glass plate negatives are breathtakingly fragile. Consult an expert at once if you come into possession of such items.

Future ramifications for photographic collections will result from the growing use of water-resistant printing paper. Kodak's **RC Papers®** are examples of this trend. Archivists are concerned because of the sensitivity of plasticized film to ultraviolet and other radiation. For long-term survival, prints made from this paper will have to be carefully protected from exposure to light. If dry mounting is planned, be sure to use dry mounting tissue compatible with water-resistant printing paper. The heat used in the dry mounting process must be carefully controlled in order to assure a good bond and yet not harm the finish of the water-resistant print. Any labeling of unmounted prints will also call for techniques suitable for the plastic surface.

The storage units used to house historic photographs are of great significance because of the effect of chemical reactions upon both negatives and prints. The most desirable housing consists of steel files with a baked enamel finish. If there is no choice but to use storage facilities made of wood, the wood should be painted with epoxy paint and allowed to "age" for a matter of weeks.

Steel map cases or acid-free print boxes made with metal edges are suitable for oversized prints. If such prints must be stored without individual envelopes, then polyester sheets or acid-free tissue should be placed between the prints.

Air conditioning with adequate filtering is recommended in the storage area to control temperature and humidity and to eliminate atmospheric pollutants.

It is wise to seek out experienced photographers who can help you with the many problems posed by historical photographs. Professional photographers are often willing to give advice. There are camera clubs even in small communities. Many schools have instructors who teach photography as a credit course or as an extra-curricular activity.

FOR FURTHER READING

Procedures for building a picture collection are discussed in **The Picture File: A Manual and a Curriculum-Related Subject Heading List (127)**, by Donna Hill. The emphasis is on school-oriented libraries.

Textbooks used in college courses on audiovisual materials are helpful in learning about such techniques as dry mounting and lamination.

For detailed information about water-resistant printing paper, write to the Eastman Kodak Company **(80)** for a free copy of **Finishing Prints on Kodak Water-Resistant Papers (Kodak Publication No. E-67)**.

The Library of Congress has announced that one of the tentative titles in preparation for its **Preservation Leaflets** series **(204)** is **Basic Preservation for Photographic Materials**. Leaflets in this series are free.

CHAPTER 10

SPECIAL FILES AND FOLDERS

In every trade there are treasured tools which spell the difference between adequate and superior performance. In the library world, these tools can take the form of special reference indexes and folders.

One of the most helpful of these devices is a card file of elusive or repeatedly used information.

FUGITIVES FILE

When you've finally come up with the answer to a devilish reference question and suspect it may be asked again someday, this card file is the place to make a notation of the answer and the sources used to find it. No wonder some librarians call this type of index a "fugitives file," since it holds the kind of information that is as hard to capture as the most legendary outlaw.

The fugitives file is also a useful place to anchor facts that are asked for repeatedly, such as the highest and lowest altitudes in the city. This handy summary will salvage time otherwise spent in repeated consultation of the original sources.

The fugitives file may also incorporate references to resource people in the community who have special talents or interests that might be tapped to answer difficult reference problems. A roster of citizens able to translate various foreign languages can form an invaluable part of this list of human resources. One word of caution! As a matter of common courtesy, check with resource people to make sure they are willing to become consultants. A local resident may be a dedicated collector of rare books, but this doesn't necessarily indicate a willingness to evaluate attic treasures for any casual caller.

PROGRAM PLANNERS FILE

A "speakers file" or "program planners file" can be a great boon to local clubs, schools, and individuals. These names are poor ones since the contents need not be restricted to speakers, nor need they be devoted entirely to formal programs. To help the harried dance chairman or the parent looking for entertainment for a children's party, the file can be expanded to include magicians, orchestras, puppeteers, square dance callers, barbershop quartets, folk dance groups, etc.

Leads for this file can be obtained from newspaper articles, especially those appearing in the social or entertainment sections. Word-of-mouth clues can also be productive. Occasionally, a local performer will place an ad in the paper asking for engagements.

It is essential to obtain clearance before adding any individual or group to the roster. A form can be developed to speed this process. As soon as the staff becomes aware of a new talent in the community, the form can be sent, explaining the file and requesting permission to add the recipient to the list. The prospect should be asked to specify:

1. The topics on which the individual will speak, in the case of speakers—or the nature of the performance, in the case of entertainers.

2. If applicable, the name of the organization being represented.

3. The estimated length of the speech or performance.

4. The audience for which the speech or performance is appropriate.

5. Time of availability.

6. Equipment needed.

7. Any conditions placed on the composition of the audience or the distance which the person or group will travel.

8. The fee, if any.

In the case of large organizations or agencies, your job may be expedited by the fact that some of these units maintain a speakers bureau or issue a list of the presentations they are prepared to offer.

A program planners file might be broadened to incorporate tours of local institutions, businesses, or other places of interest. A formal contact should be made before adding any tour possibility to the file. Details to be clarified are the name of the contact person; the nature of the tour; requirements as to size and composition of the visiting group; provisions for the handicapped; and any charges.

As you build your program planners file, remember that a logical extension of this tool would be an inventory of meeting places available for use by local groups or gatherings.

LOCAL ORGANIZATIONS DIRECTORY

One of the most popular resources in many libraries is a local organizations directory, which records the many groups active in the community. For maximum utilization, the directory should provide for access by the name of each group and also by a subject approach which reflects the nature of the organization. Such a card file can be of inestimable value to citizens planning fund-raising drives, political campaigns, or millage votes. It is also important to the patron who wants to know if there is a chess club in town that he can join or to the widow who is looking for the local chapter of Parents Without Partners.

Try to obtain the names and phone numbers of key officials or a contact person, as well as the time and place of meetings. A statement about the scope and activities of the group is helpful knowledge. The entries in the organizations file must always be dated so that the currency of the information can be judged. In many instances, elections of group officers are reported in the local newspaper but the coverage is not universal. At regular and frequent intervals, the directory must be screened for outdated cards. A form letter or postcard can be used to request the names of new officers, as well as information on any other changes in the operation of the organization.

A local organizations directory can be supplemented by a file of regional and state organizations.

Some libraries have used their local organizations files as a launching pad for an information and referral service, which attempts to match patrons with agencies, organizations, and individuals capable of assisting them with their personal problems.

INFORMATION ON COMING EVENTS

Crucial to good reference work in public libraries is the gathering of information on coming events which are of interest to the library's clientele. The heaviest concentration should, of course, be on events taking place in the local community or in neighboring regions. Scour the area newspapers for announcements and ads. Collect any flyers which are distributed to publicize area affairs. Persuade the local schools, theatrical groups, musical organizations, service clubs, churches, and civic officials to alert the library to any public events they are sponsoring.

This accumulation of information can be the jumping-off point for publishing a regular calendar of events to be distributed to groups and institutions throughout the city. Such an undertaking is both an important public service and a good publicity move for the library. In one small library where funds were not available for preparing multiple copies of a calendar of events, the librarian posted a huge homemade calendar in the library each month on which she recorded coming events in the community.

Careful attention should also be given to events scheduled for other parts of the state. In many states, there is a government agency which releases a calendar of events covering the entire state. Regional tourist associations may also publish chronologies of activities in their areas. Summaries of events in larger cities are often issued by their tourist and convention bureaus, municipal offices of public information, chambers of commerce, or arts councils. Activities in metropolitan areas may even be covered in commercially produced magazines. Some are designed to be distributed free of charge in restaurants, hotels, and motels. Others are for sale by subscription or at newsstands.

As part of your state survey, ask to be put on the mailing list for announcements of events scheduled at the outstanding auditoriums and for releases from the important art museums. If there are "big-time" sports teams in the state, obtain schedules of their games. This applies both to professional groups and to the major university teams.

In venturing beyond the boundaries of your own state, you will have to gauge your acquisitions to the requests you receive from your community. If there are major cities in nearby states that regularly attract your patrons, you will want to make every effort to obtain descriptive literature about their coming events.

Coverage on a nationwide scale should center on items of major interest. For example, many questions were sparked by the exhibits on "Treasures of Tutankhamun" and "Pompeii A.D. 79." Wise libraries collected all the information they could find on the locations and dates of the showings. The surge of interest in

Indian culture would also lead foresighted libraries to order the **American Indian Calendar (34)**, which is issued annually by the Bureau of Indian Affairs.

On the international level, free literature about coming events may be obtained from many foreign tourist agencies. Information can also be gathered from other sources. For example, **Events in the Pacific (197)** is prepared by the Pacific Area Travel Association, an organization made up of commercial travel interests and government tourist offices. This unique yearly summary is distributed without charge. Another annual compilation—now in its 61st edition—is the **World Calendar of Holidays (165)**, produced by the Morgan Guaranty Trust Company of New York. Single copies are available free to libraries.

Of course, it's to be expected that every library will have **Chases' Calendar of Annual Events, Special Days, Weeks and Months (54)** as part of its events file or readily accessible nearby.

In the process of collecting brochures about coming events, you may receive duplicate copies. Don't throw the extra copies away if they are of more than momentary value. Add them to your travel collection.

Weeding events folders poses a special problem. The first temptation is to ruthlessly eliminate anything that is past, but a little hesitation may prove profitable. Many times patrons contact the library for added information *after* they have attended an event. On the local and state level, it's good to keep seasonal lists until the new edition arrives the next year. This makes it possible to at least approximate the location and customary date of a recurring event.

SPECIALIZED REFERENCE FOLDERS

Libraries should consider creating folders for any special reference data that needs to be kept readily at hand for instant use.

For example, a folder might be established for what some librarians call "official changes." These are clippings which will eventually be used to update information in the library's basic reference books. Until the changes are recorded, the folder of clippings can be consulted to answer questions. The creation of government agencies, the outcome of elections, and the emergence of new nations are among the newsworthy items which belong in this folder.

It's also helpful to have a record of the deaths of people who are popular, distinguished, or infamous. An alternative to keeping obituary clippings in the "official changes" folder is to enter the basic information—name, identification, date of death, and the newspaper citation—on sheets of paper headed with letters of the alphabet. Clippings can then be discarded. The obituary sheets provide a quick way to determine whether a person of interest has died and, if so, when.

An excellent time-saver is a folder in which a summary of the Consumer Price Index is maintained. The recorded information needs to incorporate past index figures as well as the latest announcement. Tables keyed to various bases should be included. Such a folder is a convenient tool to use with individuals and groups negotiating salary schedules. It will also be in heavy demand to answer questions concerning labor contracts or rental agreements pegged to the Consumer Price Index. Of course, this compiled information will come in handy, too, for settling everyday arguments about the cost of living.

Every public library receives requests about the distance from the local community to other cities. It is helpful to compile a table for easy consultation which can be housed in your special reference files. In making such a table for your city, you can determine the distance to many communities by employing the guide prepared by the Household Goods Carriers' Bureau (131). This list is used by most moving companies. To establish the distance to smaller communities, you can check the official road maps of your state and neighboring states. These maps usually contain charts showing mileage between the cities and towns within a state.

Another indispensable reference folder is one which gives information about the service patterns of nearby libraries. Such a folder should cover hours, special resources, and requirements for service.

IN CONCLUSION

This paragraph is both an ending and a beginning. The ten chapters just concluded have pictured the exciting role which supplementary resources can play in library service. These chapters have also explored the practical aspects of acquiring and managing these resources. My hope is that you've garnered enough enthusiasm and know-how to make these informational aids a vital part of *your* library program. It's your turn now to experience the challenge, the fun, and the rewards offered by the vertical file and its satellites.

LIST OF REFERENCES

(1) Abbey Press, St. Meinrad, IN 47577.

(2) **Agenda.** Monthly. Press and Publications Division, Office of Public Affairs, Agency for International Development, Washington, DC 20523. Free.

(3) Agricultural Stabilization and Conservation Service, U.S. Dept. of Agriculture, 2222 West, 2300 South, P.O. Box 30010, Salt Lake City, UT 84125.

(4) Aluminum Association, Inc., 818 Connecticut Ave., N.W., Washington, DC 20006.

(5) American Association for State and Local History. **Directory of Historical Societies and Agencies in the United States and Canada.** 10th ed., 1975. American Association for State and Local History, 1400 Eighth Ave., South, Nashville, TN 37203. $20.00. New edition in preparation.

(6) American Association for the Advancement of Science Reprint Sales, Dept. ML, 1515 Massachusetts Ave., N.W., Washington, DC 20005.

(7) American Association of Petroleum Geologists, P.O. Box 979, Tulsa, OK 74101.

(8) American Bar Association, Special Committee on Youth Education for Citizenship. **Bibliography of Law-Related Curriculum Materials: Annotated.** 2nd ed., 1976. American Bar Association, Special Committee on Youth Education for Citizenship, 1155 E. 60th St., Chicago, IL 60637. $1.00.

(9) American Classical League, Miami University, Oxford, OH 45056.

(10) American Forest Institute, 1619 Massachusetts Ave., N.W., Washington, DC 20036.

(11) American Humane Association, P.O. Box 1266, Denver, CO 80201.

(12) American Map Company, Inc., 1926 Broadway, New York, NY 10023.

(13) American Music Conference. **Music USA**. Issued annually. American Music Conference, 1000 Skokie Blvd., Wilmette, IL 60091. Free.

(14) American Paper Institute, Inc., 260 Madison Ave., New York, NY 10016.

(15) American Quarter Horse Association, 2736 W. Tenth St., Amarillo, TX 79168.

(16) **American Trade Schools Directory**. Croner Publications, Inc., 211-05 Jamaica Ave., Queens Village, NY 11428. Yearly fee, $25.00, plus $2.95 postage and handling charge.

(17) **Aramco World Magazine**. Bimonthly. Aramco Services Co., Attn: S. W. Kombargi, 1100 Milam, Houston, TX 77002. Free.

(18) Argus Communications, 7440 Natchez Ave., Niles, IL 60648.

(19) Arrow Publishing Company, Inc., P.O. Box 115, Newton Upper Falls, MA 02164.

(20) Art Institute of Chicago, The Museum Store, Michigan Ave. at Adams St., Chicago, IL 60603.

(21) Artext Prints, Inc., Box 70, Westport, CT 06880.

(22) Assistant Director for Preservation, Administrative Department, Library of Congress, Washington, DC 20540.

(23) Association of Independent Colleges and Schools, Suite 401, 1730 M St., N.W., Washington, DC 20036.

(24) Aubrey, Ruth H. **Selected Free Materials for Classroom Teachers**. 6th ed., 1978. Fearon-Pitman Publishers, Inc., 6 Davis Dr., Belmont, CA 94002. $4.50.

(25) **Automobile Quarterly**. 245 W. Main St., Kutztown, PA 19530.

(26) **Background Notes**. U.S. Dept. of State. Approximately 77 revised or new **Notes** each year. For sale by the Superintendent of Documents. $0.70

each. Set of all **Background Notes** currently in stock, $31.00. Annual subscription, $31.00.

(27) Bacon Pamphlet Service, Inc., East Chatham, NY 12060.

(28) Ball, Miriam Ogden. **Subject Headings for the Information File.** 8th ed., 1956. H. W. Wilson Co. Out-of-print.

(29) Bates Manufacturing Co., Newburgh Rd., Hackettstown, NJ 07840.

(30) Bennett, Wilma. **Occupations Filing Plan and Bibliography.** 3rd ed., 1968. Interstate Printers and Publishers, Inc., 19-27 N. Jackson St., Danville, IL 61832. Book, $3.95. Book plus labels, $14.95.

(31) B'nai B'rith Career and Counseling Services, 1640 Rhode Island Ave., N.W., Washington, DC 20036.

Counselor's Information Service. Quarterly. $11.00 per year.

Occupational Brief Series. $1.00 to $1.50 each.

(32) Brown, Lloyd A. "The Problem of Maps." In **Readings in Nonbook Librarianship**, edited by Jean Spealman Kujoth, Scarecrow Press, Inc., 1968, page 269. This article appeared first in **Library Trends**, October 1964.

(33) Bureau of Engraving and Printing, Office Services Branch, U.S. Dept. of the Treasury, Washington, DC 20228.

(34) Bureau of Indian Affairs, U.S. Dept. of the Interior. **American Indian Calendar.** Published annually. For sale by the Superintendent of Documents. 1978 ed., $2.20.

(35) Bureau of Labor Statistics, U.S. Dept. of Labor, Washington, DC 20212.

Education and Job Leaflets. Series of five. Free from BLS regional offices.

Occupational Outlook Handbook. Published every other year. For sale by the Superintendent of Documents. Price of 1978-79 ed., $11.00 clothbound, and $8.00 paperback.

(35) Bureau of Labor Statistics, U.S. Dept. of Labor (cont'd)

> Reprints from **Occupational Outlook Handbook**. For sale by the Superintendent of Documents and BLS regional offices. Reprints from 1978-79 ed., $0.50 each. $8.00 for full set of 42 reprints.

> **Occupational Outlook Quarterly**. For sale by the Superintendent of Documents. $4.00 per year.

> Reprints from **Occupational Outlook Quarterly**. Free from BLS regional offices.

(36) Bureau of Land Management, U.S. Dept. of the Interior, Washington, DC 20240.

(37) Bureau of Mines, U.S. Dept. of the Interior. **Mining and Mineral Operations: Visitor Guides**. For sale by the Superintendent of Documents.

> **New England and Mid-Atlantic States**. 1976. $2.30.

> **North-Central States**. 1977. $3.25.

> **Pacific States**. 1976. $2.15.

> **Rocky Mountain States**. 1977. $2.40.

> **South Atlantic States**. 1976. $2.70.

> **South-Central States**. 1977. $4.75.

(38) Bureau of Outdoor Recreation, U.S. Dept. of the Interior. **A Catalog of Guides to Outdoor Recreation Areas and Facilities**. 1977. Single copy free from Office of Communication, Bureau of Outdoor Recreation, U.S. Dept. of the Interior, Washington, DC 20240.

(39) Bureau of Reclamation, U.S. Dept. of the Interior, Engineering and Research Center, P.O. Box 25007, Denver Federal Center, Denver, CO 80225.

(40) Bureau of the Census, U.S. Dept. of Commerce, Washington, DC 20233.

(41) Alvah Bushnell Co., 1315 Cherry St., Philadelphia, PA 19107.

(42) **Business in Brief**. Bimonthly. Economics Group, Chase Manhattan Bank, N.A., 1 Chase Manhattan Plaza, New York, NY 10015. Free.

(43) **Business Service Checklist.** Biweekly. U.S. Dept. of Commerce. For sale by the Superintendent of Documents. $9.00 per year. (Replaced in January 1979 by **Recent Commerce Publications.** Biweekly. Contact Gloria Fioravanti, Room 1411, U.S. Dept. of Commerce, Washington, DC 20230. Free to libraries that send a supply of stamped, self-addressed envelopes.)

(44) Canada Map Office, Dept. of Energy, Mines and Resources, 615 Booth St., Ottawa, Ontario, Canada K1A 0E9.

(45) **Canada Today/D'Aujourd'hui.** 10 issues a year. Canadian Embassy, 1771 N St., N.W., Room 300, Washington, DC 20036. Free.

(46) Canadian Government Dept. of External Affairs. **Publications Available Outside Canada.** Canadian Government Dept. of External Affairs, Lester B. Pearson Building, 125 Sussex Dr., P.O. Box 500, Ottawa, Ontario, Canada K1A 0G2. Free.

(47) Canadian Government Office of Tourism, 235 Queen St., Ottawa, Ontario, Canada K1A 0H6.

(48) Caplan, Frank, ed. **Parents' Yellow Pages.** By the Princeton Center for Infancy. 1978. Anchor Press/Doubleday. $7.95.

(49) Careers, Inc., P.O. Box 135, 1211 10th St., S.W., Largo, FL 33540.

Career Guidance Index. 8 issues a year. $7.25 per year.

Career Briefs. Single copies, $0.50. Complete set, $53.00. Annual subscription, $18.00.

Career Summaries. Single copies, $0.35. Complete set, $53.00. Annual subscription, $18.00.

Job Guides. Single copies, $0.35. Complete set, $16.00. Annual subscription, $3.75.

Career Reprints. Annual subscription, $3.50.

(50) **Carolina Tips.** Monthly. Carolina Biological Supply Co., 2700 York Rd., Burlington, NC 27215. Free.

(51) Cartographic Archives Division, National Archives and Records Service, General Services Administration, Washington, DC 20408.

(52) Catalyst. Booklets on careers, education, and self-guidance for women, ranging in price from $1.50 to $1.95. Write for publications list to Catalyst, 14 E. 60th St., New York, NY 10022.

(53) Changing Times Education Service, 1729 H St., N.W., Washington, DC 20006.

(54) **Chases' Calendar of Annual Events, Special Days, Weeks and Months.** Published annually. Apple Tree Press, Inc., Box 1012, Flint, MI 48501. 1979 ed., $7.95.

(55) Christianson, Elin B. "Variation of Editorial Material in Periodicals Indexed in *Readers' Guide*." **ALA Bulletin**, February 1968, pages 173-182.

(56) Chronicle Guidance Publications, Inc., Moravia, NY 13118.

> **Chronicle Career Index.** Published annually. Price of 1977-1978 ed., $10.00.

> **Chronicle Occupational Briefs.** Single copies, $1.00. Complete set, $120.00. Annual subscription, $40.00.

> **Chronicle Occupational Reprints.** Single copies, $1.00. Complete set, $25.00. Annual subscription, $12.00.

> **Filing Plan.** About 290 labeled folders, $50.00. 93 coordinated hanging folders, $75.00. Filing plan guide, $2.00.

(57) **College Blue Book: Occupational Education.** 3rd ed., 1977. Macmillan Information, A Division of Macmillan Publishing Co., Inc., New York, NY. $35.00.

(58) Committee on the Preservation of Library Materials, Resources and Technical Services Division, American Library Association, 50 E. Huron St., Chicago, IL 60611.

(59) **Congressional Directory.** U.S. Congress. For sale by the Superintendent of Documents. Price of 1977 ed., $8.50.

(60) Consumer Information Center, Pueblo, CO 81009.

Consumer Information Catalog: A Catalog of Selected Federal Publications of Consumer Interest. Issued quarterly. Free.

Lista de Publicaciones Federales en Español para el Consumidor. Issued annually. Free.

(61) **Consumer News.** Semimonthly. U.S. Office of Consumer Affairs. For sale by Consumer Information Center, Pueblo, CO 81009. $6.00 per year. Make check or money order payable to Superintendent of Documents.

(62) **Consumers Guide to Federal Publications.** Superintendent of Documents, U.S. Government Printing Office, Washington, DC 20402. Free.

(63) David C. Cook Publishing Co., 850 N. Grove, Elgin, IL 60120.

(64) Corps of Engineers, U.S. Dept. of the Army, The Pentagon, Washington, DC 20310.

(65) Craft Course Publishers, Inc., P.O. Box 280, Rosemead, CA 91770.

(66) George F. Cram Co., Inc., 301 S. LaSalle St., P.O. Box 426, Indianapolis, IN 46206.

(67) **Cumulative Index to Nursing & Allied Health Literature.** P.O. Box 871, Glendale, CA 91209. Five issues per year plus an annual cumulation which includes a list of subject headings. Yearly subscription, $45.00. **CINAHL's Subject Heading List** is also available separately for $1.00. Include mailing label.

(68) Cunha, George Martin, and Dorothy Grant Cunha. **Conservation of Library Materials.** Volume I. Rev. ed., 1971. Scarecrow Press, Inc., page 107.

(69) **Current Contents.** Six editions (plus two more scheduled for 1979). Weekly. Subscription to each edition, $135.00 per year.

(70) Daily Racing Form, Inc. **Survey on Sports Attendance.** Issued annually. Daily Racing Form, Inc., 10 Lake Dr., Hightstown, NJ 08520. Free.

(71) **Daisy**. 9 issues per year. **Daisy** Subscription Services, P.O. Box 2466, Boulder, CO 80302. $5.95.

(72) Dane, William J. **The Picture Collection: Subject Headings**. 6th ed., 1968. Shoe String Press, Inc. $6.00.

(73) Defense Mapping Agency, Office of Distribution Services, Washington, DC 20315.

(74) Demco Educational Corp., Box 7488, Madison, WI 53707.

(75) Denoyer-Geppert, 5235 Ravenswood Ave., Chicago, IL 60640.

(76) Detroit Institute of Arts, Museum Shops, 5200 Woodward Ave., Detroit, MI 48202.

(77) Dolph Map Co., Inc., 430 North Federal Highway, Fort Lauderdale, FL 33301.

(78) Dow Jones & Company, Inc. **List of Free Materials Available to Educators**. Revised annually. Dow Jones & Company, Inc., Educational Service Bureau, P.O. Box 300, Princeton, NJ 08540. Single copy free to librarians in secondary schools, colleges, and universities.

(79) Eastman Kodak Company. **Index to Kodak Information**. Revised annually. Eastman Kodak Company, Dept. 454, 343 State St., Rochester, NY 14650. $0.25. Inquire about complimentary copies for libraries.

(80) Eastman Kodak Company, Professional and Finishing Markets Division, Rochester, NY 14650.

(81) **Editorial Research Reports**. Congressional Quarterly, Inc. 48 reports each year. Congressional Quarterly, Inc., 1414 22nd St., N.W., Washington, DC 20037. $2.75 each. Annual subscription including semiannual bound compilations, $141.00 to $240.00, depending upon type of library.

(82) Educators Progress Service, Inc., 214 Center St., Randolph, WI 53956.

Educators Guide to Free Guidance Materials. Revised annually. 1978 ed., $13.00, plus $0.95 mailing charge.

(82) Educators Progress Service, Inc. (cont'd)

Educators Guide to Free Health, Physical Education and Recreation Materials. Revised annually. 1978 ed., $13.50, plus $0.95 mailing charge.

Educators Guide to Free Science Materials. Revised annually. 1978 ed., $12.75, plus $0.95 mailing charge.

Educators Guide to Free Social Studies Materials. Revised annually. 1978 ed., $13.75, plus $0.95 mailing charge.

Elementary Teachers Guide to Free Curriculum Materials. Revised annually. 1978 ed., $12.50, plus $0.95 mailing charge.

(83) Encyclopaedia Britannica Educational Corporation, 425 N. Michigan Ave., Chicago, IL 60611.

(84) **Encyclopedia of Associations.** (v.1 **National Organizations of the United States**, v.2 **Geographic and Executive Index**, v.3 **New Associations and Projects**), 12th ed., 1978. Gale Research Co., Book Tower, Detroit, MI 48226. v.1, $75.00; v.2, $55.00; v.3, $65.00.

(85) **Encyclopedia of Careers and Vocational Guidance.** 4th ed., 1978. J. G. Ferguson Publishing Company, 111 E. Wacker Dr., Chicago, IL 60601. $49.95. Distributed by Doubleday & Company, Inc.

(86) **Energy & Education.** Bimonthly during academic year. National Science Teachers Association, 1742 Connecticut Ave., N.W., Washington, DC 20009. Free under present federal grant. Subscription fee may be charged in the future.

(87) **Energy Insider.** Biweekly. Editorial Services Division, Office of Public Affairs, U.S. Dept. of Energy, Washington, DC 20545. Free.

(88) **Family Economics Review.** Quarterly. Consumer and Food Economics Institute, Science and Education Administration, U.S. Dept. of Agriculture, Federal Building 325A, Hyattsville, MD 20782. Free.

(89) Fidelity Products Co., 705 Pennsylvania Ave. So., Minneapolis, MN 55426.

(90) **Field Museum of Natural History Bulletin.** Monthly except combined July-August issue. Field Museum of Natural History, Roosevelt Rd. at

(90) **Field Museum of Natural History Bulletin** (cont'd)

Lake Shore Dr., Chicago, IL 60605. $6.00 per year. $3.00 to schools. Free to members.

(91) **Fieldstaff Reports.** American Universities Field Staff, Inc. 50 reports each year. American Universities Field Staff, Inc., The Wheelock House, P.O. Box 150, Hanover, NH 03755. $1.50 each. Annual subscription for full set of reports, $50.00. Area subscriptions available for Asia, Africa, North and South America, and Europe.

(92) **First Chicago World Report.** Bimonthly. Business and Economic Research Division, First National Bank of Chicago, 1 First National Plaza, Chicago, IL 60670. Free.

(93) Food and Drug Administration, Office of Public Affairs, 5600 Fishers Lane, Rockville, MD 20857.

(94) Ford Motor Company, Educational Affairs Dept., The American Road, Dearborn, MI 48121.

(95) Forest Service, U.S. Dept. of Agriculture, Washington, DC 20250.

(96) Frances Press, Publishers, P.O. Box 821, Greenwich, CT 06830.

Gratis en Español!–Guide to Free Informational Materials in Spanish. 1978. $2.50.

Where to Get Hundreds of Educational Materials–Free! 2nd ed., 1975. $2.00. New edition planned for early in 1979.

(97) W. H. Freeman and Company, 660 Market St., San Francisco, CA 94104.

(98) Freer Gallery of Art, Smithsonian Institution, Washington, DC 20560. Charge of $1.00 for sales catalog.

(99) **GPO Sales Publications Reference File.** Bimonthly. Superintendent of Documents, U.S. Government Printing Office, Washington, DC 20402. $50.00 per year. Supplemented by **GPO Sales Publications Reference File–Update.** Bimonthly in alternate months. Superintendent of Documents. $5.00 per year.

(100) Gale Research Company, Book Tower, Detroit, MI 48226.

(101) Gane Brothers & Lane, Inc., 1400 Greenleaf Ave., Elk Grove Village, IL 60007.

(102) Garoogian, Andrew. "Freebie Cards Get Free Documents." **Unabashed Librarian**, No. 11, Spring 1974, page 29.

(103) General Aviation Manufacturers Association. **General Aviation Educational Materials**. Revised annually. General Aviation Manufacturers Association, Suite 1215, 1025 Connecticut Ave., N.W., Washington, DC 20036. Free.

(104) Geographia Map Co., Inc., P.O. Box 688, Times Square Station, New York, NY 10036.

(105) Geography and Map Division, Library of Congress, Washington, DC 20540.

(106) George Peabody College for Teachers, Office of Educational Services. **Free and Inexpensive Learning Materials**. 19th ed., 1979. Distributed by Incentive Publications, Inc., P.O. Box 120189, Nashville, TN 37212. $4.50, plus $1.00 for shipping and handling.

(107) Giant Photos, Inc., Box 406, Rockford, IL 61105.

(108) Giganti, Carl J. "Pictures in a Small Library." **Wilson Library Bulletin**, November 1940, page 227.

(109) Gilbert, Karen Diane. **Picture Indexing for Local History Materials**. 1973. Library Research Associates, Dunderberg Rd., Monroe, NY 10950. $2.45.

(110) Goodman, Leonard H. **Current Career and Occupational Literature: 1973-1977**. 1978. H. W. Wilson Company. $10.00.

(111) Goodman, Leonard H., and Anne E. Garrett. **A "Starter" File of Free Occupational Literature**. 2nd ed., 1975. B'nai B'rith Career and Counseling Services, 1640 Rhode Island Ave., N.W., Washington, DC 20036. $2.00.

(112) Gotsick, Priscilla, and others. **Information for Everyday Survival: What You Need and Where to Get It.** 1976. American Library Association. $10.00.

(113) Gould, Geraldine N., and Ithmer C. Wolfe. **How to Organize and Maintain the Library Picture/Pamphlet File.** 1968. Oceana Publications, Inc. $5.95.

(114) Greenfield, Stanley. **National Directory of Addresses and Telephone Numbers.** 1977. Bantam Books, Inc. $9.95.

(115) Guidance Centre, Faculty of Education, University of Toronto, 1000 Yonge St., Toronto, Ontario, Canada M4W 2K8.

(116) Hagstrom Company, Inc., 450 West 33rd St., New York, NY 10001.

(117) Hammond Incorporated, Maplewood, NJ 07040.

(118) Haring, Jacqueline. "The College Arrangement." **Illinois Libraries,** March 1975, pages 226-230.

(119) Haycock, Ken. **Free Magazines for Teachers and Libraries.** 2nd ed., 1977. Ontario Library Association, 2397 A Bloor St., W., Toronto, Ontario, Canada M6S 1P6. $7.50.

(120) **Headline Focus Wall Maps.** Published biweekly during the school year (18 issues). Headline Focus Wall Map, Scholastic Magazines, Inc., 902 Sylvan Ave., Englewood Cliffs, NJ 07632. $36.00 per school year.

(121) Health Insurance Institute. **Health Education Materials and the Organizations Which Offer Them.** Revised edition to be published in 1979. Health Insurance Institute, 1850 K St., N.W., Washington, DC 20006. Free.

(122) **Health Tips,** 731 Market St., San Francisco, CA 94103. Prepared by California Medical Association. Published by California Medical Education and Research Foundation. New titles sent free to libraries on mailing list. For prices and titles of back issues, request copy of **Health Tips Index.**

(123) Hearne Brothers, 25th Floor, First National Building, Detroit, MI 48226.

(124) Hennepin County Library, Technical Services Division, 7001 York Ave. South, Edina, MN 55435.

    HCL Cataloging Bulletin. Bimonthly. $12.00 per year.

    Hennepin County Library Authority File (microfiche). Yearly subscription to four cumulations, $30.00. Single cumulation, $7.50.

(125) Hershey Foods Corporation, Park Blvd., Hershey, PA 17033.

(126) Highsmith Co., Inc., P.O. Box 25A, Highway 106 East, Fort Atkinson, WI 53538.

(127) Hill, Donna. **Picture File: A Manual and a Curriculum-Related Subject Heading List**. 2nd ed., 1978. Shoe String Press, Inc. (Linnet Books). $12.00.

(128) Hillsdale Educational Publishers, Inc., P.O. Box 245, Hillsdale, MI 49242.

(129) Hollinger Corporation, P.O. Box 6185, 3810 South Four Mile Run Dr., Arlington, VA 22206.

(130) **Hospital Literature Index**. Quarterly, with annual cumulation in fourth issue. American Hospital Association, 840 N. Lake Shore Dr., Chicago, IL 60611. $60.00 per year.

(131) Household Goods Carriers' Bureau. **Complete Listing of the Mileage Chart Section of Mileage Guide No. 11: Specific Mileages Between Key Point Cities**. Household Goods Carriers' Bureau, 2425 Wilson Blvd., Arlington, VA 22201. Price of 1978 ed., $39.50.

(132) **Information Bulletin**. Issued 3 times a year. Western Association of Map Libraries, c/o Stanley D. Stevens, University Library, University of California, Santa Cruz, CA 95064. Free with $10.00 membership.

(133) Institute for Research. **Careers Research Monographs**. Institute for Research, 610 S. Federal St., Office 703, Chicago, IL 60605. $5.75 for group of five monographs. $1.15 for individual titles. Continuation order available for new monographs.

(134) **Internal Publications Directory (Volume 5, Working Press of the Nation).** Published annually. National Research Bureau, Inc., 424 N. Third St., Burlington, IA 52601. 1978 ed., $48.00.

(135) **International Nursing Index.** Quarterly with annual cumulation in fourth issue. International Nursing Index, 10 Columbus Circle, New York, NY 10019. $50.00 per year.

(136) Ireland, Norma O. **Pamphlet File in School, College, and Public Libraries.** Rev. ed., 1954. F. W. Faxon Company, Inc. $9.00.

(137) Katz, Bill, and Berry G. Richards. **Magazines for Libraries.** 3rd ed., 1978. R. R. Bowker Company. $37.50.

(138) **LC Science Tracer Bullets.** Reference Section, Science and Technology Division, Library of Congress, 10 First St., S.E., Washington, DC 20540. Free. Requests must be by title. A list of available titles may be obtained from the Reference Section.

(139) **Lamp.** Quarterly. Exxon Corporation, 1251 Avenue of the Americas, New York, NY 10020. Free.

(140) Larousse & Co., Inc., 572 Fifth Ave., New York, NY 10036.

(141) League of Women Voters of the United States, 1730 M St., N.W., Washington, DC 20036.

(142) LeGear, Clara Egli. **Maps: Their Care, Repair, and Preservation in Libraries.** Rev. ed., 1956. Library of Congress. Electrostatic print (OP 62012) available from University Microfilms for $10.50.

(143) Library of Congress. **Free and Inexpensive Materials: A Selected List of Guides to Sources (GR & B Series, No. 3).** Rev. ed., 1977. Library of Congress, General Reference and Bibliography Division, Washington, DC 20540. Free.

(144) Library Reference Service, Box 128, Barnesville, MN 56514.

(145) **Mademoiselle.** Career and college reprints. **Mademoiselle,** Box 3389, Grand Central Station, New York, NY 10017. $0.50 each.

(146) The Malaysian Rubber Bureau, 1925 K St., N.W., Washington, DC 20006.

(147) **Man and Molecules**, P.O. Box 19210, Washington, DC 20036. Transcripts available free.

(148) Man-Made Fiber Producers Association, Inc. **Man-Made Fibers Fact Book.** 1978. Education Department, Man-Made Fiber Producers Association, Inc., 1150 Seventeenth St., N.W., Washington, DC 20036. $1.00. Inquire about a complimentary copy.

(149) **Marketing Information Guide.** Bimonthly. 224 Seventh St., Garden City, NY 11530. $12.00.

(150) Massachusetts Department of Public Health. **Sources of Free and Inexpensive Health Education Aids.** 1978. Massachusetts Department of Public Health, Division of Preventive Medicine, Office of Health Education, 600 Washington St., Boston, MA 02111. Single copy free.

(151) **Media Monitor.** 4 issues a year. Informedia, P.O. Box 1020, Pearl River, NY 10965. $10.00 per year prepaid, $11.50 with purchase order. Single issues, $2.50 each prepaid, $2.90 if billed.

(152) **Meet the Press.** Kelly Press, Inc., P.O. Box 8648, Washington, DC 20011. $0.50 plus stamped, self-addressed envelope. Yearly subscription, $23.40.

(153) Mental Health Materials Center, Inc. **Selective Guide to Materials for Mental Health and Family Life Education.** 3rd ed., 1976. Distributed by Gale Research Company. $65.00. New edition projected for 1979 will be issued in two parts, one for audiovisual materials and one for printed materials. Distribution will be by Marquis Who's Who. For details, contact Mental Health Materials Center, Inc., 419 Park Ave. South, New York, NY 10016.

(154) **Mental Health Matters.** Sponsored by the Alcohol, Drug Abuse, and Mental Health Administration. Single copies free from National Institute of Mental Health, 5600 Fishers Lane, Rockville, MD 20857.

(155) Metro Graphic Arts, Incorporated, P.O. Box 7035, Grand Rapids, MI 49510.

(156) Metropolitan Life Insurance Company. **Catalog: Health and Safety Educa-tional Materials.** 1978. Health and Safety Education Division, Metro-politan Life Insurance Company, One Madison Ave., New York, NY 10010. Free.

(157) Metropolitan Museum of Art, Box 255, Gracie Station, New York, NY 10028.

(158) **Metropolitan Museum of Art Bulletin.** Quarterly. Metropolitan Museum of Art, Fifth Ave. and 82nd St., New York, NY 10028. $11.50 per year. Free to members.

(159) Michelin Guides and Maps, P.O. Box 5022, New Hyde Park, NY 11040.

(160) Monahan, Robert. **Free and Inexpensive Materials for Preschool and Early Childhood.** 2nd ed., 1977. Fearon-Pitman Publishers, Inc., 6 Davis Dr., Belmont, CA 94002. $4.50.

(161) **Money Management Booklets.** Money Management Institute, Household Finance Corporation, Prudential Plaza, Chicago, IL 60601. $0.50 each. Set of 12 booklets, $5.00.

(162) **Monthly Catalog of United States Government Publications.** Superintendent of Documents, U.S. Government Printing Office, Washington, DC 20402. $45.00 per year.

(163) **Monthly Checklist of State Publications.** Library of Congress. For sale by the Superintendent of Documents. $21.90 per year.

(164) **Monthly Economic Letter.** Economics Dept., Citibank, 399 Park Ave., New York, NY 10022. Free.

(165) Morgan Guaranty Trust Company of New York. **World Calendar of Holidays.** Published annually. Morgan Guaranty Trust Company of New York, 23 Wall St., New York, NY 10015. Single copies free to libraries.

(166) Murphy, Patricia Lee. **A Treasury of Free Cookbooks.** 1978. Avon Books. $1.50.

(167) **NASA Report to Educators.** Quarterly. National Aeronautics and Space Administration, Washington, DC 20546. Free.

(168) National Archives and Records Service, General Services Administration, Washington, DC 20408.

(169) National Association of Trade and Technical Schools, 2021 L St., N.W., Washington, DC 20036.

(170) National Audubon Society, Educational Services, 950 Third Ave., New York, NY 10022.

(171) National Cartographic Information Center, U.S. Geological Survey, 507 National Center, Reston, VA 22092.

(172) National Center for Health Statistics, Health Resources Administration, Public Health Service, U.S. Dept. of Health, Education, and Welfare, Hyattsville, MD 20782.

Where to Write for Birth and Death Records of U.S. Citizens Who Were Born or Died Outside of the United States and Birth Certifications for Alien Children Adopted by U.S. Citizens. 1977. Single copy free.

Where to Write for Birth and Death Records, United States and Outlying Areas. 1976. Single copy free.

Where to Write for Divorce Records, United States and Outlying Areas. 1976. Single copy free.

Where to Write for Marriage Records, United States and Outlying Areas. 1976. Single copy free.

(173) National Cotton Council of America, P.O. Box 12285, Memphis, TN 38112.

(174) National Dairy Council, 6300 N. River Rd., Rosemont, IL 60018.

(175) National Forest Products Association. **Lumber and Wood Products Literature.** 1978. National Forest Products Association, Technical Services Division, 1619 Massachusetts Ave., N.W., Washington, DC 20036. Single copy free.

(176) National Gallery of Art, Publications Service, Washington, DC 20565.

(177) National Gallery of Canada. A listing of its publications is found in the **Publications Catalogue,** National Museums of Canada, Marketing

(177) National Gallery of Canada (cont'd)

> Services Division, Ottawa, Ontario, Canada K1A 0M8. Price of catalog, $1.00, plus $0.20 shipping charge outside Canada.

(178) **National Geographic World.** Monthly. **National Geographic World**, Dept. 00378, 17th and M Sts., N.W., Washington, DC 20036. $5.85.

(179) National Health Council, Inc. **200 Ways to Put Your Talent to Work in the Health Field.** Revised periodically. Latest edition March 1977. National Health Council, Inc., Box 40, Radio City Station, New York, NY 10019. Single copy free.

(180) National Home Study Council, 1601 Eighteenth St., N.W., Washington, DC 20009.

(181) National Library of Medicine. **Medical Subject Headings.** Published annually. Appears as Part 2 of the January **Index Medicus.** Also available separately for $8.00 from the Superintendent of Documents, U.S. Government Printing Office, Washington, DC 20402.

(182) National Ocean Survey, Distribution Division (C44), Riverdale, MD 20840.

(183) National Park Service, U.S. Dept. of the Interior, Washington, DC 20240.

> **National Park Service Sales Publications.** Free from National Park Service.

> **Index of the National Park System and Affiliated Areas.** For sale by the Superintendent of Documents. Price of 1977 ed., $2.30.

(184) National Safety Council, 444 N. Michigan Ave., Chicago, IL 60611.

(185) National Science Teachers Association. **Keys to Careers in Science and Technology.** 1973. National Science Teachers Association, 1742 Connecticut Ave., N.W., Washington, DC 20009. $1.00.

(186) National Vocational Guidance Association.

> **NVGA Bibliography of Current Career Information.** 7th ed., 1978. American Personnel and Guidance Association, Publications Sales, 1607 New Hampshire Ave., N.W., Washington, DC 20009. $3.50.

(186) National Vocational Guidance Association (cont'd)

        Vocational Guidance Quarterly. American Personnel and Guidance Association, Subscription Dept., 1607 New Hampshire Ave., N.W., Washington, DC 20009. $10.00 per year.

(187) National Wildlife Federation. **Conservation Directory**. Revised annually. National Wildlife Federation, 1412 16th St., N.W., Washington, DC 20036. Price of 1978 ed., $3.00.

(188) **New Publications—Bureau of Mines**. Monthly. Publications Distribution Branch, Bureau of Mines, U.S. Dept. of the Interior, 4800 Forbes Ave., Pittsburgh, PA 15213. Free.

(189) **New Publications of the Geological Survey**. Monthly. Geological Survey, U.S. Dept. of the Interior, 329 National Center, Reston, VA 22092. Free.

(190) New Readers Press, Division of Laubach Literacy International, P.O. Box 131, Syracuse, NY 13210.

(191) New York Life Insurance Company, "Careers," Box 51, Madison Square Station, New York, NY 10010.

(192) Nystrom, 3333 N. Elston Ave., Chicago, IL 60618.

(193) **Occupations in Demand at Job Service Offices**. Monthly. U.S. Employment Service, Employment and Training Administration, U.S. Dept. of Labor. Single copy free from Consumer Information Center, Dept. 39, Pueblo, CO 81009.

(194) Office for Handicapped Individuals, U.S. Dept. of Health, Education, and Welfare. **Selected Federal Publications Concerning the Handicapped**. 3rd ed., 1978. Single copy free from Clearinghouse on the Handicapped, Office for Handicapped Individuals, U.S. Dept. of Health, Education, and Welfare, Washington, DC 20201. Also for sale by the Superintendent of Documents for $2.40.

(195) Old Sturbridge Village, Publications Dept., Sturbridge, MA 01566.

(196) Oxford Pendaflex Corporation, Clinton Rd., Garden City, NY 11530.

(197) Pacific Area Travel Association. **Events in the Pacific.** Published annually. Pacific Area Travel Association, 228 Grant Ave., San Francisco, CA 94108. Free.

(198) **Panhandle Magazine.** Quarterly. **Panhandle Magazine,** P.O. Box 1642, Houston, TX 77001. Free.

(199) Perfection Form Company, 1000 N. Second Ave., Logan, IA 51546.

(200) Pharmaceutical Manufacturers Association. **Health Care and the Consumer: A Guide to Informational Materials.** 1978. Pharmaceutical Manufacturers Association, 1155 Fifteenth St., N.W., Washington, DC 20005. Single copy free.

(201) **Physical Protection of Brittle and Deteriorating Documents by Polyester Encasement.** Assistant Director for Preservation, Administrative Dept., Library of Congress, Washington, DC 20540. Free.

(202) Population Reference Bureau, Inc. **PRB Chart Series.** Population Reference Bureau, Inc., 1337 Connecticut Ave., N.W., Washington, DC 20036. Send for price list for details.

(203) **Port Guides.** Price range, $2.58 to $3.04.

For list of titles and prices, contact Human Resource Management Division, Bureau of Naval Personnel, Dept. of the Navy, Washington, DC 20370.

To order, send check or money order payable to U.S. Treasury to Commanding Officer, Naval Publications and Forms Center, Attn: CASH SALES, 5801 Tabor Ave., Philadelphia, PA 19120.

(204) **Preservation Leaflets.** Library of Congress, Attn: Assistant Director for Preservation, Administrative Dept., Washington, DC 20540. Free.

(205) **Public Affairs Pamphlets.** Public Affairs Committee, Inc. About 15 titles each year. Public Affairs Pamphlets, 381 Park Ave., South, New York, NY 10016. $0.50 each. Subscription to 15 issues, $5.50.

(206) Rand McNally & Company, P.O. Box 7600, Chicago, IL 60680.

(207) Resources for the Future, Inc., 1755 Massachusetts Ave., N.W., Washington, DC 20036.

(208) Robert Morris Associates. **Sources of Composite Financial Data—A Bibliography.** Published annually. Robert Morris Associates, Philadelphia National Bank Building, Philadelphia, PA 19107. $3.00, plus $0.50 for postage and handling.

(209) **Royal Bank of Canada Monthly Letter.** Monthly Letter Dept., Royal Bank of Canada, Box 6001, Montreal, Quebec, Canada H3C 3A9. Free.

(210) **Science Editor.** University of California, Radio Office, Los Angeles, CA 90024. Subscription to transcripts, $10.00 per year.

(211) Science Research Associates, Inc., 259 East Erie St., Chicago, IL 60611.

SRA Occupational Briefs. Complete set, $136.00. Annual subscription, $41.50. For price of individual briefs, contact SRA.

WORK Briefs. Complete set, $138.50. For price of individual briefs, contact SRA.

Occupational filing plan. Set of 212 labeled file folders, $44.50. Index, $1.20.

(212) Seal, Incorporated, 550 Spring St., Naugatuck, CT 06770.

(213) Seal-O-Matic Corporation, 272 Sussex Ave., Newark, NJ 07107.

(214) **Sears List of Subject Headings.** 11th ed., 1977. H. W. Wilson Company. $18.00.

(215) **Selected Titles: Government of Canada Publications.** Issued three times a year. Supply and Services Canada, Canadian Government Publishing Centre, Hull, Quebec, Canada K1A 0S9. Free.

(216) **Selected U.S. Government Publications.** 11 issues a year. Superintendent of Documents, U.S. Government Printing Office, Washington, DC 20402. Free.

(217) Shaffer, Dale E., 437 Jennings Ave., Salem, OH 44460.

    Career Education Pamphlets. 1976. $3.95.

    Library Picture File: A Complete System of How to Process and Organize. 1972. $1.00.

    Pamphlet Library: Use of the Sha-Frame System. 1972. $1.00.

    Posters for Teachers and Librarians. 1978. $3.50.

(218) Sive, Mary Robinson. **Selecting Instructional Media: A Guide to Audiovisual and Other Instructional Media Lists.** 1978. Libraries Unlimited, Inc. $13.50.

(219) **Small Business Reporter.** Issued irregularly. Small Business Reporter, Bank of America, P.O. Box 37000, San Francisco, CA 94137. Single issues, $2.00. Subscription to eight future issues, $10.00.

(220) Society for Visual Education, Inc., 1345 Diversey Parkway, Chicago, IL 60614.

(221) Soil Conservation Service, U.S. Dept. of Agriculture, Washington, DC 20250.

(222) **Sources: A Guide to Print and Nonprint Materials Available from Organizations, Industry, Government Agencies, and Specialized Publishers.** Edited by Patricia Glass Schuman and John Vincent Neal. 3 issues a year. Gaylord Bros., Inc., Box 61, Syracuse, NY 13201. $60.00 per year, plus postage.

(223) **State Administrative Officials Classified by Functions.** Published biennially. Council of State Governments, Iron Works Pike, Lexington, KY 40511. 1977 ed., $10.00.

(224) Still Picture Branch, Audiovisual Archives Division, National Archives and Records Service, General Services Administration, Washington, DC 20408.

(225) Stout, Chester Bernard. **Measurement of Document Exposure Time Distributions at a Small Public Library.** 1976. Dr. C. B. Stout, McKinley Memorial Library, 40 N. Main St., Niles, OH 44446. Xerox copy, $11.90; microfiche copy, $3.00.

(226) **Subject Bibliographies.** Superintendent of Documents, U.S. Government Printing Office, Washington, DC 20402. Free.

(227) **Thesaurus of ERIC Descriptors.** 7th ed., 1977. Macmillan Information, 866 Third Ave., New York, NY 10022. $9.95.

(228) Thompson, Enid T. **Local History Collections: A Manual for Librarians.** 1978. American Association for State and Local History, 1400 Eighth Ave., South, Nashville, TN 37203. $5.75.

(229) Toronto Public Library. **Subject Headings for Vertical Files.** Toronto Public Library, 40 Orchard View Blvd., Toronto, Ontario, Canada M4R 1B9. Out-of-print.

(230) U-File-M Binder Mfg. Co., Inc., P.O. Box 83, Lafayette, NY 13084.

(231) United Air Lines, P.O. Box 66100, Chicago, IL 60666.

(232) United Nations. **Information Services and Embassies in the United States of Members of the United Nations.** Public Inquiries Unit, Office of Public Information, United Nations, New York, NY 10017. Free.

(233) U.S. Civil Service Commission, Washington, DC 20415 (changed to Office of Personnel Management, January 1979).

Announcements. Distributed free of charge.

Directory of Federal Job Information Centers. Single copy free.

Federal Career Directory: A Guide for College Students. For sale by the Superintendent of Documents. Price of 1976 ed., $3.45. New edition planned for release in 1979.

Guide to Federal Career Literature. For sale by the Superintendent of Documents. Price of 1978 ed., $1.10.

Working for the USA. For sale by the Superintendent of Documents. Price of 1977 ed., $0.70.

(234) U.S. Dept. of State, Office of Media Services, Washington, DC 20520.

(235) U.S. Employment Service, Employment and Training Administration, U.S. Dept. of Labor. **Dictionary of Occupational Titles.** 4th ed., 1977. For sale by the Superintendent of Documents. $12.00.

(236) **United States Government Manual.** Revised annually. Office of the Federal Register, National Archives and Records Service. For sale by the Superintendent of Documents. 1978-79 ed., $6.50.

(237) United States Travel Service, U.S. Dept. of Commerce, Washington, DC 20230.

(238) University Prints, 21 East St., Winchester, MA 01890.

(239) **Update on Law-Related Education.** 3 issues a year. Special Committee on Youth Education for Citizenship, American Bar Association, 1155 E. 60th St., Chicago, IL 60637. $5.00 per year.

(240) **Vertical File Index.** Monthly except August. H. W. Wilson Company, 950 University Ave., Bronx, NY 10452. $16.00 per year.

(241) **Vocational Biographies.** Vocational Biographies, Inc., Service Dept., P.O. Box 31, Sauk Centre, MN 56378. Set of 700 biographies, $328.00. Series of 175 biographies, $88.50. Annual subscription, $92.50. Single biographies, $0.55.

(242) **Ward's Bulletin.** Issued three or four times a year. Ward's Natural Science Establishment, Inc., P.O. Box 1712, Rochester, NY 14603. Free.

(243) Washington National Insurance Company, Public Relations Dept., 1630 Chicago Ave., Evanston, IL 60201.

(244) Wasserman, Paul, and Esther Herman. **Festivals Sourcebook.** 1977. Gale Research Company, Book Tower, Detroit, MI 48226. $45.00.

(245) Wasserman, Paul, and Esther Herman. **Museum Media.** 1973. Gale Research Company, Book Tower, Detroit, MI 48226. $62.00. 2nd edition projected for 1979.

(246) Franklin Watts, Inc., 730 Fifth Ave., New York, NY 10019.

(247) Weber Costello, 1900 N. Narragansett, Chicago, IL 60639.

(248) Weihs, Jean Riddle, and others. **Nonbook Materials: The Organization of Integrated Collections.** 1973. Canadian Library Association. Page 82.

(249) Weinstein, Robert A., and Larry Booth. **Collection, Use, and Care of Historical Photographs.** 1977. American Association for State and Local History, 1400 Eighth Ave. South, Nashville, TN 37203. $16.00.

(250) Weisinger, Mort. **1001 Valuable Things You Can Get Free.** 10th ed., 1977. Bantam Books, Inc. $1.95.

(251) **What's New in Advertising and Marketing.** 10 issues a year. Advertising and Marketing Division, Special Libraries Association. Send subscriptions to Ruth Fromkes at Foote, Cone and Belding, 200 Park Ave., New York, NY 10017. $10.00 per year.

(252) Wheat Flour Institute, 1776 F St., N.W., Washington, DC 20006.

(253) William-Frederick Press, 55 E. 86th St., New York, NY 10028.

(254) Winch, Kenneth L., ed. **International Maps and Atlases in Print.** 2nd ed., 1976. R. R. Bowker. $42.50.

(255) **World Wide Chamber of Commerce Directory.** Published annually. Johnson Publishing Company, Inc., P.O. Box 455, Eighth and Van Buren, Loveland, CO 80537. Price of 1978-79 ed., $13.00.

(256) Zulauf, Sander W. **Index of American Periodical Verse.** Published annually. Scarecrow Press, Inc. 1976 index published in 1978. $17.50.

INDEX